Hoodoo

by Nathaniel "Nth" Bar-Fields

for dummies®
A Wiley Brand

Hoodoo For Dummies®

Published by: **John Wiley & Sons, Inc.,** 111 River Street, Hoboken, NJ 07030-5774, www.wiley.com

For general information on our other products and services, please contact our Customer Care Department within the U.S. at 877-762-2974, outside the U.S. at 317-572-3993, or fax 317-572-4002. For technical support, please visit https://hub.wiley.com/community/support/dummies.

Wiley publishes in a variety of print and electronic formats and by print-on-demand. Some material included with standard print versions of this book may not be included in e-books or in print-on-demand. If this book refers to media that is not included in the version you purchased, you may download this material at http://booksupport.wiley.com. For more information about Wiley products, visit www.wiley.com.

Library of Congress Control Number is available from the publisher.

ISBN 978-1-394-41739-1 (pbk); ISBN 978-1-394-41742-1 (ePDF); ISBN 978-1-394-41741-4 (ePUB)

SKY10159986_062326

Contents at a Glance

Table of Contents

PART 2: ROOTING AROUND IN HOODOO 77

Introduction

Hoodoo is one of America's most misunderstood spiritual traditions and, arguably, one of its most consequential. Born during the days of chattel slavery in America, Hoodoo has evolved across generations of survival and resistance. It's practiced in communities right now and resists the categories that people keep trying to assign to it. It isn't a religion, a superstition, a Hollywood invention, or simply *Black magic* in either sense of that term. It's a practical, ecologically grounded, spiritually sophisticated tradition that never stopped doing its work.

This book won't make you a Hoodoo practitioner. That happens through relationship, lineage, and time spent in real communities with real elders. What it *will* do is give you the literacy to engage with Hoodoo's history, culture, and living practitioners with understanding and respect, whether you're approaching as a curious newcomer, a student of American religious history, someone with family roots in the tradition, or a person who has already begun a practice and wants to understand the larger context of what they're doing.

About This Book

This isn't a book of spells. You'll find plenty of those elsewhere, and some of them are even accurate. This book does something harder and, I'd argue, more useful: It gives you the foundational understanding to know what you're looking at when you encounter Hoodoo in the world. It also helps you ask better questions, recognize authentic practitioners and avoid predatory ones, and engage with this tradition on its own terms rather than through the distorting lens of pop culture and historical erasure.

For Dummies books are designed for ready access. You can open to any chapter and find what you need without having to read everything before it. You can skip around and follow a thread of interest wherever it takes you. The book doesn't test you or try to act as a gatekeeper. But it does enable you to exercise your genuine curiosity and encourages a willingness to revise what you thought you knew.

Here are a few conventions worth noting throughout this book:

- When I introduce a Hoodoo-specific term for the first time, I put it in *italic* and explain it in context. Hoodoo has a rich vernacular vocabulary, and these terms carry meaning that general synonyms can't quite capture.
- I use the terms *practitioners* and *rootworkers* to refer to people who practice Hoodoo, and *elders* to refer to experienced, community-respected practitioners whose knowledge comes through lineage and long practice.
  - These terms aren't interchangeable, and elder status isn't automatic. It's a reputation the community bestows rather than one a practitioner claims. A rootworker may practice for decades and never be thought of as an auntie, uncle, mama, papa, or doc, although many will.
  - *Doc*, short for doctor, is a distinct designation in many Hoodoo lineages. Practitioners earn this title through exceptional skill that is often associated with specialized practice. The title carries its own weight independent of age or years spent working in the tradition.
  - *Mama* and *papa* function differently; they are less a formal designation than an expression of deep community affection and trust. These titles arrive through relationship rather than reputation alone.
- Web addresses appear in `monofont`. If you're reading a digital version of this book on a device connected to the internet, you can click the web address to visit that website directly.

To make the material as accessible as possible, I've organized it into six parts:

- **Part 1, "Getting Started with Hoodoo,"** covers the scope of the tradition, its history, its cultural roots, and the frameworks scholars and practitioners use to understand it.
- **Part 2, "Rooting Around in Hoodoo,"** delves deeper into how Hoodoo actually works: the mechanics of rootwork, the practitioner's mindset, spirit work, and divination.
- **Part 3, "Living Hoodoo,"** explores how Hoodoo functions as a lived practice and describes its relationship to faith, personal spiritual power, community life, and justice work.
- **Part 4, "Embracing the Craft of Hoodoo,"** gets specific about materials, methods, and the four primary modes of rootworking.
- **Part 5, "Checking Out Hoodoo Now and Next,"** situates Hoodoo in the contemporary world: its role in health and medicine, its presence in modern culture and entertainment, and where the tradition is headed.

- **Part 6, "The Part of Tens,"** presents ten insights that indicate you may have grown up with Hoodoo and ten historical examples of Hoodoo in action.

Foolish Assumptions

Every author makes assumptions about the book's readers, and honest ones admit it. Here are my two assumptions about you:

- **You're curious about Hoodoo and want accurate information,** not sensationalized accounts or hollow reassurances. You may be approaching the tradition through family stories, academic interest, popular culture, or a spiritual search. Something real has drawn you here. You don't need prior knowledge of Hoodoo or African American folk traditions, but if you have some, you'll find material here that extends beyond the introductory.
- **You're approaching in good faith,** even if some of your current assumptions turn out to need revision. And I'm assuming you're an adult who can understand nuance: Hoodoo is a living tradition with real practitioners, real communities, and real protocols around who teaches what to whom. This book honors that, which means it describes some things without full details. Those limits are intentional.

What I haven't assumed is that you're African American, that you're a spiritual person, that you intend to practice Hoodoo, or that you'll agree with everything I say. None of those things are required to get genuine value from this book.

Icons Used in This Book

Throughout this book, icons in the margins highlight certain types of valuable information that call out for your attention. Here are the icons you'll encounter and a brief description of each.

TIP

The Tip icon marks practical suggestions for engaging with Hoodoo, its communities, and its practitioners more effectively.

REMEMBER

Remember icons flag the key conceptual anchors: the points that, if you take nothing else from a section, you want to carry with you.

TECHNICAL STUFF

The Technical Stuff icon marks information that goes deeper into history, scholarship, or cultural context than the surrounding material requires. Feel free to skip it on a first read and come back later if you want.

WARNING

The Warning icon alerts you to common mistakes, misconceptions, and situations where getting things wrong has real consequences for real people.

Beyond the Book

In addition to the material in these pages, you get access to more help and resources online at `Dummies.com`. Check out this book's online Cheat Sheet, which collects some of the most useful quick-reference material from across the book. Just go to `www.dummies.com` and search for "Hoodoo For Dummies Cheat Sheet."

Where to Go from Here

This book is designed as a reference, not a linear read. If you're entirely new to Hoodoo, Chapter 1 is genuinely the right place to start because it gives you the big picture before the details arrive. But if you have a specific thread of interest pulling at you, follow it. Curious about the historical roots of Hoodoo? Start with Chapter 2. Want to understand how rootwork actually operates? See Chapter 5. Interested in spirit work and ancestor veneration? Try out Chapter 7. Trying to find your footing as a potential practitioner? Chapters 10 and 13 are a must for you.

Wherever you start, the tradition will still be here when you circle back to what you skipped.

1 Getting Started with Hoodoo

IN THIS PART . . .

Explore the full scope of Hoodoo as a living tradition that weaves together science, spirit, and everyday life, and find out how to engage with it wisely.

Discover the African roots of Hoodoo, follow its journey through slavery and freedom in the US, and find out who leads the charge for keeping Hoodoo alive and well.

Uncover the many cultural threads — African, European, Native American, and beyond — that converged to shape Hoodoo into the distinctly American tradition it is today.

Examine how scholars and practitioners classify the study of Hoodoo, and discover what those frameworks illuminate about the tradition's nature and its place in the wider world.

IN THIS CHAPTER

» **Understanding what Hoodoo is and isn't**

» **Tracing Hoodoo's African foundations and multicultural influences**

» **Grasping why decentralization is a feature, not a flaw**

» **Seeing how spirit work forms the heart of Hoodoo practice**

» **Engaging wisely with this living tradition**

Chapter 1
Seeing the Breadth and Depth of Hoodoo

When some people hear the term *Hoodoo*, they picture Hollywood stereotypes: dolls stuck with pins, curses muttered in darkness, and scary voodoo magic. But what's the reality? Hoodoo is sophisticated spiritual technology developed by enslaved Africans and their descendants; it's a tradition of healing, protection, empowerment, and justice that's been practiced for more than four centuries in America.

This chapter gives you the big picture of the Hoodoo tradition. You can find out what Hoodoo is, where it came from, how it works, and, most importantly, how to approach this living tradition with understanding and respect. Think of this chapter as your orientation to a rich, complex world that African Americans have inhabited for generations.

Recognizing the Roots of Hoodoo

Hoodoo is a practical African American spiritual tradition focused on solving real-world problems through work with roots, herbs, prayers, spirits, and resourcefulness. The traditional practices developed in the American South when the enslaved Africans from multiple ethnic groups synthesized their various spiritual systems into something new. They took West African spirit work, Central African conjure bundles, and Islamic prayer traditions and fused them with materials and knowledge found in America. The tradition also draws on Jewish and Christian prayers, Native American herbs, and European folk magic.

The result of this combining and infusing became a distinctly African American practice built for survival and resistance under brutal conditions. Other names for Hoodoo practice that you may encounter include *rootwork* (which emphasizes the aspect of herbal and botanical knowledge), *conjure* (which emphasizes spiritual work), and simply the *Work* (which is what some Hoodoo insiders call it).

Knowing what Hoodoo isn't

Hoodoo can be confused with a lot of other things. Following are a few examples of other religions, practices, and traits that are distinct from Hoodoo but may be linked in people's minds:

- **Voodoo (Haitian Vodou).** Both Hoodoo and Voodoo descended from African spiritual systems, but they developed separately. *Voodoo, or Vodou*, is an organized religion with temples, priesthood, and specific spirits (for example, *lwa*, intermediary spiritual messengers or deities). Hoodoo is decentralized folk practice without formal clergy. In New Orleans, these two traditions met and blended into Louisiana Voodoo, but elsewhere they remained distinct.
- **Santería.** *Santería* (also called Lukúmí) is a Cuban religion preserving Yoruba traditions with elaborate initiations and worship of Orisha (divine spirits or deities). Hoodoo shares African roots with Santería but developed differently. It's less formally organized, more thoroughly Christianized, and shaped by North American rather than Caribbean circumstances.
- **Generic witchcraft.** European witchcraft traditions come from their own cultural contexts. Hoodoo comes from African spiritual systems filtered through the Black American experience. The techniques, the spirits, and the cultural logic are all distinctly African American.

» **Evil, malevolent, or devil worship.** This unfortunate — and completely wrong — stereotype comes from white supremacist fear-mongering and the Christian demonization of African practices. Historical Hoodoo practitioners were often deeply devout Christians who used the Bible as their primary working text. The tradition's origin is fundamentally about protection, healing, and justice.

Exploring the African trunk

Before addressing what Hoodoo absorbed from other cultures, I want to describe the origins that started it. Hoodoo's foundation is African. Specifically, it's West and Central African spiritual systems that enslaved people carried across the Middle Passage. (See Chapter 7 for information about the Middle Passage as part of the journey from Africa.)

Multiple West African ethnic groups contributed. Yoruba people brought understanding of *Orisha* (divine spirits governing natural forces) and the spiritual potency of iron and crossroads. The Fon and Ewe peoples contributed reverence for water spirits and the understanding of rivers and crossroads as spiritually charged places. Mandinka and Bambara peoples brought gris-gris, protective charm-sacks filled with herbs, minerals, and prayers, which became Hoodoo's mojo bags. Many of these West African Muslims also demonstrated that written sacred words carry spiritual power, preparing the way for Psalm magic.

If West Africa provided Hoodoo's cosmology, Central Africa — especially the Bakongo people of Congo and Angola — provided its material technology. Over 40 percent of enslaved Africans brought to North America came from this region. Their *minkisi* (spirit-filled bundles made for specific purposes) are direct ancestors of every Hoodoo conjure bag, bottle spell, and buried charm. The Kongo *Cosmogram* (explained in Chapter 2), a cross within a circle representing the boundary between living and dead, shaped Hoodoo's understanding of crossroads as power centers where worlds meet.

REMEMBER

What enslaved Africans could not carry in their hands, they carried in their memory. When everything else was stripped away, including languages, names, families, and freedom, they held onto their traditional practices because they worked.

Recognizing a multicultural synthesis

Hoodoo didn't develop in isolation. Enslaved Africans encountered other cultures, and each encounter left its traces on the development of the Hoodoo tradition.

Native American influences

Native Americans shared botanical knowledge that proved essential, although the relationship was complicated. Some Native peoples sheltered escaped enslaved Africans and exchanged knowledge freely; others participated in the slave trade. Practitioners learned which North American plants carried the properties they needed through whatever contact was available. Native American peoples' influence came from their proximity to plantations, through trade, and by genuine alliance in maroon communities (see Chapter 12) where escaped enslaved people and Native peoples lived and built together.

The Hoodoo practitioners used the local tobacco for offerings, cedar for cleansing, and sassafras for money work. The spiritual framework for how to use these resources remained African; what changed was the *pharmacopoeia*, or the documented formulas.

European impact

European influence came primarily through Christianity, and it came by force. But what was imposed on the Africans became weaponized. The enslaved people took the Bible and turned it into a working text, with the following uses:

- Psalm 23 for protection from overseers and oppressive living conditions
- Psalm 35 for justice against enemies
- Psalm 91 for strong cover during dangerous work or spiritual battle

Similarly, European grimoires (magic manuals) like *The Sixth and Seventh Books of Moses* circulated through 19th-century mail-order catalogs, and Hoodoo practitioners took what was useful from the grimoires and discarded the rest. They might *pull a seal* (copy a specific symbol from a grimoire) that worked and tuck it into a mojo bag with High John root rather than perform the elaborate ritual the European text prescribed.

Hebrew mystical elements

The Sixth and Seventh Books of Moses title alone signals a deeper thread because the text is steeped in Jewish Kabbalistic tradition. This tradition is part of a broader Hebrew mystical current whose reverence for sacred names, written text as power, and practical spiritual work found natural resonance in Hoodoo's own understanding of the written word as living force. The Jewish thread in Hoodoo runs deeper than most people realize; Chapter 3 explores it further.

The resulting combination

The genius isn't in any single element borrowed from another culture or tradition. It's in the synthesis: Hoodoo grabbed whatever was useful from any available source and transformed it on African terms, for African American purposes, into something that's 100 percent African American regardless of what else was mixed in.

TECHNICAL STUFF

The multicultural nature of Hoodoo sometimes is used to argue that it belongs to everyone. This interpretation misunderstands the purpose of Hoodoo's synthesis. American jazz draws on African rhythms, European harmonics, and blues traditions, but no one argues that jazz isn't a Black American art form. Hoodoo's multicultural influences don't dilute its African American identity; they demonstrate its creative genius.

Establishing Hoodoo as Science and Magic

At its heart, Hoodoo answers one question: How do I handle this situation or circumstance I'm faced with when official channels don't work or were designed to work against me?

The situation might be an abusive boss threatening your livelihood, a sickness that medicine can't cure, a legal case where the system is rigged, a love that needs working (a romantic situation requiring a spell or rootwork ritual to bring it to the desired outcome), or a child who needs protecting. Hoodoo developed as practical problem-solving for people with limited resources facing enormous challenges.

REMEMBER

Enslaved people couldn't call the police because the police were their oppressors. They couldn't sue in court because they weren't legally recognized as human. They couldn't openly organize or resist. But they could work roots. They could pray. They could call on ancestors. They could make protective charms, heal with herbs, and divine the future.

This practical, results-focused nature remains Hoodoo's defining characteristic. You didn't come to Hoodoo seeking enlightenment or cosmic mystery. You came because your rent is due, your child is sick, or someone is trying to harm you, and you need results. Survival and protection may address different situations for today's practitioners, but practicality of purpose is Hoodoo's origin and deserves to be remembered.

Hoodoo also refuses to separate the material from the spiritual. Herbs have both chemical properties and spiritual properties, not as two different realities, but as two aspects of the same one. Prayer isn't just psychological comfort; practitioners expect it to produce measurable outcomes. This integration of science and spirit isn't a contradiction; it's the tradition's distinctive epistemology, forged under conditions where people couldn't afford to keep those realms separated.

Getting the Right Mindset

What often confuses newcomers to the practice is that Hoodoo has no central authority, no official doctrine, and no standardized practices. Ask 10 rootworkers how to work a particular root, and you'll get 12 different answers. The results are similar if you ask how to make collard greens or other traditional African American dishes. This decentralization is both the tradition's greatest strength and its most persistent challenge. Consider this:

- **Decentralization is a strength because it enables survival.** You can't destroy Hoodoo by raiding a temple or killing a high priest because Hoodoo has no temples or hierarchies. The knowledge lives in thousands of families, passed through generations, hidden in plain sight. Without fixed dogma, practitioners could innovate and adapt. When traditional African herbs weren't available, they substituted American plants; when new materials became accessible, they incorporated them.
- **Decentralization is a challenge because it means no consensus.** Terms aren't standardized. For example, a mojo bag (see Chapter 5) is also called a gris-gris, a hand, a trick, and a conjure bag. Quality of roots and magical items varies widely. Debates about authenticity and who has the right to practice continue without resolution. And because no central authority exists to settle them, the debates about the tradition will persist.

REMEMBER

Hoodoo's lack of central structure isn't a flaw waiting to be fixed. It's the architecture that kept the tradition alive for four centuries under conditions designed to destroy it.

The book that you're holding is a map, not the territory. It provides the foundational understanding — history, principles, techniques, and cultural context — you need to engage with Hoodoo wisely. It helps you recognize authentic practitioners, distinguish the tradition from its Hollywood distortions, and approach living communities with respect. What this book can't do is replace elders, community, or direct spiritual relationship. Those can't be delivered in print.

TIP

The Appendix covers red flags for identifying fraudulent practitioners and guidance for finding legitimate teachers. If you're planning to seek out a rootworker or begin a practice, read that material before you engage.

Understanding How Hoodoo Is Practiced

Hoodoo encompasses four main areas of practice. Understanding these helps you recognize what practitioners are doing and why. These four domains interweave constantly, and a typical working might combine all of them at once:

- **Changemaking (Fixin' or Workin')** is what most people associate with magic, the practical work to alter circumstances. In Hoodoo, you can make a mojo bag to attract money, burn candles to open roads and remove obstacles, use *foot track magic* (working roots or powders into the ground where a target will walk, so the magic enters through the feet) to influence someone's behavior, and create *bottle spells* (workings placed inside a sealed bottle or jar) to either trap and confine or sweeten, bind, or protect. Honey jars are the most familiar contemporary form of bottle spells.
- **Divination** involves reading signs and understanding what's coming or is unseen and in play, as you can read in Chapter 8. Methods for divination include using standard playing cards, tarot, bones, dream interpretation, and *bibliomancy,* which means letting the Bible fall open to reveal answers. Some practitioners are *two-headed* — gifted seers who perceive both the material and the immaterial dimensions of a situation simultaneously.
- **Personal power development,** as I describe in Chapter 10, involves practitioners building their spiritual strength and authority through regular spiritual baths and cleansings, cultivating discernment, and maintaining spiritual hygiene. The goal is to keep yourself clear of influences that would compromise your work.
- **Spirit work** is the foundation that supports everything else. You can read about it in Chapter 7. Honoring ancestors, maintaining relationship with spiritual forces, making offerings, and learning to receive guidance from the dead are all part of spirit work.

Reaching the Heart of Hoodoo

If one practice defines Hoodoo more than any other, it's spirit work, particularly ancestor veneration. Everything else in the tradition ultimately serves this relationship between the living and the dead, the material and the immaterial.

In African cosmology, which Hoodoo maintains, death isn't an end. The dead become *ancestors*: guides and guardians that have powers and remain actively involved in the living world. When enslaved Africans lost everything — freedom, family, homeland, and language — they didn't lose their dead. Ancestors couldn't be sold away or beaten into submission. That bond persisted across the Middle Passage and through every generation of oppression.

Modern Hoodoo practitioners may pour libations, leave food offerings at graves and ancestor altars, petition ancestors for help with specific problems, use graveyard dirt to carry ancestral power, and speak to the dead regularly, not metaphorically, but as actual presences who can and do intervene in material reality.

Hoodoo without spirit work is just herbalism. A practitioner can memorize every root correspondence, mix perfect oils, and burn candles in the correct colors. But if they're not honoring ancestors and maintaining right relationship with the spirit world, they're not practicing Hoodoo. Practitioners consistently express a version of the same wisdom: Spirit connection isn't optional. It's what makes the work *work*.

REMEMBER

Honoring ancestors and worshiping ancestors aren't the same thing. Hoodoo venerates ancestors — shows respect, maintains relationship, and asks for help — without elevating them to divine status. This distinction matters especially for Christian practitioners who worry about idolatry. Chapter 7 explores this in depth.

Knowing Hoodoo's Place in Society

Hoodoo is accessible by design. The tradition carried no priestly gatekeeping, and its benefits extended beyond the community. Even outsiders sought out rootworkers for healing, protection, and counsel. That democratic accessibility was both practical necessity and spiritual principle. The tradition existed to serve people's actual needs, not to restrict who could receive the service. Whether that same openness extends to deciding who may practice Hoodoo — rather than who may seek help — remains a lively and unresolved conversation within contemporary Hoodoo communities (see Chapter 2 for more about this conversation).

This focus on serving actual needs hasn't changed. The 21st century has brought a renaissance led primarily by African American women — publicly reclaiming traditions that white supremacy and patriarchal forces tried to erase, and sharing knowledge through books, workshops, and online communities. Information that was once passed along in whispers is increasingly visible. That visibility brings debates about authenticity, cultural appropriation, and who has the right to practice Hoodoo. The tradition's decentralized nature means those debates will never have a single authoritative answer. (See the section "Getting the Right Mindset" earlier in the chapter.)

TIP

Without a central authority, the development of the Hoodoo tradition helps clarify the debate about who should practice and how. Hoodoo emerged from African American life, was preserved through African American determination, and continues to serve African American communities. That's Hoodoo's home, its center of gravity, and the context without which you can't properly understand it. The ancestors preserved Hoodoo practices across four centuries of sustained effort to erase them. This book is your guide to understanding what they preserved and why it still matters.

IN THIS CHAPTER

» Discovering Hoodoo's African roots

» Watching Hoodoo's development during slavery in the US

» Following Hoodoo through Reconstruction, migration, and modern revival

» Debating about who can practice Hoodoo

» Understanding Black women's central role as keepers of tradition

Chapter 2 Exploring Hoodoo's History

You can't understand where Hoodoo is going without knowing where it's been. Hoodoo's history reveals its genius: born from African spiritual technology, forged under slavery's brutality, adapted through every era's challenges, preserved by Black women's dedication, and revived today as cultural reclamation. Understanding this history isn't optional; it's essential for respecting the tradition, recognizing its sophistication, and appreciating the ancestors who kept it alive when everything worked against them. The essence of Hoodoo wasn't folk superstition. It was and is African American survival science, spiritual resistance, and generational wisdom encoded in roots, prayers, and practice.

In this chapter, I go beyond telling you about dates and dead people, which would likely bore you and cause you to miss out on valuable context and insight. Instead, I tell you about the ingenuity, resilience, and sheer audacity of the ancestors who built a spiritual tradition under impossible conditions. Hoodoo didn't emerge from comfortable circumstances or ivory towers. Although this chapter doesn't go out of its way to traumatize readers, it also doesn't sugarcoat or delete uncomfortable parts of the narrative that are important for understanding how Hoodoo developed. The practice was forged in the crucible of slavery, refined through Reconstruction's broken promises, tested during Jim Crow's brutality, and carried forward by people who refused to let Hoodoo die.

The information in this chapter helps you understand that Hoodoo isn't just folk magic; it's also African American cultural technology, spiritual resistance, and practical ingenuity wrapped into one living tradition.

Exploring Origins in West and Central African Roots

Knowing the origin and history of Hoodoo development does three things:

- **Shows you why Hoodoo works the way it does** — why it's pragmatic, secretive, adaptable, and fiercely focused on results.
- **Connects you to a lineage of practitioners** who faced challenges that make modern problems look manageable. And they still found ways to protect, heal, and empower their communities.
- **Clarifies who Hoodoo belongs to and why that matters** — not to gatekeep, but to honor the specific historical experience that created it.

REMEMBER

The term *Hoodoo* most likely comes from *vodu* (spirit or deity), a word shared across the Gbe languages of the Ewe, Fon, and related peoples of West Africa. This word reached American English through the Louisiana Creole term *houdou*. You'll sometimes see claims that the term *Hoodoo* comes from an Ewe word *hudu*, which means spirit work, but no such religious term is documented in primary Ewe-language sources. The closest match in the linguistic record is *Wudu* (also spelled *Hudu*), which describes a small Gbe-speaking people in Togo, not a practice. What's certain is this: The word itself is African in origin, just like the practices it describes.

Hoodoo's deepest roots lie in West and Central Africa. Between the 16th and 19th centuries, human traffickers enslaved millions of Africans and forced them across the Atlantic. The Africans came from diverse ethnic groups — Yoruba, Fon, Ewe, Igbo, Kongo, Mbundu, Mandé, Wolof, and dozens more — but their spiritual worldviews shared common threads that would form Hoodoo's foundation.

West African cosmological foundations

The Fon and Ewe peoples of the former Slave Coast (modern-day Benin, Togo, and Ghana) brought Vodun (voodoo) beliefs to their new lives in the Americas. These beliefs included a reverence for powerful spirits called *vodun*, practices of voluntary spirit possession, and the use of sacred herbs in ritual. The Yoruba of southwestern Nigeria contributed knowledge of *Orisha* (divine spirits), *Ifá* (divination systems), and an understanding that spiritual and material worlds constantly interact.

These belief systems weren't religions in the Western sense. In other words, they didn't necessarily worship a superhuman power, or a god. But the beliefs represented complete *cosmologies*, which are metaphysical frameworks that attempt to explain how the worlds worked. In these cosmologies,

- **Spirits existed everywhere:** They inhabited rivers, trees, crossroads, and storms, for example.
- **Ancestors remained active:** The dead weren't gone; they guided and protected the living.
- **Herbalism was spiritual:** Plants had both medicinal and mystical properties.
- **Ritual created change:** Humans worked with spiritual forces to alter reality through prayer, offerings, dance, and sacrifice.

REMEMBER

Many West Africans brought by enslavers were Muslim, particularly from Senegambia and Mali. These enslaved scholars carried Islamic mystical traditions, such as the use of written verses as protective amulets, numerology, and sacred geometry. In West African Islam, *gris-gris charms* — small bags containing Quranic verses, herbs, and minerals — protected against harm. This practice of written spiritual protection blended seamlessly into Hoodoo, in which Bible verses written on paper and carried in mojo bags serve the same function.

Central African (Kongo) foundations

Scholars estimate that between a quarter and a third of enslaved Africans brought to North America came from Central Africa. They primarily came from the Kingdom of Kongo and surrounding regions, including the modern-day countries of Angola, Congo, and Democratic Republic of Congo. The Bakongo people profoundly shaped Hoodoo's structure and symbolism.

The Bakongo people, in particular, contributed foundational elements that are still visible in Hoodoo practice today:

- **The Kongo Cosmogram** (Yowa cross) represented the cycle of life, death, and rebirth. The symbol is a circle intersected by a cross. It showed the world of the living, the physical world, above a horizontal line. The world of ancestors, the spiritual world, was below the line. See Figure 2-1 for a depiction of the Kongo Cosmogram.

  The crossroads, where the lines meet, became a *liminal space* — a transitional space not meant for prolonged occupation — where living and dead could communicate. The crossroads remain so significant in Hoodoo because they're portals between worlds: places to leave offerings, make deals with spirits, or dispose of spiritual work. For example, suppose that you want to remove negative energy. You'd put your written concern in a small packet with some dirt, bury it at a crossroads at midnight, and walk away. The crossroads is the doorway between worlds, so you'd be handing your problem to the spirit world. Done.

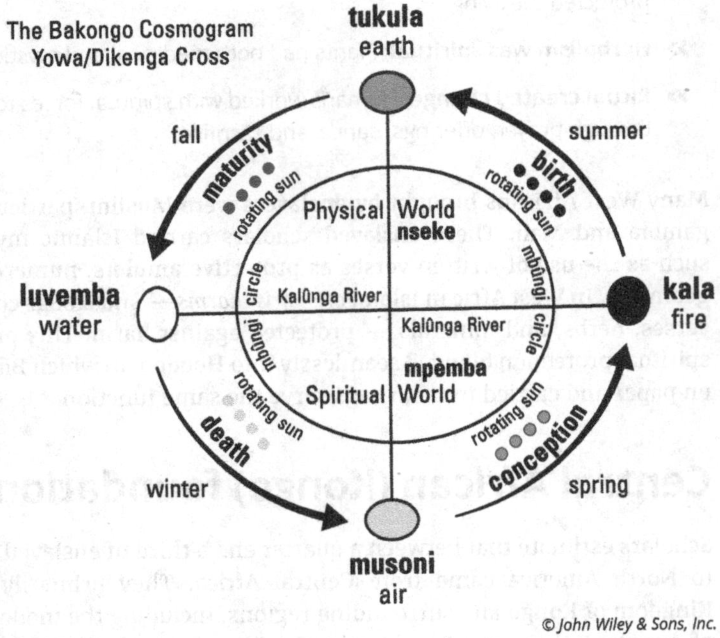

FIGURE 2-1: The Kongo Cosmogram.

- **Minkisi** (singular: nkisi) were sacred bundles or containers — cloth bags, clay pots, carved figures — that held empowered combinations of herbs, roots, bones, graveyard dirt, and other materials. Each nkisi housed a spirit bound to serve specific purposes, such as healing, protection, justice, love, or harm. The Hoodoo *mojo bag* is a direct descendant of the nkisi.

REMEMBER

Archaeologists have found concealed *conjure bundles* (another name for mojo bags) under slave cabin floorboards. The bundles contain iron nails, coins, roots, bones, and other items arranged exactly like Kongo minkisi. These conjure bundles weren't coincidental items; they were deliberate spiritual technologies, transported and adapted for use in Hoodoo.

- **Water spirits** (like Simbi) in Kongo cosmology dwelled in rivers and streams, offering wisdom and power. Enslaved Kongolese people maintained this reverence for water, secretly invoking Simbi during Christian baptisms and seeking to syncretize African water deities with Christian water rites. Rivers, oceans, and crossings of water became spiritually significant in Hoodoo practice.
- **Ancestor veneration** was non-negotiable. The wisdom that deceased family members could guide, protect, and empower the living formed Hoodoo's spiritual backbone. You didn't just work alone. You worked with your ancestors.

What they brought with them

Enslavers did everything possible to strip away African culture by forbidding languages, traditional religion, drumming, and gatherings. But no one can erase what lives in the mind and spirit of people. On plantations, Africans from different regions shared their knowledge, creating something new from combined traditions. What emerged wasn't purely Yoruba or purely Kongo. It was *African American*, forged from multiple sources but adapted to a new and brutal reality.

When the first enslaved Africans reached North American shores in 1619, they carried these cultural beliefs and physical items related to them:

- Knowledge of hundreds of herbs and their spiritual/medicinal uses
- Understanding of how to communicate with and petition spirits
- Techniques for divination, dream interpretation, and reading signs
- Methods for creating protective charms and offensive hexes
- Belief in the power of spoken words, prayers, and incantations
- Systems for calling on ancestors and maintaining relationships with the dead

I cover how Hoodoo involves these beliefs, items, and practices in Part 2 of this book.

Journeying through Slavery's Effects in the US

Hoodoo's history is ultimately one of hope and resistance. The practice was born from the need to survive and forged by enslaved Africans who refused to surrender their spirits. Along the way, Hoodoo absorbed pieces from every source that could help — African, European, Native American, Christian, Islamic — and became a rich, syncretic tradition that sustained the enslaved people when nothing else would.

Finding survival, secrecy, and resistance in the slavery era

During the era of slavery (1619–1865) in what is now the US, the enslaved people were forced or pressured to convert to Christianity. Many didn't abandon African beliefs. Instead, they hid them inside Christian forms.

This action of integration wasn't deception as much as it was strategic adaptation. If survival meant appearing Christian while maintaining African practice, practitioners did both. The result was a unique synthesis in which Bible and roots, prayer and conjure, and church and Hoodoo became inseparable.

But everywhere, the essential focus remained: to use spiritual means to endure and escape slavery's conditions.

Syncretism with Christianity

Moses became more than a prophet in the manifestation of Hoodoo. The African American slaves reenvisioned him as a powerful conjurer who turned his staff into a serpent, brought plagues on Pharaoh, and parted the Red Sea. He was a magician who freed his people. The Psalms weren't just scripture; they were spells. Psalm 23 was for protection. Psalm 37 was for justice against enemies. Psalm 91 was for safety. Recited with conviction and spiritual intention, these Psalms became incantations.

The *invisible church* — secret prayer meetings called *hush harbors* and held in the woods at night — provided cover for spirit communication, Hoodoo teaching, and African-style ring shouts. *Ring shouts* were spiritual dance and religious rituals. Enslaved preachers delivered Biblical sermons while teaching protection techniques. The Christian God and African Creator merged, saints paralleled spirits, and everything operated in code.

In other words, the religious activities changed — new names, new prayers, new rituals — but the underlying African worldview remained. The mechanics of how spiritual work operated stayed fundamentally the same, just expressed through Christian vocabulary.

Secrecy and community protection

Legal suppression of African spiritual practices began well before the most dramatic uprisings. The 1724 French Code Noir in Louisiana explicitly banned any religion except Catholicism, and Anglo-American slave codes similarly forbade unsanctioned gatherings, especially at night. Events like the Stono Rebellion in South Carolina in 1739 only intensified that crackdown.

As a result of these laws and codes, practitioners of African spiritual activities went underground. They met in woods after dark, drummed on overturned pots to muffle sound, and turned iron kettles upside down to catch prayers so they wouldn't carry through air. Despite the danger of being caught in illegal activities, conjure doctors — called *rootworkers* (a term for practitioners of Hoodoo), *two-headed doctors*, or *Hoodoo men/women* — emerged in every slave quarter. These conjure doctors were community healers and spiritual warriors, often elders who'd gained reputations for effective healing work.

Enslaved communities fiercely protected their rootworkers. If authorities discovered their activities, punishment was severe. Yet paradoxically, some enslavers grew wary of enslaved people who were known to conjure, fearing that they'd suffer illness or misfortune if they caused offense. Even in secrecy, Hoodoo provided subtle leverage, a way for the powerless to invoke fear in the powerful.

Some regions allowed slightly more openness. For example

- **In New Orleans under French/Spanish rule,** enslaved people gathered Sunday afternoons in Congo Square to dance African dances, drum, and trade herbs, keeping traditions semi-visible.
- **On isolated South Carolina and Georgia sea islands,** the Gullah people maintained particularly strong African customs due to relative isolation from white oversight.

Asserting Hoodoo as resistance

Every act of Hoodoo under slavery was quiet revolt — asserting African agency in a system designed to strip a slave's identity.

Sometimes resistance was direct. The 1712 slave revolt in New York was led by Peter the Doctor, an African conjurer who prepared magical powder for conspirators to rub on their bodies and clothes, believing it would protect them from harm. The rebels did carry out a fierce uprising. Whether the powder worked magically or, instead, psychologically emboldened them wouldn't have mattered to them; it served its purpose, getting the desired result.

More often, resistance was covert and took the following forms:

- Charms to make cruel overseers fall ill
- Powders to poison an enslaver's food
- Talismans to help someone escape enslavement successfully
- Mojo bags for protection from physical or sexual abuse from slave owners or overseers

TECHNICAL STUFF

Some mysterious slaveholder deaths were likely conjure justice. Symptoms of common hex work, including *wasting illness* (involuntary loss of more than 10 percent of body weight), sudden misfortune, and unexplained death, match documented accounts of poisoning using plants available on plantations. Some historians argue that numerous deaths attributed to disease or accident among enslavers were, in fact, acts of deliberate conjure or chemical resistance, carried out by enslaved people who had extensive knowledge of toxic plants.

The *Underground Railroad*, a network of secret routes and safehouses used by enslaved African Americans to escape to freedom, had a spiritual dimension. Runaways carried protective mojo bags filled with powerful roots and graveyard dirt from ancestors' graves. A famous trick was to use cemetery soil when fleeing to throw off bloodhounds. You'd "confuse the dogs" and break the scent trail by rubbing your feet with graveyard dirt or sprinkling it behind you. Numerous enslaved people's narratives recounted using this trick. Whether this method was magic or folk science mattered less than the fact that it worked. Hoodoo practitioners advised fugitives on which woods to travel through and which herbs to carry for concealment. One former Alabama enslaved person said of a successful escape: "Dey calls hit Hoodoo-in' de dogs."

Moving through post-emancipation and reconstruction

Emancipation from slavery, which President Lincoln proclaimed during the American Civil War in 1863, brought legal freedom, but it didn't bring safety or justice for newly freedpeople. During *Reconstruction*, the nation's rebuilding period following the Civil War, and the violent backlash that followed from 1865 to 1900, Black communities encountered new struggles. Hoodoo remained essential as bedrock support for *freedpeople* — people formerly enslaved and now free — who were building lives under Jim Crow's emerging shadow. See the section "Jim Crow era and civil rights" later in the chapter for information about the Jim Crow era.

Maintaining continuity and evolution

Formerly enslaved *root doctors* — healers who used naturally derived treatments — carried their knowledge into freedom. Because freedpeople had little access to doctors or legal justice, conjure doctors became community pillars as healers, advisors, and spiritual protectors. They treated freedpeople's ailments with herbs, set up house protections, and made charms for sharecroppers' luck in hard times.

REMEMBER

Many Black churches quietly tolerated and benefited from Hoodoo. Some preachers were also skilled rootworkers. Congregations generally saw no contradiction between their theology and Hoodoo practices because one dealt with religion and the other dealt with everyday matters of concern. So someone might attend a church service on Sunday and then visit the root doctor on Monday for help with a sick child or for a prosperity spell. Christianity provided collective hope and moral framework, but Hoodoo offered immediate, personalized solutions.

Documenting Hoodoo's existence

This Reconstruction era saw Hoodoo enter into written records. Paschal Beverly Randolph, a free Black man and occultist who taught freed slaves in Louisiana after the Civil War, encountered New Orleans Voodoo and Hoodoo practitioners. In 1870, he published *Seership, The Magnetic Mirror*, containing the first known appearance of the word *Hoodoo* in English print. In the book, he correctly identified Hoodoo as African-derived and noted that many practices associated with what were then broadly termed *Voodoo rites* had survived under new guises. These guises often reinterpreted and relabeled the rites within Hoodoo, which the author distinguished from Voodoo as less ceremonial, more practical, and rooted in personal magical work rather than communal religious ritual.

Randolph recounted a story of two rival conjure men engaging in a magical battle in Mobile, Alabama, in 1860. These rivals were reportedly Africans from the last illegal slave ship, the *Clotilda*, which arrived in the same year. Each conjurer used Kongo charms to try to get the best of the other. Publishing this duel-of-Kongos tale in 1870 shows that Congo African magic remained vibrant nearly a decade after slavery ended.

Examining Hoodoo's commercial beginnings

The late 19th century brought early commercialization to the practice of Hoodoo. Enterprising individuals, both Black and white, began selling spiritual supplies to meet Black community demand. For example, Mattie Sampson, an African American woman in Georgia, ran a mail-order Hoodoo business that sent remedies and luck charms to clients in the 1890s.

White-owned Southern drugstores, realizing profit potential because of demand, began stocking *High John roots* (roots primarily from the Ipomoea jalapa plant, which is related to morning glories) and occult items such as lodestones and sulfur. Rootworkers, Black customers seeking remedies and protection, and a smaller number of non-Black buyers all contributed to that demand. By 1900, you could find mass-produced dream books for lottery gambling and Hoodoo almanacs, often published by white entrepreneurs but marketed to Black audiences.

REMEMBER

When Southern drugstores began stocking High John root in the late 19th century, many white proprietors understood it as a profitable curiosity. Their Black customers knew exactly what they were buying and why. The commerce was new; the meaning was ancient. See the sidebar "High John the Conqueror: The Man, the Legend, the Root."

HIGH JOHN THE CONQUEROR: THE MAN, THE LEGEND, THE ROOT

High John the Conqueror occupies a singular place in Hoodoo lore: He is at once a legendary folk hero, a spiritual force, and a physical root sitting on a botanica shelf. Understanding both dimensions reveals something essential about how Hoodoo encodes resistance.

The folk figure predates the root's commercial popularity by generations. In African American oral tradition, High John was said to be an African prince — enslaved and brought to America — who could never be broken in spirit regardless of what slavery inflicted on his body. He outwitted overseers, slipped between worlds, laughed when he should have wept, and always, always landed on his feet. He wasn't powerful because he was physically strong; he was powerful because no one could own what lived inside him. Zora Neale Hurston, writing in 1943, described him as the source of laughter and song that kept enslaved people from spiritual destruction. He was the force that said, "We will survive this, and we will do it with our dignity intact."

That spirit became literally embodied in the root. High John the Conqueror root, botanically identified with *Ipomoea jalapa* and related morning glory species, is used in

Hoodoo work for luck, personal power, success in legal matters, love drawing, and general domination of difficult circumstances. Practitioners carry it as a mojo, dress it with condition oils, or incorporate it into baths and floor washes. The root is considered especially potent for men, though practitioners of any gender work with it.

The name attached to the root isn't coincidental. Naming a plant after a trickster hero of liberation is itself a Hoodoo act: It encodes meaning, anchors the root's purpose in collective memory, and ensures that every time someone reaches for the root, they are, however unconsciously, reaching toward that legacy of unbreakable spirit.

Louisiana Hoodoo also incorporated Catholic saint products and glass-encased novena candles labeled for specific purposes and with names such as Fast Luck and Court Case. Regional Louisiana Hoodoo repurposed these items from Catholic devotional practices for use in conjure spells.

Solidifying regional Hoodoo styles

Each regional style of Hoodoo that developed after emancipation adapted to local resources, but all maintained three core principles: work with spirits, use what's available, and get results. These different regional areas (Chapter 3 offers more information about each area) developed distinct Hoodoo styles:

- **Lowcountry (Sea Islands)** maintained the most "African" Hoodoo, with strong ancestor veneration and water spirit reverence.
- **New Orleans** blended Hoodoo with Voodoo and Catholicism into unique Creole conjure.
- **Appalachia** saw European and African folk magic cross-pollinate.
- **Texas and Oklahoma** incorporated influences from Indigenous Plains tribes of Native Americans.

TIP

A formerly enslaved Virginia root doctor described his work simply: "I gives de people what dey need — de herb for de fever, de prayer for de hope, an' a little conjure to scare off de bad." That philosophy carried Hoodoo into the 20th century.

Finding a Foothold in Freedom

Formerly enslaved people faced new battles: sharecropping that kept them in poverty, Jim Crow laws that stripped rights, lynch mobs that terrorized communities, and social systems designed to keep them powerless. Hoodoo didn't disappear when slavery ended. It adapted. Root doctors became community pillars, publications featured Hoodoo practices for the first time, and regional Hoodoo styles solidified. Through it all, Black Americans used the spiritual tools that their ancestors gave them to survive a freedom that looked a lot like bondage wearing different clothes.

The Great Migration and urban adaptation

Between 1916 and 1970, approximately six million Black Americans moved from the rural South to the urban North and West. Millions of Black families relocated to Chicago, Detroit, New York, Philadelphia, Los Angeles, and other cities to seek better opportunities. They brought Hoodoo with them, and this Great Migration transformed Hoodoo from primarily rural practice to urban phenomenon. And city life demanded Hoodoo adaptation.

Facing urban challenges and innovations

Traditional rituals involved going to wild crossroads, rivers, or graveyards at midnight. In crowded cities, that was harder. Practitioners adapted by

- **Performing spells in back alleys,** on rooftops, or at city parks after dark
- **Using bathtubs instead of creeks** for ritual baths
- **Flushing spiritual items down toilets** as a modern substitute for rivers
- **Burning candles in closets** to simulate swamp darkness

Without readily accessible wild herbs in the city, reliance on spiritual supply shops increased. By the 1920s, storefront *botanicas* (small stores selling traditional remedies and other items used for religious or spiritual purposes) and occult shops in Black neighborhoods sold dried roots, ready-made oils, candles, incense, sachet powders, and mail-order spell kits.

Black herbalists ran some shops by using traditional formulas. White, Jewish, Italian, or Latine merchants who saw profitable niche markets ran others. A white Jewish pharmacist in Chicago might stock *Devil's Shoe Strings* (protective vine root) or *Goofer Dust* (harmful powder) because Black customers requested them. Some providers also integrated items from Kabbalah or Jewish mysticism of questionable accuracy but marketed as having exotic spiritual power to Black and white customers alike. These included mezuzahs, psalms written in Hebrew, and King Solomon products such as oils and powders; see Figure 2-2, which shows an anointing oil available for sale online at Amazon (`www.amazon.com`).

FIGURE 2-2: A selection of King Solomon products available from online sellers.

Entire companies formed to mass-produce spiritual products. Valmor Products in Chicago and King Novelty in Memphis manufactured condition oils with colorful labels like Money Drawing Oil, Love Me Powder, and Fast Luck Incense. By the 1930s, Hoodoo advertisements appeared in Black newspapers, disguised as dream interpreters or herbal remedy offers.

Hoodoo and the Blues

Early 20th-century blues music brims with Hoodoo references, reflecting how common the practice was. Blues songs mentioned mojos, jacks (divination tools), and roots, for example. These cultural expressions kept Hoodoo imagery alive nationwide, spreading it beyond the South through music.

The song "Got My Mojo Working," later popularized by Muddy Waters, speaks of using a mojo bag to attract love. Lyrics in the song include: "I'm going to Louisiana to get me a mojo hand; I'm gonna have all you women right here at my command."

Many blues musicians consulted root doctors. Robert Johnson allegedly went to a crossroads to gain supernatural guitar skill. This story conflates Hoodoo practice (leaving offerings at crossroads for spirits) with European Faustian legend (selling one's soul to the devil).

Adapting to new needs

Moving to northern cities brought new challenges, including job discrimination, race riots, overcrowded housing, and police harassment. Rootworkers adjusted their services accordingly to include the following:

- » Charms for finding factory employment
- » Powders to ward off abusive landlords
- » Protection spells for those working in bootlegging during Prohibition
- » Lucky hands for winning numbers games (gambling) during the Depression

REMEMBER

Hoodoo's focus on practical needs included urban survival and helping people navigate systemic oppression. A Chicago rootworker might provide a charm for Black people to carry when traveling, ensuring that the bearer won't be unjustly arrested.

Achieving academic notice

The 1930s brought significant scholarly attention. Beginning at that time, academic works by various authors validated Hoodoo as a legitimate subject of study and influenced practitioners who could see their culture documented and analyzed with respect rather than dismissed as ignorance. Examples include

- » **Zora Neale Hurston,** African American writer and anthropologist, was initiated into Hoodoo practice by New Orleans Hoodoo doctor Luke Turner. In 1931 she published the book-length scholarly article "Hoodoo in America," and in 1935 the book *Mules and Men*. Both contained vivid firsthand accounts of rituals, formulas, and spoken ceremonies. Hurston preserved knowledge that might otherwise have been lost, illuminating Hoodoo's richness for readers who'd dismissed it as superstition.
- » **Harry M. Hyatt,** a folklorist, traveled the South in the late 1930s and interviewed hundreds of rootworkers, compiling a massive five-volume collection of their spells and beliefs that was published in the 1970s. This documentation ensured mid-century Hoodoo practice was recorded for posterity.
- » **Katrina Hazzard-Donald,** a more recent scholar, provides rigorous academic analysis to the study of Hoodoo. Her 2012 book *Mojo Workin': The Old African American Hoodoo System* offers a bold reconsideration of Hoodoo belief and practice, examining it as a coherent system rather than random superstitions. This modern scholarship builds on earlier documentation while bringing contemporary analytical frameworks to understanding Hoodoo's cultural significance and internal logic.

Jim Crow era and civil rights

From Reconstruction's end through the Civil Rights era (roughly 1877–1968), during legally enforced segregation and intense racial violence, Hoodoo continued providing refuge, empowerment, and sometimes clandestine resistance.

Protection and empowerment

Jim Crow was a period, primarily in the Southern US, in which state and local laws enforced racial segregation and discrimination. Under it, Black people faced daily threats of lynchings, police brutality, economic exploitation, and unjust laws and courts. Root doctors commonly prepared protection talismans for clients who were dealing with the dangerous situations of this era. The root doctors assisted by

» **Helping clients avoid harm:** A mojo bag might contain High John root (described in the section "Examining Hoodoo's commercial beginnings" earlier in the chapter), snake skin, and silver dimes, which were prayed over and hidden in clothing. These items sought to help someone escape harm or win a court case against odds. Oral histories describe people using such charms to turn away unjust officers or keep lynch mobs from finding homes.

» **Bolstering courage and watchfulness:** Whether charms worked literally, bolstered courage and hypervigilance needed to survive, or did both, they gave an edge in terrifying circumstances to people who greatly needed every edge they could get.

» **Securing economic opportunities:** Rootworkers might tell job seekers to sprinkle powdered sugar and salt in a boss's office as a sweetening spell or provide dressed (ritually prepared) green candles to burn while praying for money. These personal rituals filled gaps left by systemic injustice.

Conflict and acceptance

As the Black church grew in influence and sought to assimilate into white America, many congregations that once benefited from Hoodoo began preaching against "conjure" as witchcraft or superstition. Educated African Americans seeking respectability distanced themselves from rootwork publicly as well. This desire to be accepted by the dominant culture while still relying on Hoodoo to solve certain problems created in many African Americans *cognitive dissonance*, mental stress stemming from conflicting beliefs and actions. They continued practicing Hoodoo techniques but were incapable of acknowledging them as such, instead calling them ordinary Christian traditions or folk wisdom.

Many Christian African Americans still quietly believed in and used Hoodoo. It wasn't either/or. Anyone could sing in the church choir on Sunday and visit Aunt

Caroline Dye (circa 1843-1918, a renowned Hoodoo rootworker based in Arkansas) on Monday if trouble arose. Church mothers might disapprove of working roots but still practice it themselves without recognizing what they were doing; they may

- Randomly open the Bible to reveal scriptural answers to pondered questions
- Anoint doorframes with olive oil in the sign of the cross for protection
- No longer have *the sight* (clairvoyance), but now "God tells them things"

These weren't just Christian practices; they were Hoodoo techniques wearing Christian clothes.

REMEMBER

Other Hoodoo customs continued while the historical understanding was lost across generations. Families painted porch ceilings *haint blue* because "that's just what folks do." But they no longer recognized the purpose was to ward off or confuse the problematic spirits. This practice and others survived even as their meaning faded.

External pressure from societal forces existed, but it was less consistent than internal church criticism. Law enforcement occasionally arrested root doctors for fraud or fortune-telling, though generally Hoodoo flew under the radar. Within Black communities, practitioners remained respected figures even as the church officially condemned their work. Sometimes that respect came with a touch of fear.

Civil rights connections

Hoodoo's presence surfaced in the struggle for justice in subtle ways. Prayer meetings and spirituals had parallels to old ring shouts and conjure prayers, calling on divine power for justice. Some meeting organizers privately carried charms. Accounts exist of Mississippi activists wearing small mojo bags sewn into clothes for protection when entering Klan-dominated areas. This practice wasn't publicized because the movement emphasized Christian imagery, but the cultural undercurrent of Hoodoo belief was present.

By the 1950s/60s, as younger urban Black Americans embraced modern identity, Hoodoo was less openly discussed. Some of them viewed Hoodoo as a relic, but it persisted within families. Many recall grandmothers burning incense or secretly burying a Bible at the doorstep for protection. These acts blended Christian faith with folk magic. Families casually discussed dreams that gave warnings or revealed where to find lost items, not recognizing that this dream interpretation was part of the Seer/Reader tradition within Hoodoo.

Hoodoo had gone somewhat underground again, not from legal threat but from cultural shifts and assimilation desires. But it never died. Devoted practitioners kept the flame alive, quietly passing knowledge to the next generation.

Modern renaissance and revival

After the civil rights era's social upheaval, African Americans began reclaiming pride in all heritage aspects, including marginalized spiritual practices. The result was a Hoodoo renaissance.

Reclaiming Black culture

Starting around the 1970s and intensifying in the 1990s–2000s, more Black Americans explored Hoodoo and other African diaspora traditions as sources of cultural identity and empowerment. This exploration paralleled the Black Arts Movement and *Afrocentric turns*, which are shifts in thought and culture that centralize African history and values. People wanted to know "What did my great-grandmothers practice?"

An earlier generation kept Hoodoo practices quiet, but younger people were inspired by scholars such as Hurston or contemporary authors to explore them proudly. (See the section "Achieving academic notice" earlier in the chapter.) Workshops on rootwork, Hoodoo-themed books, and shops owned by Black practitioners appeared.

Black women entrepreneurs led this revival's forefront, opening spiritual supply stores and botanical shops in Black neighborhoods and online to serve communities. They tapped into Hoodoo's health and wellness facet, branding it as self-care and self-determination in modern times, teaching ancestral herb use for healing trauma or cleansing rituals for coping with racism-induced stress. See the section "Recognizing the Backbone of Hoodoo: Black Women as Keepers of the Flame" later in this chapter for more about Black women's influence on Hoodoo.

The internet enabled practitioners nationally and globally to connect, share knowledge, and correct misconceptions. African American-led online forums, YouTube channels, and workshops now teach authentic Hoodoo practice, reclaiming narrative away from old stereotypes or non-Black commercialization.

Garnering academic and artistic recognition

Modern scholarship vindicated Hoodoo's importance. Historians such as Tony Kail and Katrina Hazzard-Donald traced Hoodoo's development and showed that what may be dismissed as superstition is a complex spiritual system with deep cultural significance. Such scholarship framed Hoodoo as a national treasure of African American folklore and religion.

Kail's Memphis research linked local practices directly to Kongo and West African traditions, demonstrating Africa-to-America continuity. Sociologist Sterling Stuckey argued that African cultural practices such as the ring shout and conjure formed Black American identity's core and fueled liberation movements.

Artists also engaged Hoodoo themes. Visual artist Renee Stout created acclaimed works that incorporated conjure symbols and tools. See, for example, *The Rootworker's Table*, 2017 in the online archive of `newmuseum.org` at `https://archive.newmuseum.org/images/12121`. Writers from Ishmael Reed to contemporary poets have alluded to Hoodoo lore, destigmatizing it and presenting it as a source of creative strength.

Taking a role in social justice

Unsurprisingly, Hoodoo and African spirituality found places in modern activism movements such as Black Lives Matter. Organizers acknowledged the need for spiritual grounding for fighting systemic racism.

After police violence incidents, some community gatherings incorporated libation ceremonies, pouring water to honor the dead. They also incorporated altars at tragedy sites adorned with candles, flowers, and personal items. In Ferguson, Missouri, after the unrest in 2014, activists cleansed streets with burning sage and laid offerings. These are acts rooted in ancestral Hoodoo traditions.

TIP

Recognize this full circle of Hoodoo influence. Ring shouts and Hoodoo prayers that formerly helped people endure slavery have become energies that descendants of slaves now consciously invoke to confront contemporary injustice. This cycle underscores that Hoodoo has always been about Black freedom, survival, and well-being.

Answering the Hard Questions: Who Can Practice Hoodoo?

The increasing popularity of Hoodoo brings challenges in keeping it true to its roots. Internet openness means that many non-Black enthusiasts have appropriated Hoodoo spells, for example, by selling Hoodoo kits without understanding the cultural context or the history that created them.

The question of who can practice Hoodoo is contentious. Some practitioners say it's closed to non-Black people. Period. Others say it's not closed but requires deep respect and understanding that this is Black ancestral technology, not a spiritual buffet. This book won't settle that debate, but it will give you knowledge to engage in the conversation honestly.

Here are some points foundational to the debate:

- **Many Black practitioners emphasize that Hoodoo is African American heritage first, not simply a magical system that anyone can pick up.** Ongoing conversations about cultural respect involve elders admonishing seekers to approach with humility and learn history before attempting practice.
- **Younger African Americans proudly share how they discovered a grandparent's mojo bag in a drawer or realized mom's "tea" for bad dreams was actually a rootwork remedy.** These revelations bring families closer to ancestry. Hoodoo is no longer a shameful secret. It's increasingly seen as a badge of cultural resilience.

For everyone else? The conversation continues. Approach with humility. Learn the history. If you're interested in practicing Hoodoo, examine what you're asking for and why. Recognize that good intentions don't erase power dynamics or historical context.

TIP

Understand that some people may say "No, this isn't for you," and that boundary deserves respect. Others will say, "Of course you belong here. Welcome." Don't make them regret it.

Knowing what African American means in this context

Hoodoo is undeniably Black, but specifically African American. It was created here in the US by people whose descendants would become known as American Descendants of Slavery. Some use the term ADOS to distinguish Black Americans whose ancestors were enslaved in the US from more recent Black immigrants.

REMEMBER

This ADOS distinction matters because Hoodoo's practices aren't 100 percent African. As I mention throughout this chapter, enslaved Africans learned folk medicine and folk magic from European settlers and Native Americans — sometimes as allies, sometimes as fellow enslaved people, and sometimes through force. So the heritage being protected isn't pure African. It's African American synthesis, forged in specific historical circumstances.

Nearly all Black Americans who descend from the Transatlantic Slave Trade have European ancestry or Native American ancestry. This shared ancestry isn't just genetic. It's cultural. Hoodoo synthesized knowledge from multiple sources because survival demanded it and proximity produced it.

Considering where to learn Hoodoo practices

Hoodoo's African American synthesis raises complicated questions:

- Would a modern ADOS practitioner be wrong to learn about Central or West African cosmology — the spiritual seed of Hoodoo — from a Central or West African person who isn't ADOS?
- How about learning regional herbalism from a Native American instructor of a local tribe?
- Who would know more about Irish folk magic than an Irish or Irish American family that has practiced it for generations?
- If it's okay to learn from Native Americans and Irish descendants, is it okay for them to learn Hoodoo?

These questions aren't rhetorical. They're real tensions that practitioners of Hoodoo navigate.

Approaching the spiritual core of the debate

The spiritual component of Hoodoo tends to be the core point of contention, and for good reason. Consider these points of Hoodoo practice:

- **Venerating ancestors:** If Hoodoo's spirit work centers around veneration of ancestors who were enslaved or descended from the Transatlantic Slave Trade, which ancestors would someone without that lineage venerate? That piece gets lost when people treat Hoodoo like just another magical system to add to their collection.

  Asking "Which ancestors empower your work if you don't have those ancestors from the Transatlantic Slave Trade?" isn't gatekeeping. It's a genuine metaphysical question about how the practice functions.
- **Claiming an inheritance:** If Hoodoo is a magical inheritance that ancestors bestow on their descendants to help them gain edges against the many

disadvantages their new world and its institutions imposed on them, is it fair to ask for part of their inheritance if it isn't yours?

Is it fair to claim the protective power of Hoodoo without inheriting the hardships that come from being ADOS in the US?

These questions cut to the heart of why some practitioners say Hoodoo is closed. It's not gatekeeping for gatekeeping's sake. It's asking whether you can separate a survival technology from the people who needed it to survive, and whether taking it without living the context dishonors those who built it.

TIP

THINKING THROUGH AN ANALOGY

Consider a family that, across several generations of hardship, developed a body of knowledge: which herbs healed which ailments, which prayers warded off which dangers, how to read certain signs, how to call on their ancestors when trouble came. That knowledge was encoded and passed down specifically because the family needed it to survive. It kept them alive. It was also, in a very real sense, a gift from each generation to the next.

From one perspective, that knowledge belongs to the descendants of the people who created it. It wasn't developed in comfortable circumstances; it was forged in response to specific historical conditions. If the practice functions by calling on those particular ancestors, a practitioner who doesn't share that lineage isn't just culturally adjacent to the tradition; they're working with spiritual connections they don't actually have. And to claim the practice as their own, or profit from it, dishonors the people whose survival created it.

From another perspective, some practitioners argue that Hoodoo's own history as a *syncretic tradition*, one that absorbed knowledge from every available source and pragmatically used what worked, suggests the tradition has always been adaptive rather than rigidly bounded. These practitioners may welcome non-Black people into the practice under specific conditions: coming through a lineage holder who explicitly invites them, approaching with deep humility and historical grounding, and never positioning themselves as authorities or commercializing what they've been given. Proximity to the tradition through a practitioner who vouches for you, they argue, is its own form of lineage.

Neither of these positions is unreasonable. The debate is real, ongoing, and lived by practitioners, not just argued by academics. What most practitioners across both sides of the debate tend to agree on is this: Approach Hoodoo with humility, learn the history first, listen to ADOS voices, and examine honestly what you're seeking and why.

Retaining the community service tradition

Retaining Hoodoo's tradition of community service is where the questions about the practice become less complicated. Hoodoo has a long history of practitioners helping everybody who needed it. Root doctors served Black, white, and Native people — whoever came to them with a need. Marie Laveau, a renowned herbalist and midwife, worked with clients across racial lines. Dr. Buzzard, also known as Stepheney Robinson (sometimes spelled as Stephaney), who was well known for healing, curse-breaking, and fortune-telling, helped anyone who paid. The Hoodoo tradition has always been pragmatic about serving community needs, and the term *community* often meant the whole community, not just Black folks. That is Hoodoo's history and will likely be its future.

TIP

Despite the debate about who can learn and claim the practice of Hoodoo, there should be no debate about who practitioners can help, given the centuries-long history that answers that question. If you're an authentic Hoodoo practitioner, you can help yourself, help your community, and help whoever needs it.

Accepting multiracial, biracial, and adoptive family realities

All families don't present a simple lineage, which raises questions about who can and should practice Hoodoo. In fact, many configurations of families and their connections to Hoodoo exist:

- **Biracial Americans who have ADOS on one side of their family and something else on the other, say, Kenyan or Mexican-American.**
- **Interracial unions in which one partner is ADOS and practices Hoodoo, and the other isn't ADOS.** You have these questions:
  - Does the non-ADOS partner learn Hoodoo as part of family life?
  - If an ADOS practitioner teaches their non-ADOS spouse protective work or healing techniques for their household, is that cultural sharing within a family or transmission to someone outside the tradition?
  - If an ADOS practitioner wants to share Hoodoo knowledge with a non-ADOS parent or partner, how do they handle that?
- **Someone multiracial who's raised by a Black grandparent who taught them rootwork or biracial children of one ADOS and one non-ADOS parent.**

- Are they practicing their own heritage or appropriating their ancestors' heritage?
- Do they have access to Hoodoo as part of their ADOS heritage, even though it's only from one side?
- Are they "ADOS enough" if only one parent is? And who decides?

» **Children adopted by ADOS parents who raise them in the ADOS culture, teach them family practices, and help them participate in family spiritual life.**

- Are those children practicing their family's tradition or learning something that isn't theirs?
- Does cultural transmission through upbringing count differently than biological inheritance when the tradition is so tied to ancestral bloodlines?

These family configurations aren't fringe cases. They're increasingly common realities in families where Hoodoo has been passed down.

REMEMBER

KEEPING THE HOODOO CONVERSATION GOING

You won't find easy answers to the debate over who can and should practice Hoodoo. The community can discuss, listen, share, and grow on this topic, adapting as the practice itself always has.

What you can do to continue seeking answers:

- Study the history so you understand what you're engaging with
- Understand techniques and the Hoodoo knowledge base
- Embrace respect, context, and responsibility
- Listen to ADOS practitioners, especially elders
- Examine your own motivations and relationship to the tradition

The community is actively working to preserve Hoodoo's integrity while welcoming back African Americans whose families may have forgotten the old ways. That's where the clearest consensus exists. If Hoodoo is in your lineage, reclaim it.

Recognizing the Backbone of Hoodoo: Black Women as Keepers of the Flame

Across all developments in the history of Hoodoo, one theme stands out: Black women are the backbone of Hoodoo's survival and transmission. While men practice Hoodoo, it was often women — mothers, grandmothers, and aunties — who quietly kept traditions alive in families and communities.

Because of them, Hoodoo exists today as more than anthropological curiosity. It survives as the vibrant, evolving practice of folk spirituality — one that continues empowering and protecting Black communities.

Knowing why women became primary keepers

In African American culture, as in many others, women historically were primary healers, midwives, and caregivers. Enslaved women particularly were often herbal doctors on plantations, using knowledge to care for both Black and white people.

These women passed down remedies and rituals to children under the guise of "old custom" or "women's wisdom." After emancipation, the conjure woman or granny healer remained vital, especially in rural areas where medical access was scarce and Black people faced hospital segregation.

Hoodoo became part of cultural inheritance that mothers gave their children as a protection means in a hostile world. As one practitioner writes: "In our community, intergenerational wealth is hard to come by, so the practices passed down act as a different sort of currency to support us through life. The guardians and preservers of this wealth are mostly women, of course."

Children learned to sweep evil out the door or place water by the bed to catch bad dreams because an older female relative insisted. Such small acts, repeated over generations, kept Hoodoo lore alive without fanfare.

Exploring women's role in Black church and community leadership

Black women's Hoodoo role intertwines with their role in Black church and community leadership. While 20th-century literature often sensationalized male conjure doctors, the day-to-day reality is that women were doing much of rootwork. They prepared healing teas in kitchens, said prayers over children, sewed mojo bags into clothes, and taught about signs and omens to heed.

As folklorist Kameelah Martin writes: "Our mothers, grandmothers, and aunts teach us the rules to living productively with the dead." She's referring to how elders instruct the young about honoring ancestors and respecting spiritual forces.

REMEMBER

The spiritual aspect of Hoodoo at its core involves maintaining relationships with ancestors, spirits, and forces. Women have been the primary mediators, whether as mediums, dream interpreters, or ritual leaders in family ceremonies.

Seeing modern women leading the revival

Today, Black women entrepreneurs lead the forefront of Hoodoo's resurgence. They open businesses and online shops and teach others, much like their foremothers, but with new platforms:

- Authors such as Katrina Hazzard-Donald and Yvonne Chireau have researched and written about Hoodoo's history and meaning.
- Younger practitioners — calling themselves *conjure women* or *Hoodoo sisters* — emphasize that Hoodoo is African American family heritage, not a commodity, and encourage reconnection with ancestral practices.
- The rise of movements like #BlackLivesMatter depicts Black women healers conducting ceremonies for community healing and protection. These ceremonies include prayer circles, candle vigils for violence victims, and libation rituals at tragedy sites.

I can't overstate Black American women's special role in Hoodoo. From slavery-era root doctors to Appalachian granny witches to urban church mothers, women secretly carried the fire through generations. They kept recipes, told stories, preserved taboos and customs, and ensured Hoodoo remained a living tradition.

As one modern rootworker recalls: "I saw Hoodoo practitioners who were mainly Black women. Black women played a role in their communities as midwives, healers, and conjure women for their clients."

The grandmothers and aunties of Hoodoo truly deserve honor as the keepers of the flame.

IN THIS CHAPTER

» Understanding Hoodoo as resistance magic at its foundation

» Discovering how African traditions shaped values and women's authority in rootwork

» Learning how enslaved people weaponized forced Christianity for liberation

» Seeing how different cultures contributed to Hoodoo's character and values

» Knowing why cultural roots matter for choosing when to work with Hoodoo

Chapter 3
Examining Hoodoo's Cultural Roots

I want you to consider these questions regarding the nature and practice of Hoodoo:

» Why does Hoodoo treat women rootworkers as equals or even leaders when the broader culture doesn't?

» Why is the Bible used as a spell book and talisman instead of just a devotional text?

» Why does Hoodoo say "use what works" instead of following rigid orthodox rules?

The answers to these questions lie in Hoodoo's cultural roots. And when I use the word *roots*, I'm not just talking about where natural ingredients and remedies came from; I'm including the values that different peoples brought when shaping how Hoodoo operates.

This chapter isn't about ethnic shopping lists in the form of "Africans contributed X and Europeans contributed Y." It's about understanding what makes Hoodoo *authentic*. It's the cultural DNA that makes it different from other magical traditions. In this chapter, I show you how the element of resistance shaped the backbone of Hoodoo, how multiple cultural influences fused into a new practice, and why these roots matter when you're deciding whether using Hoodoo is right for your situation.

Embracing the Foundation of Resistance Magic

Everything in Hoodoo flows from one core reality: It was born as resistance magic. When I say Hoodoo is *resistance magic*, I mean that it was created by enslaved people (primarily in the southern US) who were facing brutal oppression. This basis of Hoodoo isn't empowerment in the modern self-help sense. It involves resistance against subjugation, survival methods, and fighting back.

Hoodoo didn't focus on abstract spirituality. This practice was life-or-death problem-solving. The enslaved people who developed Hoodoo needed spiritual power to do the following:

- **Escape physically** by laying confusion tricks on roads and crossroads to disorient slave catchers and their dogs
- **Protect themselves** by deflecting violence, making overseers overlook them, and constructing spiritual shields
- **Harm oppressors** by poisoning brutal enslavers, sending spiritual attacks, and creating justice when existing laws couldn't
- **Maintain identity** by keeping African spiritual practices alive despite forced Christianity
- **Empower psychologically** by providing courage workings, as Henry Bibb documented when he sought conjurers before escape attempts
- **Survive impossible circumstances** by getting physical healing when medical care was denied and helping each other when institutions excluded them

When enslaved people synthesized Hoodoo from multiple cultural sources, they chose every element strategically. Their choices weren't random mixing of methods and traditions but, instead, embodied *resistance engineering:* building a spiritual technology from whatever tools were available.

The founding engineers of Hoodoo used various elements to construct a solid base:

- **African spirit work** because they needed power that white enslavers couldn't control
- **Christian Bible verses** that turned the oppressor's religious weapon into liberation magic
- **Native American plant knowledge,** which helped source local materials for healing and resistance
- **Jewish Kabbalistic texts** that offered written formulas when literacy became accessible
- **Islamic amulet traditions,** particularly the West African practice of sealing sacred written texts into carried pouches, which shaped the mojo bag's basic logic
- **European grimoires** whose spells and invocations they adapted to work for their needs (discarding the parts of these books that didn't work)

REMEMBER

Understanding Hoodoo as resistance magic isn't just historical trivia. It tells you when Hoodoo is especially suited: when you're facing systemic injustice, when you need to fight back spiritually, when you're surviving with limited resources, and when you need power despite material powerlessness.

TIP

If you're looking for gentle manifest-your-dreams spirituality, Hoodoo might not be your best fit. But if you need to resist something, Hoodoo was built for exactly that.

Exposing African Matriarchal Roots and Communal Values

When you walk into any Hoodoo community, you'll see women rootworkers treated as equals or leaders. Whether they're two-headed doctors who deal with both natural medicine and spiritual forces, root doctors who offer natural healing, spiritual mothers who provide wisdom and guidance, or queens who lead and take strategic action, women hold authority in the practice of Hoodoo. (Chapter 2 gives you more information about women as the backbone of Hoodoo.)

This recognition of women's importance and leadership didn't exist in broader American society, especially during slavery and the Jim Crow era. (Get more information about Hoodoo during Jim Crow in the section "Looking at African communal values" later in this chapter.)

So why was the position and authority of women respected in Hoodoo? The next section explains the root of this respect in African tradition.

West and Central African matriarchal traditions

Many of the African peoples brought to America came from cultures in which women held significant spiritual and social authority. This is particularly true of Yoruba, Fon, Ewe, and various Central African groups. Women were active in the following roles:

- **Priestesses:** In Vodun traditions, women served as powerful priestesses, not just assistants.
- **Healers:** Herbal medicine and midwifery were often women's domains.
- **Business operators:** Market women in West Africa controlled commerce and wealth.
- **Spirit mediums:** Possession and channeling spirits was often women's expertise.

REMEMBER

Also, some African groups traced *matrilineal descent*, or tracing their lineage through mothers. This, too, gave women structural power in society. These positions and activities for women weren't just beliefs; they were operational social structures that carried over into Hoodoo practice.

Why the traditions survived in Hoodoo and influence modern practice

Hoodoo developed somewhat separately from mainstream American institutions, which meant African values about women's authority could persist. Consider Marie Laveau, the famous New Orleans Voodoo Queen. She wasn't an exception; she was an example of a long tradition of powerful women practitioners of African descent.

The resistance nature of Hoodoo (see the section "Embracing the Foundation of Resistance Magic" earlier in the chapter) meant that competence mattered more than gender. Spiritual power didn't require male institutional approval, and rootwork was based on community, meaning it wasn't institutionally controlled. Because enslaved communities needed every capable person to work, they couldn't afford to ignore women's talents and expertise in herbs, midwifery, and healing.

For the modern practice of Hoodoo, the African matriarchal heritage means that

- Women practitioners aren't trying to "break barriers" in Hoodoo. They're continuing tradition.
- Female rootworkers often trace lineages through their mothers and grandmothers.
- Gender hierarchy isn't built into Hoodoo's spiritual structure.
- Both men and women can be "queens" or "kings." It's about spiritual power, not gender.

TIP

If you're a woman interested in rootwork, understand that you're entering a tradition where women have always held authority. You're not an outsider asking for acceptance; you're coming home to a practice that was often carried by women. And if you're a man? Respect the heritage of women in Hoodoo. Some of your best teachers will be women.

Looking at African communal values

Individual success matters in Hoodoo, but that success is framed within community survival. (Chapter 12 offers a closer look at the individual and community faces of Hoodoo.) This dual approach reflects African communal values that persist in Hoodoo despite the prevalence of American individualism.

Here's a glimpse of the African communal orientation, how it shaped Hoodoo tradition, how it supported community during transitions, and how it affects modern Hoodoo practice.

Many African societies operated on communal rather than individualistic principles, such as these:

- Extended family structures that go beyond nuclear families
- Shared resources with the goal being what benefits one, benefits all
- Collective responsibility so that the village raises the child
- Mutual protection to ensure community defense, not just individual safety
- Shared spiritual practice in which ceremony is communal event

Rootworkers traditionally served their communities, not just individual clients. For example, they provided the following:

- Protection work for the whole neighborhood
- Healing available to those who couldn't pay
- Training for the next generation of practitioners
- Sharing of knowledge within the community
- Community rituals to address shared concerns

REMEMBER

This community focus is why some older rootworkers say that modern commercial Hoodoo feels wrong. It's too individualistic, transactional, and disconnected from community. To them, if you are not answering to a community, you are not really practicing Hoodoo.

During slavery and Jim Crow, Hoodoo was part of larger mutual aid networks:

- Rootworkers worked with midwives, healers, and community organizers.
- Spiritual protection supported Underground Railroad work.
- Crossing powders protected escaping people from *night riders,* which were patrols that tried to interfere with escape.
- Healing work compensated for Black people being excluded from medical care.
- Community defense was spiritual and practical.

For modern Hoodoo practitioners, the community-focused heritage suggests that you should commit yourself to five things:

- Practicing Hoodoo to benefit more than just yourself
- Considering how your work affects your community
- Supporting other practitioners rather than hoard knowledge
- Sharing what you learn appropriately
- Remembering that you stand on the ancestors' shoulders

TIP

The shift from community-focused to individual-focused Hoodoo is relatively recent (post-1980s commercialization). Original Hoodoo was about collective survival and mutual aid. When you practice today, consider whether your work serves just you, or your community. Both focuses can be valid uses of Hoodoo, but knowing the traditional communal roots helps you practice with integrity.

Exploring the Influences of Religion on Hoodoo Roots

The developmental roots of Hoodoo incorporated tools and practices from various forms of religion and spirituality. Resistance engineers used these elements to fill their arsenal. In this section, I cover the influences of Christian and Jewish theologies that you find in the practice of Hoodoo.

Using the Bible as a resistance tool

Enslavers forced Christianity on enslaved Africans to (supposedly) make them docile. Instead, enslaved people took the Bible, weaponized it, and turned it into liberation magic. This is one of Hoodoo's most brilliant cultural moves.

Forced Christianity and strategic response

White enslavers thought teaching Christianity would make enslaved people submissive. Their message was to obey your masters, accept your lot, and wait for heaven. Fortunately, the enslaved people embraced the Bible's contents and heard completely different messages:

- **Moses and exodus:** The enslaved became the Israelites, the enslavers became the Egyptians, and God liberated the oppressed.
- **Psalms as power:** These anthems weren't just prayers; they were formulas for protection and justice.
- **Jesus as liberator:** The enslaved didn't choose the turn-the-other-cheek version of Jesus. Instead, they opted for the Jesus who overturned tables and challenged authority.
- **Old Testament justice:** The early Hoodoo practitioners turned to the eye-for-an-eye, plagues on oppressors, and divine retribution forms of biblical justice.

REMEMBER

The Bible became the ultimate Trojan horse inside the slave system. The enslaved could carry the Bible openly, quote it freely, and use it for resistance while enslavers assumed it was making them compliant.

Psalms became spells

Jewish Kabbalistic influence (which you can read about in the next section) integrated beautifully with the Bible's book of Psalms. When books like *Secrets of the*

Psalms became available through Jewish mail-order merchants in the 1930s and 1940s, they brought with them the idea that specific Psalms had specific magical purposes:

- Psalm 23 was a spell for protection.
- Psalm 35 was for defeating enemies.
- Psalm 91 was for safety.
- Psalm 109 was for cursing oppressors.

Rootworkers didn't need permission to recite Psalms because that practice reflected "being Christian." But they were doing magic. The Bible prayer book became a spell book hidden in plain sight.

Hoodoo is Christian-compatible but not Christian-submissive

The biblical roots and Christian heritage associated with Hoodoo mean that Hoodoo practitioners can be devoutly Christian *and* practice rootwork. They treat the Bible as a powerful magical text, not just devotional reading material.

Liberation theology is baked into Hoodoo's interpretation of the Bible. The message isn't "obey authority." Instead, the takeaway is "God liberates the oppressed." You can practice Hoodoo as a Christian or not. Most practitioners do. But the Christianity involved in Hoodoo is liberation Christianity and resistance Christianity, not the obedience version enslavers tried to force.

WARNING

Don't mistake Hoodoo's use of the Bible for Christian fundamentalism. When rootworkers use Psalms and Bible verses, they're not literalists worried about biblical correctness; they're practitioners using powerful texts that work for them. The Bible is a respected and effective tool in Hoodoo that itself is treated as a talisman, but it doesn't restrict the practice to narrow doctrinal boxes.

Text-heavy magic: The Jewish Kabbalistic contribution

In the 1930s and 1940s, the same forces that put Jewish refugee scholars in historically Black colleges and universities (HBCUs) also put Jewish merchants in Black communities via spiritual supply shops. In these shops, the mystical, esoteric methods of *Jewish Kabbalistic tradition* (aimed at growing closer to God and repairing the world) became available to Hoodoo practitioners. This integration introduced a more literate, text-heavy dimension to Hoodoo.

Here's what Jewish mysticism brought to Hoodoo's development:

- **Written formulas** that documented spells and procedures.
- **Psalm magic** that tied specific Psalms to specific purposes.
- **Angel names** used to call on specific spiritual entities by name.
- **Sacred geometry** represented by seals, sigils (magical symbols), and diagrams that have power. In the Jewish Kabbalistic tradition, sacred geometry symbols include the Star of David.
- **Systematic documentation** that provides written magical systems versus strictly oral tradition.
- **Logos magic,** which is the power of the written word itself.

How Jewish mysticism entered Hoodoo practice

Jewish merchants and publishers sold Kabbalistic texts to the Hoodoo community. In addition to spiritual shops, they advertised in Black-owned newspapers such as the *Chicago Defender* and offered mail-order spiritual supplies.

Harry Middleton Hyatt's interviews with 1,600 Hoodoo practitioners in the 1930s documented that Memphis rootworkers specifically named these books as sources that could supplement resistance magic:

- ***Secrets of the Psalms*** (Godfrey A. Selig), which presents ways to connect with higher consciousness and past lives, became hugely popular.
- ***Sixth and Seventh Books of Moses***, in its various compilations, is a grimoire that contains Jewish mystical elements.

This integration of structured tools attempted to create a more scholastic, literate branch of Hoodoo in which some practitioners embraced written formulas and systematic study over maintaining a purely oral tradition. But many practitioners combined both aspects: They learned from elders *and* read books.

The incorporation of the literate branch of Hoodoo may have created some tension between traditional (oral) and book-learning approaches, but the developing practice of Hoodoo became big enough to encompass both experiential/oral and textual/scholarly aspects.

Why incorporating literacy matters

Modern Hoodoo benefits from both the oral wisdom of lineage holders and the documentation that makes learning about Hoodoo accessible. The integration of a more scholarly approach that happened with the Jewish Kabbalistic influence shows Hoodoo's openness to literacy and documentation when it serves practitioners by the following:

- Recognizing value in written knowledge, but not seeking legitimacy from Hoodoo outsiders
- Preserving formulas, ensuring consistency in practices, aiding the teaching of Hoodoo, and applying the use-what-works core culture to written as well as orally kept knowledge

TECHNICAL STUFF

The 1930s and 1940s overlap between Jewish HBCU professors and Jewish spiritual merchants isn't coincidence. Both reflected the same historical moment: Jewish refugees fleeing Nazi persecution found solidarity with African Americans facing Jim Crow. Some refugees became professors at Black colleges. Others became shopkeepers and publishers serving Black spiritual communities. These were parallel manifestations of mutual recognition between persecuted peoples.

Ecstatic Worship, Spirit Possession, and Pragmatic Practice

Have you ever wondered why Black church services look and feel different from white Protestant services? Why "getting happy," speaking in tongues, being "slain in the spirit," and full-body worship are normal? Those elements of worship are African spiritual technology carried through Hoodoo culture.

West African possession traditions

In Vodun, Orisha worship, and other African traditions, spirit possession was central to worship and reflected the idea of the full body participating in the ritual.

Spirit possession wasn't demonic or scary; instead, it served to connect the participants with the divine.

During spirit possession, the spirits would mount practitioners (literally riding them like horses) and tag along with their physical expression of spirit through dancing, shouting, speaking differently, falling, and so on. Also, these traditions include the community witness and support of the possession that happens in group contexts.

REMEMBER

This spirit possession wasn't losing control; it was a sophisticated spiritual technology for communication with divine forces.

In this list, you can find aspects of African worship traditions that have been adopted and adapted as Hoodoo developed, the aspects of Hoodoo that require the physical side of these African traditions, and the core Hoodoo value that places results above doctrine:

- **When African spiritual practices were forbidden, they went underground or became integrated into acceptable Christian worship.** For example,
  - *Possession* became receiving the Holy Ghost.
  - *Dancing* became shouting.
  - *Spirit communication* became prophesying.
  - *Ecstatic trance* became getting happy.

  The form looked Christian, but the technology was African.
- **Hoodoo isn't just intellectual knowledge. It's also a practice, an embodiment, and a relationship with spiritual forces.**
  - Spirit work in Hoodoo isn't abstract; it's experiential, embodied, and intense.
  - Rootworkers may enter altered states to commune with spirits or ancestors.
  - Physical sensations such as tingling, heat, and chills are signs of spiritual presence.
  - The boundary between church and rootwork is porous, and many practitioners move between them.

» **A core Hoodoo value sets it apart from many spiritual traditions: Results matter more than orthodoxy.** When you're enslaved and fighting for survival, you don't have the luxury of doctrinal purity:

- You can't afford to reject some tool or method just because it's not traditional.
- You need every tool that produces results.
- You must adapt to circumstances that change constantly.
- You must recognize that community survival matters more than individual correctness.

Hoodoo's pragmatism in practice

Pragmatism is why Hoodoo has survived four hundred years. Rigid systems can break under pressure, but adaptive systems evolve. When you practice Hoodoo, you're inheriting this adaptability. But use it wisely. The mantra *use what works* doesn't mean that you can completely ignore lineage, heritage, and collective wisdom. Instead, you must learn from those who came before, test your methods honestly, and refine your work based on results. Hoodoo says to understand the principle and then work with what you have. The resistance mindset — improvise, adapt, and overcome — is baked into the practice itself.

TIP

Pragmatism doesn't mean that anything goes. You have principles, lineages, and respected practices to draw from when you practice Hoodoo. But you don't have orthodoxy police telling you "that's not real Hoodoo."

Check out Table 3-1, which contrasts Hoodoo adaptiveness and pragmatism with rigid magical systems.

TABLE 3-1 Hoodoo versus Rigid Magic

Hoodoo Says	Rigid Magic Demands
If unique Christian prayers work, use them.	Specific magic wording must be exact.
If herbs from another tradition are effective, incorporate their use.	Rituals have precise steps that can't vary.
If modern materials (magnetic sand) can replace traditional ones (lodestone), use what's available.	Materials must be authentic.
If a new technique produces better results, switch your technique.	Deviation from the ceremony means failure.

Infusing the Cultures of Regional Hoodoo

Although it's unified by common African American core beliefs, Hoodoo isn't monolithic. Over centuries it evolved into distinct regional styles influenced by local environment, cultural mix, and time period. These branches didn't emerge simultaneously. Some are older, maintaining closer ties to African origins, while others developed later as Hoodoo spread and adapted.

TECHNICAL STUFF

The terms and categories you find in this section — *Lowcountry Hoodoo, Louisiana Hoodoo, Appalachian Hoodoo,* and so on — aren't universally codified names. Many practitioners have never heard of these labels. However, these categorizations are gaining traction among scholars, authors, and contemporary practitioners because they organize and visualize how, where, and when Hoodoo spread and adapted across America. Think of them as useful frameworks for understanding diversity within the tradition, not rigid boxes that every practitioner can fit into.

Lowcountry Hoodoo (coastal Carolinas and Georgia)

Lowcountry Hoodoo is often regarded as the oldest and most "African" form. It's been around since the 1600s and has deep Gullah-Geechee culture roots. In swampy lowlands and Sea Islands, enslaved Africans were relatively isolated on rice or cotton plantations beginning in the late 1600s and continuing through the 1800s. The high ratio of African-born people and isolation allowed West and Central African spiritual customs to survive with less dilution than anywhere else in North America.

Key features of this cultural impact on Lowcountry Hoodoo include

- Strong emphasis on ancestor veneration and spirit communication
- Incorporation of Kongo Cosmogram (which I introduce in Chapter 2) and reverence for water spirits
- Use of rivers, oceans, and marshes as powerful conduits for spiritual work, echoing African water spirits and the importance of crossing water for cleansing and hex-breaking

Lowcountry conjure is often seen as a *way of life* — inherited folkways to cope with hardships rather than a separate mystical vocation. This branch of Hoodoo retains a proud sense of African heritage and autonomy that's relatively uninfluenced by mainstream American culture.

Louisiana Hoodoo (New Orleans and Gulf Coast)

In Louisiana — especially New Orleans — Hoodoo took unique Creole character beginning in the French colonial period of the early 1700s. The character intensifying through Spanish rule and the influx of Haitian refugees after the Haitian Revolution that lasted from 1791 to 1804. Often called *New Orleans Hoodoo*, this branch developed in a cosmopolitan port where African, French, Spanish, Caribbean, and Native American cultures collided over centuries.

Lines between Hoodoo and Voodoo blurred because of the culture collision. New Orleans Voodoo is a religion derived from Haitian Vodou and African spirituality; New Orleans Hoodoo typically focuses on the spell-craft and rootwork side of Hoodoo practice. Following are three key features of this Hoodoo branch:

- ***Gris-gris***, which are small charm bags or packets containing roots, herbs, minerals, written prayers for luck, love, protection, or *cursing* (a term for spell-casting from the African Mandé language)
- **Catholic saints, candles, and icons** incorporated into spells alongside traditional conjure curios such as graveyard dirt or black cat bones
- **Elaborate rituals** that use colored glass prayer candles, veve-like symbols (which represent and invoke specific spirits) drawn in powders, and midnight ceremonies at crossroads or cemeteries

Louisiana Hoodoo retains ceremonial flair and syncretic nature. It's not unusual for practitioners to also identify as Vodou priests and priestesses or Catholic devotees.

Appalachian Hoodoo (mountain folk magic)

Also called *Appalachian folk magic* or *granny magic*, this branch of Hoodoo developed in rural Appalachia (eastern Kentucky, Tennessee, West Virginia, western North Carolina) primarily during the 1800s as the region was settled by various groups. It's the least African-influenced branch. Some experts debate whether the practice should be called *Hoodoo* at all.

The Appalachian region was populated largely by Scots-Irish, English, German settlers, Cherokee and other Native peoples, and comparatively fewer African Americans. Mountain folk healers were often elderly women called *granny witches*. They drew on European folk magic (British Isles herbal lore, midwifery, and German powwow) and Native American plant knowledge.

When Native Americans taught enslaved Africans about local plants, they didn't just share what plants to use. They shared information about how to work with plants and reinforced the culture of establishing a whole relationship to the land. In addition to local plant knowledge, such as which plants heal, which can harm, and what grows where, they offered advice regarding the nature of local territories, harvesting responsibly, shared resistance, and mutual aid strategies for isolated communities.

Over time, Appalachian folk magic incorporated some elements from African American Hoodoo based on knowledge shared by Black people who moved into the mountains or escaped slavery via the Underground Railroad. However, African contributions were relatively limited.

Southern Plains Hoodoo (Texas, Oklahoma, and Kansas)

A less-discussed branch of Hoodoo developed among African Americans in Southern Plains states during the late 19th and early 20th centuries. After the Civil War, Black communities formed here from groups such as *Exodusters* (Black people migrating to the plains states from the South), *Black freedmen* formerly enslaved among Native American nations in Oklahoma (forced there during Indian Removal), and many Black Texans remaining post-emancipation.

The practice of Southern Plains Hoodoo incorporated African-derived formulas in combination with the use of cornmeal and sage (learned from the neighboring Native Americans) and the rich diversity of flora and fauna not found in the East, including pecans, chili peppers, cotton bolls, rattlesnake rattles, and coyote bones. The practice is closely integrated with Black church life. Many practitioners never called it *Hoodoo*; to them, it's just the way Grandma prayed.

Urban and commercial Hoodoo

The Great Migration brought Black people from the rural South to urban centers across the North, Midwest, and West. Hoodoo came with them, and city life shaped it into something new. Commercial suppliers emerged. Mail-order catalogs and shops offered condition oils, incense powders, candle kits, sachet powders, and curios. Some were legitimate Black herbalists using traditional formulas. Many were white, immigrant entrepreneurs with no Hoodoo background who saw a profitable niche and marketed exotic-sounding items with flashy labels.

This commercialization changed the practice. Where old-time conjure doctors personally gathered and prayed over each root, now many bought ready-made preparations. Hoodoo spell books were often written by white authors under exotic pseudonyms. They gained popularity but distorted Hoodoo by focusing on quick-fix spells disconnected from deeper spiritual context.

REMEMBER

Authentic Hoodoo survives in urban environments within invisible institutions such as Christian prayer groups, spiritualist churches, and home circles. Practitioners adapted: If you couldn't sacrifice a chicken in your backyard, you could use eggs or store-bought meat symbolically; if you had no river to throw ritual items into, you could use crossroads at midnight or flush things down the toilet.

Diasporan and solo practitioners

Beyond geographic branches of Hoodoo exists a vast, often invisible network of practitioners who don't fit neatly into a category. These are individuals and families all over the US and abroad whose ancestors retained fragments of Hoodoo knowledge but lost the full context.

You can find these solo and diasporan practitioners everywhere the African American diaspora reaches. In other words, they're worldwide. A Black British family descended from Caribbean immigrants might have Grandmother's old ways that trace back through the Caribbean to the African American US South. A Black family in Paris might have practices brought by great-grandparents who migrated during WWI or WWII. A family in California might have techniques that came west during the Dust Bowl migrations.

Diaspora refers to the spread of a people outside their homeland.

This diffuse, decentralized knowledge reflects Hoodoo's resilience, culture of heritage, and adaptive nature. It didn't require institutions to survive. It encoded itself in families, in a common sense, in the-way-we-do-things approach. When someone in Seattle who's never heard the term *Hoodoo* puts a glass of water by their bed because Grandma always did it, they're part of this invisible branch.

REGENERATIVE VERSUS EXTRACTIVE HERBALISM

Modern rootworkers face a challenge: Many traditional plants used in Hoodoo practice are now endangered in part because of over-harvesting for commercial Hoodoo supplies. Honor the Native American contribution by practicing Hoodoo herbalism *regeneratively*. That is, grow your own plants when possible, source plants sustainably, never strip a plant bare, and give back to the land that feeds your practice.

Note the differences between the extractive (European) and regenerative (Native American) approaches to herbalism:

Extractive Approach	Regenerative Approach
Harvest maximum amount	Harvest sustainably
Plants are resources to exploit	Plants are relatives and allies
Relationship is transactional	Relationship is reciprocal
How much can I get?	How do we both thrive?

The regenerative approach isn't just nice. It's also practical. If you destroy your herb sources, you can't practice. The regenerative practice ensures long-term access.

Seeing Why Cultural Roots Matter for Your Practice

In the previous sections of this chapter, you can find out about Hoodoo's cultural DNA and all the pieces that go into it. Understanding these cultural roots is important and can influence your practice of Hoodoo's resistance magic.

Respecting the cultural roots involves understanding why Hoodoo developed the way it did. You embrace the core values that Hoodoo's development and culture have set for you, including these:

- **Resistance to systemic forces** that direct you to face oppression, confront injustice, and oppose institutions that harm you and the community
- **Fierce spiritual power** that goes beyond gentle light and love, to embrace the power to fight back

- **Survival magic** in which you can work with limited resources, make do, and improvise
- **Results-focused work** that targets what you need and not just what feels good
- **Maintaining dignity under pressure** to invoke spiritual strength when material power is denied
- **Protection that includes an offense** so you can defend yourself and combat those who seek to harm you
- **Pragmatic spirituality,** which dictates that you use what works, discard what doesn't, and adapt to circumstances

REMEMBER

You don't have to be African American to benefit from Hoodoo. The tradition has always adapted and included allies. But you do need to understand and respect the cultural roots. This practice is resistance magic built by brilliant people under brutal oppression. Treat Hoodoo accordingly: Learn the history and culture, honor the ancestors, and use it wisely and well.

The cultures that built Hoodoo didn't contribute ingredients to a recipe. They contributed the values of resistance, pragmatism, community, and survival. Those values are the practice. Everything else — the roots, the psalms, the regional variations — is how those values take physical form.

IN THIS CHAPTER

» Understanding the folk science and folk engineering aspects of Hoodoo

» Exploring how rootworkers observe, test, and refine through empirical methods

» Discovering the technologies that practitioners engineer from available materials

» Finding out how systematic knowledge is documented and transmitted

» Balancing empirical observation with spiritual openness in your practice

Chapter 4
Classifying the Study of Hoodoo

When Frederick Douglass was a teenager enslaved under brutal conditions on a Maryland farm, a fellow enslaved man named Sandy Jenkins gave him a root to carry in his pocket. It was High John the Conqueror root, the ultimate protective charm in Hoodoo. Douglass, ever the rationalist, was skeptical. But he carried it anyway.

What happened next changed his life. Armed with the root, Douglass stood up to his tormentor for the first time, fought back, and won. Years later, writing about the incident across three separate memoirs spanning 50 years, Douglass remained uncertain: Was it the magic in the root? Or was it the belief in himself that the root gave him? "I saw in Sandy too deep an insight into human nature, with all his superstition, not to have some respect for his advice," he wrote.

Here's what Douglass knew for certain: Having the root worked. Whether through spiritual power, psychological empowerment, or both, that root helped a terrified boy become a man who would never be enslaved in spirit again.

That's Hoodoo. It doesn't require you to believe one explanation over another. It requires results. And the practitioners who developed this tradition — the innovators, the experimenters, the clever engineers of survival — built a practice that's sophisticated enough to produce those results across four centuries.

This chapter examines how Hoodoo operates as folk science and folk engineering. Some practitioners use their powers of observation, experimentation, evaluation of methods and results, and process improvement strategies to improve the practice of Hoodoo. These aspects of Hoodoo point to a structured science and engineering mindset.

Not every practitioner works this way. Many operate on faith, and that faith is psychologically powerful and valid. But the Hoodoo tradition itself was built by people who observed carefully, tested systematically, and engineered brilliant solutions to impossible problems. That's the lineage you're learning from.

Defining Hoodoo's Roots in Science and Engineering

Before diving into how Hoodoo operates as folk science and folk engineering, I want to explain what these two terms mean and why they fit the practice of Hoodoo without diminishing the spiritual power of the tradition.

REMEMBER

The terms *folk science* and *folk engineering* don't make Hoodoo less spiritual or magical. They reveal another facet of sophistication. Hoodoo's innovators — the people who built and refined this tradition — were careful observers, systematic experimenters, and creative engineers. Honoring the ancestors means recognizing their genius and respecting their methods. They built solid knowledge systems when educational institutions excluded them, and they built these systems well enough to work for four hundred years.

Hoodoo as folk science

Folk science is community-based knowledge built through long observation, systematic testing, and continuous refinement. It involves the empirical production of knowledge that happens outside universities and laboratories but follows the same basic principles: observe, hypothesize, test, refine, transmit verified results.

Here's what makes the practice of Hoodoo folk science. Its design and methodology have these characteristics:

- **Empirical:** They're based on observation and experience, not just theory.
- **Testable:** The claims regarding results can be examined and verified through practice.
- **Replicable:** Results are examined for consistency when practice conditions are repeated.
- **Refinable:** The knowledge gained improves through continued testing and correction.
- **Transmittable:** The shared knowledge is document, passed on, and improved over generations.
- **Community-validated:** Multiple practitioners work in conjunction to confirm what works.

Folk science simply operates outside universities, corporate labs, and institutional gatekeeping. The scientific part is no less rigorous, but it's accountable to different communities and measured by different metrics.

Hoodoo's early practitioners and innovators were folk scientists. They weren't sloppy and disorganized, instead, they practiced and improved their craft carefully by doing three things:

- **Experimenting with plants** to identify which ones poisoned oppressors effectively and which ones healed their own communities.
- **Observing the stars and planets** and using astronomy and astrology interchangeably (they didn't distinguish) to determine optimal timing for the application of their work.
- **Testing combinations of ingredients,** refining formulas, and passing on verified knowledge.

The boundary between agricultural science and rootwork was often nonexistent. The same person who knew which crop rotation could restore soil also knew which roots could restore a person's luck.

Hoodoo as folk engineering

Folk engineering is hands-on invention and practical design that focuses on building devices, processes, and work-arounds by using whatever materials are available. The engineering involves creative problem-solving that produces functional technologies (tools, systems, methods) without the benefit of formal training or institutional resources.

Here's what makes the tradition of Hoodoo folk engineering. The ongoing practice is marked by the following characteristics:

- **Problem-focused:** It starts with real needs that the community must solve for.
- **Resource-adaptive:** Hoodoo remedies and charms work with whatever materials are available.
- **Iterative:** Practitioners build, test, and improve formulas and methods through cycles of refinement.
- **Functional:** It measures results by whether the remedies work.
- **Creative:** The progress of Hoodoo requires innovation and improvisation.
- **Practical:** Hoodoo engineers design their works for real-world conditions, not laboratory perfection.

Early Hoodoo innovators embraced the folk engineering role and focused their efforts on these practical results:

- **Designing acoustic systems in praise houses:** These structures amplified sound inward so the community could worship loudly while muffling it outward so overseers couldn't hear.
- **Engineering the Underground Railroad as a communication and navigation system** that used coded songs, quilt patterns, and astronomical navigation with instructions such as "follow the Drinking Gourd north." The Drinking Gourd was their name for the Big Dipper constellation.
- **Developing botanical chemistry for both healing and resistance,** creating medicines that saved lives and poisons that ended the lives of brutal oppressors.

Hoodoo's Empirical Foundations: The Science

As I mention earlier in the chapter, not every Hoodoo practitioner operates empirically. Many work on pure faith when they trust the formula because Grandmother taught it. They believe in the spirits without needing proof, and they carry a mojo bag because faith in its power is what they need psychologically. That approach to Hoodoo is completely valid.

But the tradition itself — the formulas, techniques, and knowledge that's passed down — was built by a variety of innovators, including those who observed, tested, and refined. Those innovators created a knowledge system that works whether you understand the mechanisms or not. This section explores how that empirical foundation operates.

Observation and pattern recognition

The innovators in Hoodoo were (and are) keen observers of the natural, social, and spiritual worlds. These observations form the foundation of their knowledge:

» **Natural patterns:** The innovators seek knowledge by asking and answering questions. Which plants grow where? When do they bloom? What conditions affect their potency? Which plants heal and which ones kill?

  For example, generations of rootworkers noted that High John the Conqueror root grows in specific conditions, that they must gather certain herbs at particular times, and that moon phases affect plant properties.

» **Astronomical patterns:** Practitioners observed the stars and planets carefully, using an integrated knowledge that's currently separated into astronomy and astrology. For example, they tracked lunar phases for timing their work, used the Big Dipper for navigation on the Underground Railroad, and noted seasonal patterns for gathering materials.

» **Botanical chemistry:** Through careful observation and testing, practitioners learn which plants contained compounds that could poison oppressors, which ones healed illness, which ones induced abortion or contraception, and which ones altered consciousness. This process produces a practical chemistry through systematic experimentation that tests dosages, observes effects, and refines methods.

» **Social and psychological patterns:** Innovators observe human psychology and social dynamics as carefully as they observe plants. They seek to discover

  - What behaviors consistently lead to what outcomes?
  - If someone carries themselves with confidence, do others treat them differently?
  - Does having something to believe in (like a mojo bag) give people courage to act?

As I also recount in Chapter 2, numerous accounts from escaped enslaved people documented the practice of rubbing graveyard dirt on their feet or sprinkling it behind them when fleeing to evade tracking dogs.

TECHNICAL STUFF

Rootworkers weren't particular about whether their successful escapes were due to the spiritual properties of cemetery soil, unusual scent compounds that disrupted the dogs' ability to track, psychological confidence that made people move differently, or a combination of all three. What they documented was the pattern and a technique that they could associate with successful escapes. That observation, repeated across multiple accounts, became transmitted knowledge. The mechanism mattered less than the outcome.

Experimentation and testing

Observation alone wasn't enough. Hoodoo's innovators actively tested their hypotheses to find the most effective and repeatable solutions. They included these testing and experiment methods:

- **Botanical testing:** For healing, they tried out different plant combinations. For poisons, they tested dosages carefully because a dosage that was too small allowed the oppressor to survive and retaliate, and a dosage that was too large could make the death look suspicious rather than natural. For all testing, they adjusted timing and preparation methods and documented the practices that produced better results.
- **Formula refinement:** A rootworker would prepare similar protective charms but vary one ingredient to find out whether a substitution worked as well, better, or worse. They also tested formulas under varied conditions and tracked the outcomes.
- **Timing experiments:** Practitioners looked at shared traditional knowledge with a questioning eye. Did working during a waxing moon improve drawing work? Did midnight spirit work produce different results than dawn work? Did certain days of the week align with certain types of work? They tested the traditional claims rather than accepting them blindly.
- **Engineering prototypes:** When designing acoustic systems for praise houses, builders tested different structural designs and materials to determine two things about them:
  - Which materials and designs amplified sound inward best?
  - Which materials and designs most effectively muffled the outward sound?

  They built, tested, and refined designs to incorporate their findings.

» **Communication systems:** The Underground Railroad's coded song system was tested and refined. Failed communication meant capture and death, so the system had to work reliably. Hoodoo practitioners had to be sure everyone understood that the song "Wade in the Water" meant to travel in streams to throw off tracking by dogs. And "Follow the Drinking Gourd" needed to successfully guide people north.

Cause-and-effect thinking

Rootwork innovators thought systematically about causation, and Hoodoo's innovators applied cause-and-effect reasoning to spiritual work. They did so not because they doubted that spirits exist, but because even spiritual forces operate according to patterns that they can learn and work with. So, to gather information about cause and effect, Hoodoo practitioners can take some measures:

» **Apply if-then reasoning:** If I use this poison plant in this way under these conditions, I should get this result without detection. If the result doesn't occur as expected, something in the practitioner's understanding must be wrong, and they need to examine the dosage, the preparation method, the timing, or the delivery system.

» **Isolate variables:** When a formula doesn't work as expected, innovators isolate variables in the materials and process to find out which one might be causing the less-than-desirable effect. They look at the ingredients, the preparation, the timing, the spiritual approach, and even the practitioner's state of mind. Then they change one variable at a time to identify what affects the outcome.

» **Understand mechanisms involved:** While practitioners didn't always explain why in scientific terms, they developed working models. They understood basic properties of ingredients, such as that some herbs were hot (stimulating), others were cool (calming), and certain plants contained compounds that were toxic to humans but not animals. They also grasped that they could use elements such as iron for both protection and harm, depending on how they included it in their work.

» **Respond to astronomical causation**: Practitioners observe that certain celestial events correspond with certain outcomes. They don't separate the concept of moon phases causing certain effects or aligning symbolically with specific Hoodoo work; instead, they observe the correlation and use it for its effect.

WARNING

Don't confuse empirical, cause-and-effect thinking with *materialism*, which is a focus on the tangible world. Testing whether and how a prayer works isn't disrespecting the divine; it's taking Hoodoo work seriously enough to do it well. Acknowledging that faith itself has psychological power doesn't reduce magic to just psychology. Instead, it demonstrates your recognition that psychology, spirituality, and material reality interact.

Replicability and consistency

Good Hoodoo formulas work consistently when conditions are replicated. Experienced and serious practitioners work to achieve reliable and consistent results by using the following:

- **Reliable formulas:** Traditional formulas such as Van Van oil, Fast Luck formula, or Crossing powder work for multiple practitioners across generations because they're based on consistent principles and well-tested combinations.
- **Documented procedures:** Experienced rootworkers document their methods, including what ingredients they use, in what proportions, with what preparation steps, and at what time. By working this way, they can replicate successes and teach others. Their documentation might be oral (passed along through apprenticeship), written (in personal notebooks), or demonstrated (in teach-by-doing settings).
- **Verification through community:** When multiple practitioners independently report that a formula or technique works, that's community verification. High John root's reputation for protection didn't come from one person's experience; it came from generations of practitioners confirming its effectiveness.
- **Adaptation for variation:** While formulas should work consistently, practitioners understood that circumstances vary. A formula might need adjustment for differences in people, problems, or materials. Consistency doesn't mean rigidity. Instead, *consistency* means understanding core principles well enough to adapt your work intelligently.

Hoodoo's Creative Problem-Solving: The Engineering

If science is about understanding how things work, engineering is about building things that work. Hoodoo's innovators were engineers who designed systems and technologies to solve real problems they encountered under brutal living conditions.

Hoodoo practitioners engineered not only objects and formulas, but also processes that involved sequences of actions designed to produce specific results. Beyond individual objects, formulas, and processes, Hoodoo's innovators thought systematically about how multiple elements interact to create effective solutions.

The mark of a good engineer isn't just following specifications. A good engineer solves problems creatively when circumstances change. Hoodoo practitioners are experts at creative problem-solving, as demonstrated in how they tackled these problems:

- **Disguising community worship:** Enslaved people needed to worship loudly by singing, shouting, undergoing voluntary spirit possession, and voicing ecstatic prayer. But doing so openly meant punishment by enslavers or worse. The solution to this problem was acoustic engineering.
- **Providing safe passage for those escaping captivity:** The Underground Railroad was an engineering marvel. It comprised a vast communication and navigation network designed to move people from slavery to freedom despite constant surveillance and pursuit.
- **Experiencing the absence of medicines for health and survival:** Enslaved people developed impressive knowledge of plant chemistry for both survival and resistance. The engineering of remedies for ailments and poisons for resistance involved practical chemistry accomplished through experimentation and careful observation.

Hoodoo practitioners' achievements for solving their real-world problems represent folk engineering at its finest and follow this general process:

- **Identifying a problem:** They needed to worship without detection and supply medicine to the community.
- **Understanding available materials, physics, and chemistry:** They had to understand how sound travels, what absorbs it, what plants work for what illnesses, and so on.
- **Designing a solution:** They needed to find specific structures and positioning, plan escape routes, and create working formulas.
- **Testing the solutions until they work reliably:** They did this through trial and error.

TIP

The best rootworkers are spiritual MacGyvers because they mimic the adaptive creativity of the star of the former TV series of the same name. They can solve almost any problem with whatever materials are at hand because they understand scientific principles, not just recipes. You can build this skill by learning why formulas work, not just how to make them. When you understand the underlying logistics, you can improvise brilliantly.

Check out Table 4-1 for the characteristics of the tools, methods, and processes involved in folk engineering as they relate to the practice of Hoodoo.

TABLE 4-1 Folk Engineering in Hoodoo

Category	Includes	Examples
Technologies	Acoustic engineering	Designing praise houses to direct sound inward; turning over iron pots or kettles to catch sound
	Communication and navigation	Coding songs as travel instructions; quilting patterns with embedded escape information; using astronomical knowledge for directions
	Botanical chemistry	Sourcing plants for medicine or poisons; identifying formulas and dosages; delivering formulas discretely
Processes and systems	Multi-stage work	Defining steps and sequence
	Timing	Identifying starting and stopping points for work and disposal of used materials
	Ritual structure	Positioning the specific practice for effectiveness
	System integration	Ensuring that the technologies, timing sequence, and ritual structure work together
	Community protection	Regularly watching for threats, conducting protective rituals, spreading warnings, and advising about response protocols
	Layered spiritual defense	Incorporating multiple systems such as spiritual baths, protective powders, and elements at specific positions; using mirrors to reflect negativity; integrating ancestor altars for maintaining blessings
Improvisation and adaptive design	Material substitutions	Substituting herbs by function, using household items, and working with found materials
	Adapting to available resources	Using what you already own, employing natural resources that are free to everyone, and embedding messages into well-known communications (like songs)
	Customizing for circumstances	Adapting formulas for specific people or situations, customizing the approach to delivery, and timing the work for various urgencies

Modern Validation: When Institutional Science Catches Up

REMEMBER

You don't need institutional science to validate Hoodoo. The tradition validated itself through four hundred years of effectiveness. The Underground Railroad, poisons, medicines, coded songs, and protective charms worked.

But when institutional science confirms traditional knowledge, it's a reminder that folk science *is* science. Communities that lacked laboratories and degrees nonetheless produced reliable knowledge through careful observation and systematic testing.

Increasingly, institutional science validates what traditional practitioners already knew. Here are some examples:

- **Ethnobotany:** Research on traditional plant medicine often confirms that communities correctly identified therapeutic plants and effective preparation methods through observation and testing over generations. Cayenne pepper is now widely accepted as a supplement for relieving pain or digestive discomfort. Some of the poisons that enslaved people used for nerve and joint pain are now recognized by toxicology as exactly what practitioners knew them to be.
- **Psychoneuroimmunology:** Studies such as Koenig, Duke University (`https://pubmed.ncbi.nlm.nih.gov/11253254`) report that psychological and spiritual states affect physical health, which validates what rootworkers always knew about the mind-body-spirit connection. The High John root's effectiveness for Douglass, whether through magic or psychology, demonstrates this integration.
- **Acoustic engineering:** Practitioners proved that using wet blankets and overturned pots in some praise houses functioned to amplify sound inward while dampening it outward.
- **Environmental psychology:** Research compiled and presented at the National Library of Medicine (`https://pmc.ncbi.nlm.nih.gov/articles/PMC8125471`) supports the idea that people's surroundings affect their mental and emotional states. This affirmation supports Hoodoo practices of keeping living and working spaces clean, orderly, and spiritually charged.

Documenting Hoodoo as Systematic Knowledge

Folk traditions preserve knowledge differently than institutional science, but no less systematically. Specifically, Hoodoo knowledge has been systematically collected and transmitted through several channels, which include oral tradition, written records, and apprenticeship.

Inherent documentation methods

Hoodoo practitioners pass on their knowledge of formulas, work techniques, and scientific principles to students by direct teaching, storytelling, and demonstration. Although having written documentation of formulas and methods may be more reliable in some ways, the oral transmission of Hoodoo knowledge often includes context, warnings, and practical wisdom that written documentation may not.

Many written records take the form of personal notebooks of the rootworkers. They documented formulas that worked, client cases and outcomes, observations about timing and materials, dream records, and divination results. These personal writings probably weren't published, but they were systematic documentation.

Apprenticeship involves learning by doing under guidance. The apprentice observes, assists, practices under supervision, receives correction, and gradually builds great skill with the craft. This hands-on transmission ensures that the knowledge stays practical and testable.

Following are three other methods of preserving Hoodoo knowledge:

- **Songs and stories:** The Underground Railroad's coded songs weren't only communication tools, but documentation. For example, "Wade in the Water" preserved navigation knowledge, and "Follow the Drinking Gourd" documented astronomical navigation. Stories about successful escapes documented which routes and methods worked.
- **Community verification:** When multiple practitioners independently confirm that certain formulas or methods work, that knowledge is preserved and transmitted. What doesn't work reliably is filtered out over generations.
- **Commercial formularies:** Products such as Van Van oil, Crown of Success powder, and Uncrossing Bath have become standardized because they work consistently. For all its problems, the commercial spiritual supply industry has preserved and spread working formulas.

The Carver model: Integrating inquiry and reverence

Although no records document that the African American botanist Dr. George Washington Carver claimed to practice Hoodoo, his approach to knowledge embodies the same integrative ethos that the tradition was built on. Carver, who grew up in the post-Civil War South and spent his career at Tuskegee Institute, described his systematic laboratory work as inseparable from prayer and spiritual communion with the natural world. He reportedly told students that he would ask a plant to reveal what it had to offer before he began investigating its properties. Figure 4-1 is a photograph of Carver from the Tuskegee University archives as presented on the National Park Services website at `www.nps.gov/people/george-washington-carver.htm`.

FIGURE 4-1: George Washington Carver.

Carver's posture of approaching material inquiry with spiritual openness — rather than treating the two as mutually exclusive — produced some of the most practically generative botanical chemistry of the 20th century. For example, Carver devised hundreds of uses for peanuts and sweet potatoes, which were developed specifically to serve impoverished Southern communities that had limited resources.

REMEMBER

Whether Carver would have recognized the term *folk engineering*, the principles he used were identical. He started his research with materials that communities had available, understood the underlying properties deeply, and engineered solutions to real problems. Spirit and science, in Carver's hands as in Hoodoo's, weren't competing vocabularies. They were complementary instruments for the same investigation, which he conducted and documented scientifically.

Practicing Hoodoo Scientifically and Technically (without Losing the Magic)

How do you bring empirical rigor and engineering creativity to your practice of Hoodoo without reducing mystery or losing spiritual power?

TIP

Scientific rigor and mystery work together when you use traditional knowledge as your foundation, empirical observation to refine your practice, an engineering mindset to solve problems creatively, and spiritual intuition to know when to follow rules and when to break them. For example, development and operation of the Underground Railroad required both precision (astronomical navigation and tested routes) and intuition (knowing when to deviate from the plan and how to sense danger).

You can observe the material reality of the world around you systematically while remaining open to spiritual reality. Sometimes empirical observation tells you one thing and spiritual intuition tells you another. Both aspects matter for your practice of Hoodoo. Learn when to follow evidence and when to follow spirit-guidance.

Stay open to mystery. Some Hoodoo formulas and charms work in ways you can't fully explain. That's fine. In any case, to keep a base in the empirical approach, track the results of your Hoodoo work honestly by keeping records of what you do and what happens. Note when your work succeeds, when it fails, and when results are unclear. This isn't reducing magic to data; it's respecting your practice enough to learn from it.

WARNING

Respect faith-based Hoodoo practice. Not everyone needs to completely understand scientific mechanisms. Many practitioners work on pure faith, and that faith is psychologically and spiritually powerful. Don't impose empirical thinking on those who operate differently. The tradition is big enough for both approaches.

Table 4-2 includes information about documenting, systematically practicing, and monitoring precision versus intuition in Hoodoo. These aspects of the practice will protect both the scientific and the magical sides of the craft.

TABLE 4-2 Systematic Hoodoo Practices

Method	What to Do	How and Why You Do It
Documenting carefully	Record what happened beyond what you expected.	Note surprising results, unexpected timing, and unique synchronicities. These might reveal patterns you wouldn't see otherwise.
	Include context.	Record more than perfunctory information. Note timing, circumstances, and personal actions and contributions. Context reveals why some works succeed and others fail.
	Track failures.	Record failed work as carefully as successes. Be specific about what went wrong, whether materials and ingredients, quantity, delivery, or timing. Learning from failure makes you a better practitioner.
	Practice discretion.	Keep records without violating individual and community privacy. Use codes specific to Hoodoo, change identifying details, or keep certain work off the record entirely if needed.
Retaining tradition	Learn traditional formulas first.	Practice with proven formulas and charms that are proven to work. Traditional formulas are traditional because generations have tested them.
	Understand performance before making changes.	Understand why traditional formulas work before making changes. Substitutions should maintain function and not just foster convenience.
	Test modifications carefully.	Test your innovations systematically. Don't assume your new approach works as well as the traditional one until you've confirmed it.
	Pass on reliable changes.	If you develop a formula or method that works consistently, document it and share it appropriately to help the tradition evolve.
Embracing precision	Create safe formulas.	Avoid making formulas that could be dangerous if done wrong, like working with poisons or toxic materials.
	Monitor the sequence of activity.	Regulate complex multi-stage work where sequence is crucial.
	Work for others' benefit.	Recognize and enable those who are depending on you for results.
	Understand significance.	Effectively engineer systems for which failure can mean capture, harm, or death.
Applying intuition	Face unprecedented situations.	Improvise when no specific formula exists.

(continued)

TABLE 4-2 *(continued)*

Method	What to Do	How and Why You Do It
	Receive spiritual guidance.	Go with your gut when it contradicts conventional approaches.
	Act instinctively.	Figure out how to work in emergency situations that require you to improvise.
	Develop personal practice.	Create methods that serve your unique spiritual path.

2

Rooting Around in Hoodoo

IN THIS PART . . .

Understand the mechanics of Hoodoo magic, from the spiritual logic underlying rootwork to how practitioners direct intention through material means.

Develop the practical, strategic mindset that guides Hoodoo practitioners when they assess a situation, set an intention, and move from problem to work.

Enter the world of ancestor veneration and spirit relationships, the living foundation beneath all Hoodoo practice and the source of its deepest power.

Discover how Hoodoo practitioners use cards, bones, and oracular devices to receive spiritual guidance and clarify the path forward.

IN THIS CHAPTER

» Deciphering the magic in Hoodoo practice

» Discovering six core principles of rootwork

» Meeting the four domains of Hoodoo work

» Exploring questions of effectiveness and safety in rootwork

Chapter 5 The Magic of Hoodoo: How Rootwork Works

If you're honest with yourself, the topic of this chapter — discovering how rootwork works — is probably why you picked up this book.

You may find the history of Hoodoo development in Chapter 2 to be fascinating. You may appreciate learning about Hoodoo as medicine and a mindset. But perhaps what you really want to know is this:

- **How does the magic work?** How do Hoodoo practitioners make things happen? How do rootworkers change reality, protect themselves, draw love, secure money, or read the future?
- **What makes objects like mojo bags and formulas powerful?** Why does crossing someone's doorstep with particular powders cause them trouble?
- **And, perhaps most importantly, does Hoodoo magic actually work?** The answer depends on your starting assumptions. But if the answer is simply no, it's hard to explain why millions of people across four centuries kept coming back to the practice, or why so much of Hoodoo eventually found its way into mainstream science and medicine.

This chapter delivers answers to these questions, but not in the way you might expect. I don't hand you a shopping list and a recipe and send you on your way. Instead, I give you something more valuable: I help you understand how Hoodoo practitioners think about magic, what principles guide their work, and why they choose the materials and methods they do. After you understand the logic of rootwork, you won't need a spell book for every situation. You'll be able to think like a rootworker.

Understanding What Magic Means in Hoodoo

Before diving into how Hoodoo magic works, you need to understand what practitioners mean by magic in the realm of Hoodoo practice.

In Hoodoo, *magic* isn't some supernatural force that defies the laws of nature. It's more like a technology: a set of techniques for influencing outcomes by using material resources and spiritual principles that operate within the world, not outside it. Rootworkers don't try to break reality; they work with reality's hidden aspects that most people don't perceive or don't know how to manipulate.

Think of this analogy: Before people understood electricity, flipping a switch on the wall to make light appear would have seemed magical. The physical elements and forces that make up electricity were always there; people just didn't know how to work with them. Many Hoodoo practitioners would say the same thing about the spiritual forces that they use. They're not creating something from nothing. They're directing, focusing, and amplifying influences that already exist.

This spiritual existence is why Hoodoo has always coexisted comfortably with Christianity for most of its practitioners. Many rootworkers see their work as cooperating with God's creation, using the properties they believe God put into roots, stones, and words. Prayer is central to Hoodoo work, not as a substitute for magic but as part of the magic. When rootworkers pray the 23rd Psalm over a protection mojo, they're not hoping God will override the magic. Instead, they're activating it through divine power.

REMEMBER

Scholars may debate the interconnection of magic, religion, and superstition endlessly, but here's how most Hoodoo practitioners would frame these debate elements and their relationship:

- Religion is your relationship with the divine.

» Magic is your method for engaging forces to solve practical problems.

» Superstition is doing something *just because*, without understanding why.

Hoodoo practitioners generally reject the label *superstition* for their work. They know exactly why they're doing what they're doing, even if outsiders don't understand the reasoning.

REMEMBER

If you're hoping for a mystical tradition shrouded in vague symbolism and mysterious energy, you may be disappointed with the information in this chapter. Remember, Hoodoo is practical, direct, and results-oriented. It's about solving problems, seizing opportunities, and protecting what's yours. As I establish in Chapter 4, if practices don't get results, they're not Hoodoo.

Working with Core Principles of Rootwork

Hoodoo magic operates on several key principles that I present in this section. After you understand these, individual spells and formulas start to make sense as tangible applications of these principles. And the principles help you see the patterns behind the practice of Hoodoo.

The six core principles of Hoodoo magic direct its practice and make the following declarations:

» **Like affects like.** This statement is the foundation of most magical systems worldwide, and Hoodoo is no exception. The principle is simple: Things that resemble each other are spiritually connected, and acting on one affects the other.

» **Once connected, always connected.** Spiritual bonds don't break the way physical ones do. Things that were once joined remain spiritually linked even after physical separation, which is why a person's hair, handwriting, or worn clothing carry weight in the work.

» **The worker's power matters.** Here's where Hoodoo differs from purely mechanical magic. It's not enough to assemble the right ingredients and say the right words. The rootworker's focused intention, spiritual authority, and force of will are crucial to the work.

» **You're not alone.** The rootworker's personal power is crucial, but most practitioners don't work alone. Hoodoo engages with spiritual allies: ancestors, saints, angels, and other helping spirits.

- **When and how you work matters.** Effective rootwork pays attention to timing and the worker's spiritual state. When you work and what your state of mind is can be as important as what you do.
- **Magic is pragmatic.** Remember the foundational saying: If it doesn't get results, it's not Hoodoo. This principle means that practitioners must evaluate their work based on outcomes, not aesthetics or theory.

Using sympathy and correspondence: Like affects like

The effect of sympathy and correspondence of like things is why a *poppet* — a doll, usually hand-crafted — dressed to represent a specific person can be used to influence that person for healing and protection according to Hoodoo thought. The doll doesn't just symbolize the target of the Hoodoo magic. In the spiritual logic of Hoodoo, the doll is that person for magical purposes after it's properly prepared and named. What you do to the doll happens to the person literally or symbolically.

Similarly, colors correspond to intentions: Red is for passion and power, green is for money and growth, black is for protection and banishing, and white is for purity and blessing. When you burn a green candle dressed with money-drawing oil while praying for financial increase, you're not just thinking about prosperity. You're working with the spiritual frequency of prosperity itself.

Applying contagion: Once connected, always connected

This connection principle involves *personal concerns*, which are the most powerful ingredients in Hoodoo spellwork. Hair, nail clippings, worn clothing, bodily fluids, handwriting, and photographs aren't just helpful identification tools; they're parts of the person. In spiritual terms, getting someone's hair gives you a piece of their essence, and working on that hair is working on them, no matter how far away they are.

This connection also applies to footprint dirt — soil from someone's footstep — and items that people have touched. These are valued ingredients in rootwork. The connection persists. You can lay down a powder where someone walks and affect them as surely as if you'd fed them a potion because their foot touching that powder creates a spiritual link.

WARNING

The power of personal concerns is precisely why Hoodoo practitioners are cautious about what they leave behind. You don't throw away hair from a haircut or let just anyone handle your photographs. In communities where Hoodoo is taken seriously, disposing of personal concerns properly isn't paranoia; it's common sense. Honoring this principle is why rootworkers guard or dispose of their own personal items carefully.

Focusing intention and will: The worker's power matters

Two people can make identical mojo bags by using the same recipe, and one bag will be powerfully effective while the other does nothing. The difference? It's likely that the rootworker who made the powerful mojo bag meant it. They put their will into the bag, charged it with focused intention, prayed over it with conviction, and believed in their own power to make the mojo bag work.

This principle of intention is one reason why Hoodoo practitioners often work in private, in a focused mental state. They're not just following instructions. They're directing spiritual force through their actions. Distraction, doubt, or half-hearted effort weakens the work. To gain focus, many rootworkers fast, pray, or otherwise prepare themselves spiritually before doing major rootwork. They're building up their own power.

Some rootworkers describe this focus and will as *having the gift* or *having the power in you.* Others see it as faith: the kind that the biblical Jesus talked about when he said that faith the size of a mustard seed, when genuine, could move mountains. Either way, the role of the practitioner isn't passive. They're the engine that drives the work.

Engaging spiritual assistance: You're not alone

Historically, most Hoodoo practitioners are Christian. The idea of engaging spiritual assistance might mean praying to specific saints known for certain kinds of help, such as St. Expedite for urgent matters, St. Joseph for employment and home matters, or St. Michael for protection. Asking for spiritual support might also mean calling on the Holy Spirit for guidance or asking guardian angels for assistance.

For other practitioners, spiritual assistance means working with the ancestors: the beloved dead who watch over their descendants and have a vested interest in the family's well-being. A rootworker might set up an ancestor altar, make offerings, and petition the ancestors for help with major work.

A spectrum exists for the type of rootwork taking place. Some work is purely *natural magic*; it uses the inherent spiritual properties of herbs, stones, and words without calling on external spirits. Most people note no difference between this "natural magic" and herbalism. Other work is deeply relational, involving petition, offering, and sometimes negotiation with spiritual beings. Both ends of the spectrum exist within the scope of Hoodoo, and many practitioners use the entire spectrum, depending on the situation.

REMEMBER

This comfortable integration of magical work and Christian faith confuses outsiders, but it makes perfect sense to practitioners. God created the world and everything in it, so why wouldn't plants have spiritual properties? If Jesus gave his followers power to heal the sick and cast out demons, why wouldn't that power extend to protection work and blessing? The Bible itself is full of magical objects and acts involving stories about Moses's staff, anointing oil, and the hem of Jesus's garment. For most Hoodoo practitioners, rootwork doesn't happen instead of faith. It's faith in action.

Choosing timing and condition: When and how you work matters

Many practitioners observe moon phases for different uses. A new moon is for starting things, a full moon is for bringing things to completion (fullness), and a waning moon works is for banishing and removing. Days of the week also have traditional associations listed in this mini-table.

Day of the Week	Hoodoo Work
Monday	Psychic work
Tuesday	Conflict
Wednesday	Communication
Thursday	Abundance
Friday	Love
Saturday	Binding and protection
Sunday	Success

Certain hours during the day, especially sunrise and sunset hours, matter too. They represent *liminal times* when the veil marking the boundary between material and spiritual worlds is thin. Midnight is powerful for certain kinds of work, such as crossroads work and communing with the dead, and high noon (when shadows disappear) is good for revealing hidden things.

Beyond external timing, internal condition also matters. Most rootworkers will tell you not to do work when you're emotionally scattered, spiritually compromised, or physically depleted. Some traditions require fasting, bathing, or sexual abstinence before major work. This idea of specific preparations isn't arbitrary; it's about ensuring that rootworkers are in the right condition to direct spiritual force effectively.

REMEMBER

What makes Hoodoo different from many other magical traditions is that it was forged under the worst possible conditions. Enslaved people didn't have the luxury of waiting for the perfect spiritual state or ideal timing. They worked magic while exhausted from fieldwork, terrified of being caught, separated from loved ones, and living under constant trauma. And it still worked. See Chapter 2 for more information about the history of Hoodoo's development.

Because of the origin of Hoodoo in less than ideal conditions, the techniques developed tend to be robust and reliable. They're closer to chemistry than to the fickle, temperamental magic of popular imagination. A formula that only works when you're perfectly centered and the stars align isn't useful to someone who may need protection right now. Hoodoo had to work under adverse conditions, so it was refined over generations to be dependable even when nothing else was.

Evaluating results and adjusting: Magic is pragmatic

If a formula doesn't work, a rootworker asks: Did I use the wrong ingredients? Was my intention unclear? Did I work at the wrong time? Is there blockage or interference? Do I need spiritual cleansing first? Should I try a different approach entirely?

This results-oriented mindset makes Hoodoo adaptable. When rootworkers discovered they couldn't get certain African roots in America, they found local substitutes. When commercial oils and powders became available, practitioners tested them and kept what worked. When new situations arose, they developed new formulas.

TIP

The tradition of Hoodoo isn't frozen in time. It evolves because effectiveness matters more than purity. If adding a new ingredient makes the work more powerful, add it. If an old formula stops working, modify or replace it.

Practicing the Four Domains of Hoodoo Work

Hoodoo's guiding principles, presented under the section "Working with Core Principles of Rootwork" earlier in the chapter, apply throughout its practice. But four domains help to sort Hoodoo rootwork into major categories of magical work.

The following sections give you the big picture, the landscape of Hoodoo's magical domains. The remaining chapters in this part explore specific techniques used in each domain of practice.

Changemaking: Working magic to alter circumstances

Also called *fixing*, *laying*, or simply *rootwork*, *changemaking* is what most people think of as *spellwork*. It's doing magic to make something happen, to change a situation, or to influence outcomes. This work involves drawing and attracting desired things, banishing and removing unwanted influences, compelling and commanding people or situations, binding and fixing to prevent harm, and working with relationships through reconciliation or separation.

All changemaking involves principles discussed earlier, such as sympathy, contagion, intention, and often spiritual assistance. The rootworker assembles ingredients that correspond to the goal, incorporates personal concerns when possible, charges the work with focused will, times the work appropriately, and petitions spiritual helpers as needed.

Divination: Seeing what's hidden

Hoodoo isn't just about making things happen. It's also about knowing what's going to happen or what's happening in situations that you can't directly observe. *Divination*, also called *seeing* or *reading*, involves insight that helps rootworkers diagnose problems, predict outcomes, and receive spiritual guidance.

Common Hoodoo divination methods include these:

- **Playing card reading:** Hoodoo readers historically use a standard 52-card deck (not tarot, although many modern practitioners use tarot today), with each card carrying specific meanings drawn from the tradition. The ace of spades signals death or major change; the queen of hearts often represents a kind woman.
- **Looking for signs and omens:** Spirits and circumstances send messages through the world around you: a bird flying into the house, a recurring or insightful dream, unusual animal behavior, or coincidences too pointed to ignore.
- **Reading candles:** When you burn a candle for spiritual work, the flame, smoke, soot, and wax patterns tell you how the work is progressing. A tall, steady flame suggests strong forward motion; heavy black soot often signals obstacles being cleared.
- **Practicing pendulum work:** A weighted object hung on a chain or string responds to subtle spiritual cues, swinging in patterns the worker has agreed on for yes, no, and maybe. It's especially useful for locating things and pinpointing where energy is blocked.
- **Conducting spirit communication:** Rootworkers consult ancestors, saints, and other helping spirits directly through prayer, dreams, sitting at altars, or mediumistic practice. Answers come through subtle nudges, intuitive flashes, or unmistakable confirmations.

These methods aren't fortune-telling entertainment. Divination is diagnostic work. Before doing major magic, a rootworker might divine to check for whether they're planning the right approach, to find any blockages, to discover the root cause for a problem, or to flush out hidden enemies.

Building personal power: Strengthening your spiritual foundation

Effective magic requires a strong spiritual foundation. You can't pour power into your work if you're spiritually depleted, blocked, or compromised. And so, personal spiritual maintenance is central to Hoodoo practice.

Personal power work includes cleansing and uncrossing to remove negative influences, adding protection and shielding against harm, feeding your head to strengthen your spiritual antenna, maintaining altar space to support your practice, and right living to preserve your spiritual power.

If changemaking and divination are the engine, think of your personal power as the infrastructure that supports everything else. You maintain your tools, tend your spiritual relationships, keep yourself clean and protected, and build your own authority. Then when you need to do major work, you have the power to back it up.

Engaging spirit work: Connecting with the invisible world

Working with spirits is qualitatively different from working with herbs and personal concerns alone. Spirit work includes venerating ancestors, petitioning the saints, working with guardian angels, building relationships with spirit guides and helpers, calling on the dead in magic, and using music and song as spiritual technology.

REMEMBER

Basic spirit work — praying to God, petitioning your ancestors, asking your guardian angel for protection — is accessible and relatively safe for beginners. But deeper spirit work requires knowledge and caution. Spirits can have their own agendas, and not all spiritual beings are helpful. Traditional Hoodoo strongly emphasizes working with your own ancestors and the Biblical God first. Only after you have those relationships established should you consider more complex spirit work.

Addressing Common Questions and Concerns

If you're encountering Hoodoo for the first time, two questions probably sit close to the surface: Does it actually work, and should you be afraid of it? The next two sections take on each question and offer answers grounded in how practitioners themselves talk about the tradition.

Examining effectiveness: Does the magic actually work?

Skeptics are fond of asking whether Hoodoo magic actually works. And the question deserves an honest answer — or rather, several honest answers — depending on what perspective you're taking. Here are those perspectives:

» **From the practitioner's perspective:** Yes, Hoodoo absolutely works. Hoodoo practices exist because generation after generation found that they produced results and served their needs. If they didn't work, the practices wouldn't have survived 400 years of practice. The empirical evidence of success, from the practitioner's standpoint, is overwhelming: The money comes in, the lover returns, the enemy stops their harassment, and the sick person recovers.

» **From the outside skeptic's perspective:** Maybe what looks like magical results is actually psychology, coincidence, placebo effect, or natural outcomes misattributed to magic. Maybe confirmation bias makes people remember the hits and forget the misses. Maybe giving people a sense of control in hopeless situations is the real value, not literal magical results.

» **From the middle ground:** Perhaps the question of whether Hoodoo works itself is too simple. Does prayer work? Does therapy work? Is the placebo effect useful and real? If a woman carries a mojo bag and subsequently feels more confident, makes bolder decisions, and consequently gets the job she wanted, did the mojo work? The rootworker would say yes. The skeptic might say it was just psychology. But the woman got the job either way.

Here's what's not in question: Hoodoo practices do something. They affect the people who use them, whether that's because spiritual forces are real and magic genuinely alters outcomes, the human mind is powerful and belief creates measurable effects, or some combination or the two. Reasonable people can disagree. But dismissing Hoodoo as pure delusion or fraud doesn't match the historical evidence. Too many people over too long a time have found Hoodoo valuable, and dismissing it as fraud just doesn't make sense.

For purposes of this book's content, I present Hoodoo on its own terms, explaining what practitioners believe and do. You can decide for yourself what perspective makes sense to you. The techniques work the same for those that Hoodoo touches, regardless of your explanation for why they work.

Understanding safety: Should you be afraid of Hoodoo?

The short answer to the question of whether you should fear Hoodoo is no. But to unpack the common fears, check out the following:

» **Fear of being cursed or hexed:** Movies and sensationalized media have convinced people that rootworkers are lurking around every corner ready to put a fix on them. The reality is much less dramatic. Yes, some Hoodoo work is adversarial, but this isn't casual or common. Most rootwork is protective, healing, prosperity-focused, or relational. Enemy work exists, but it's usually targeted and typically happens in response to specific conflicts, not randomly.

If you're not involved in serious conflicts with people who practice Hoodoo, you're extremely unlikely to have Hoodoo work against you. And if you think you're the recipient of negative practices, note that Hoodoo also has strong uncrossing and protection traditions that are specifically designed to counter hexes and remove bad work.

- **Fear of *black magic* or evil:** This fear often has racist roots. In reality, Hoodoo is morally neutral. It's a technology that can be used for various purposes. Yes, you can harm with it. But you can also heal, protect, and help with it. The ethics depend on the practitioner's choices, not the tradition itself.

  Consider this: People use chemistry to create not only life-saving medicines but also deadly poisonous drugs. But you don't call chemistry evil, and there's no concept of "white chemistry" or "black chemistry." You recognize it as a neutral science whose good or bad results depend entirely on the practitioner's intent and choices. Hoodoo works the same way.

- **Fear of spiritual danger:** If you plan to practice Hoodoo yourself, a little caution is wise. Spirit work can be powerful and isn't the best fit for everyone at every stage of life. Many seasoned conjurers say the safest starting point is your own spiritual lineage — your ancestors or long-trusted allies — rather than unfamiliar entities. They also recommend everyday grounding habits such as daily prayer, mindful breathing, or checking in with a trusted elder or teacher.

TIP

But should you be afraid of Hoodoo as some kind of inherently dark or dangerous force? That type of fear isn't warranted. Hoodoo is a spiritual technology developed by oppressed people for survival, healing, and empowerment. Treat it with respect, learn properly, and understand what you're doing just like you would with any powerful tool.

IN THIS CHAPTER

» Meeting the fundamental Hoodoo mindset

» Applying the mindset as practical problem-solving and spiritual practice

» Cultivating the Hoodoo mindset through practical exercises

» Integrating magical thinking into everyday life

Chapter 6
Thinking Like a Rootworker

Hoodoo isn't just a set of techniques you perform. It's a way of thinking and a mental orientation that shapes how you perceive problems, evaluate solutions, and move through the world. Hoodoo emerged when naturally clever people were forced into circumstances that demanded even more cleverness. (See Chapters 2 and 3 for more information about how Hoodoo developed.) The result is a tradition that doesn't just teach you what to do; it trains you how to think so you can figure out what to do when the situation is new, the old formulas don't apply, or you have to work with whatever's at hand.

This chapter explores what I call the *Hoodoo mindset*: the particular combination of pragmatism, creativity, resourcefulness, and strategic thinking that characterizes effective rootwork. This mindset defines the difference between someone who memorizes steps and formulas and someone who can adapt, improvise, and solve problems others can't see solutions for.

Whether you approach Hoodoo as religion, culture, or technique, the Hoodoo mindset is what makes you effective. It doesn't replace or explain away the spiritual reality of rootwork, and instead, works with it. But the Hoodoo mindset can also stand on its own; for some practitioners, the trickster consciousness *is* the practice.

And like with any mental skill, you can develop the mindset. In this chapter, I lead you through the fundamental aspects of the Hoodoo mindset and help you understand how to integrate them into your approach to problem-solving specifically and your everyday perception of the world in general.

Identifying the Aspects of Hoodoo's Mindset

Some people are born with the Hoodoo mindset. They naturally see opportunities where others see obstacles, connections where others see randomness, and solutions where others see dead ends. Others develop the mindset through necessity. Survival in hostile environments can force creative problem-solving, and oppression teaches you to work around, through, or against systems designed to keep you powerless.

In this section, you find out about the fundamental aspects of the Hoodoo mindset and how they work together to offer magical and practical power.

Applying pragmatism over philosophy

The first and most fundamental aspect of the Hoodoo mindset is radical pragmatism that focuses on results rather than theories. Hoodoo doesn't waste time philosophizing about whether some Hoodoo practice is magic or just science. The question that matters is: Does it work?

Suppose that a rootworker develops a hair cream that uses certain herbs, oils, and specific preparation methods. Also suppose that the cream makes people's hair healthy and helps it grow longer. The rootworker doesn't sit around debating whether the observed effectiveness comes from the chemical properties of the ingredients, the spiritual properties of the plants, the intention infused during preparation, or some combination of all three. The hair cream works to grow long, healthy hair, and that's what matters.

The Hoodoo mindset constantly evaluates and adapts based on outcomes. If the methods and ingredients provide successful, consistent results, you keep them. If they don't, you adjust or discard them. This type of evaluation creates a self-correcting system that filters out ineffective work over time and refines and passes on the successful work.

REMEMBER

This pragmatic approach to evaluating results isn't anti-intellectual or dismissive of understanding mechanisms. But it prioritizes effectiveness over classification. You can study why something works after you've confirmed that it does. But getting caught up in theory before confirming results is backward to the thinking of most Hoodoo practitioners.

Because the focus of rootwork is on results rather than purity or orthodoxy, Hoodoo practitioners readily adopt whatever works:

- If Christian prayers work, use them.
- If an herb from another tradition proves effective, incorporate it.
- If a new technique produces better results than the old one, switch them out.
- If modern materials work as well as traditional ingredients, use what you have available.

This focus isn't cultural appropriation or loss of Hoodoo tradition. Instead, it's the tradition's core operating principle: Use what works, discard what doesn't, adapt to circumstances.

Embracing strategic cleverness

The second major aspect of the Hoodoo mindset is strategic cleverness: the willingness and ability to use misdirection, creativity, and guile to achieve goals when direct power isn't available. Rootworkers apply this cleverness in part by engaging with the trickster tradition that's prevalent in African and African American folklore. The *trickster* is a figure who survives and thrives not through direct force (which they may lack) but through wit, creativity, and strategic deception.

Understanding the trickster archetype

Br'er Rabbit is the most famous example of a trickster in African American folklore. He's small, physically weak, and constantly threatened by predators who aren't so small and weak. But Br'er Rabbit consistently outsmarts his predators through clever tricks, misdirection, and understanding weaknesses that his opponents have.

When Br'er Fox catches Br'er Rabbit and is about to kill him, Br'er Rabbit doesn't fight. He'd lose. Instead, he begs Fox not to throw him in the briar patch — anything but that! Fox, thinking the briar patch must be torturous, throws Rabbit in. Rabbit escapes easily because he was born in the briar patch. He tricked Fox into doing exactly what he wanted by pretending to want the opposite.

TIP

The tale of Br'er Rabbit outfoxing Br'er Fox represents quintessential Hoodoo thinking: Assess the situation accurately, understand your opponent, use psychological misdirection, turn apparent weakness into advantage, and achieve your goal through cleverness rather than force.

Applying Hoodoo's cleverness aspect

The strategic cleverness aspect of the Hoodoo mindset has served African Americans in the past and still serves them today in current oppressive circumstances. Here are examples:

- Enslaved people and those working to free them used the trickster cleverness to outsmart and work around enslavers. Harriet Tubman, for example, disguised herself to lead people to freedom and used elaborate deception to throw off pursuers.
- Frederick Douglass escaped slavery in part by using deception and disguise to obtain forged papers and impersonate a free Black sailor. You can find more examples of strategic cleverness in the sidebar "Recognizing Historic Use of the Hoodoo Mindset."
- When modern healthcare systems fail to serve and nurture the Black (and other racially marginalized) populations, communities create informal health networks in which they sharing knowledge about herbs, home remedies, and wellness practices that don't require insurance or doctor access.
- Black entrepreneurs are sometimes blocked from traditional startup funding. In this case, people with the Hoodoo mindset create alternative economies that include mutual aid networks, barter systems, community investment circles, and crowdfunding that bypass traditional banking structures.

REMEMBER

The strategic cleverness aspect of the Hoodoo mindset isn't a substitute for systemic change, but it's how people survive and fight effectively while working toward that change. During COVID-19, when government systems failed Black and marginalized communities catastrophically, people created mutual aid networks that distributed food and resources, protected eviction-vulnerable people, shared information about healthcare access, and organized distribution of protective equipment. These efforts weren't charity; they represent strategic community survival accomplished by using the Hoodoo mindset.

Understanding magic as practical problem-solving

If the Hoodoo mindset's problem-solving is magic, it's like street magic, which involves prestidigitation, or sleight of hand, and misdirection. Having the Hoodoo mindset is like being a trickster, a street magician, and an innovative problem-solver. While the mindset may not be magical in the occultic sense of the word, you can apply it to the magical aspects of Hoodoo or use it as its own force.

The Hoodoo mindset doesn't involve supernatural forces. Street magicians don't violate the current understanding of the laws of physics. They create the appearance of impossibility through these mechanisms:

- **Misdirection:** Street magicians are experts at making you look where they want you to.
- **Preparation:** Practiced magicians set up the situation and props in advance.
- **Understanding psychology:** Good magicians know how people think and what they'll likely overlook.
- **Skill and practice:** Savvy magicians must execute their techniques smoothly so that they're believable.
- **Confidence and presentation:** Experienced magicians sell the illusion to achieve their goals.

Hoodoo can work similarly to street magic. Not because Hoodoo is fake or just uses tricks, but because effective magic often operates through psychological, social, and strategic means as much as (or more than) through direct spiritual force.

When rootworkers fix a situation (perform their magic), they might use

- **Social engineering** by getting information, influencing people, creating appropriate circumstances
- **Psychological manipulation,** in which they play on people's fears, desires, and assumptions
- **Strategic timing** by acting when their opponents are distracted
- **Misdirection** by appearing to do one thing while doing another
- **Social or spiritual authority** to make people believe they have power, so that the people act accordingly

Does using the trappings of street magicians mean that the spiritual components of Hoodoo practice are fake? No. It means that effective rootwork combines spiritual and practical/psychological methods.

REMEMBER

The best rootworkers understand human nature, social dynamics, and strategic thinking as well as spiritual forces. The spiritual work amplifies and guides the practical work. The practical work grounds and manifests the spiritual work. They're not separate; they're integrated.

RECOGNIZING HISTORIC USE OF THE HOODOO MINDSET

Throughout American history, African Americans demonstrated this mindset in survival and resistance.

Harriet Tubman didn't just lead people to freedom through courage. She used strategic deception, misdirection, and psychological manipulation. She disguised herself, used drugs to quiet crying babies, carried a gun not primarily to fight but to threaten escapees who might give up and endanger the group, and employed elaborate deception to throw off pursuers. Her success rate — never losing a "passenger" — came from thinking like a Hoodoo practitioner: assess the situation, use whatever tools are available, and outthink your opponents.

Frederick Douglass escaped slavery partly through obtaining forged papers and impersonating a free Black sailor — using deception and disguise. Later, his oratory and writing didn't just argue for abolition directly; they strategically deployed emotional appeals, logical arguments, and moral pressure customized to different audiences. He understood his opponents and crafted approaches that would work on them.

The Underground Railroad itself was a massive exercise in Hoodoo thinking: coded language (songs with double meanings), misdirection (false trails), use of natural and spiritual signs (moss on trees, quilts with patterns indicating safe houses), and community networks operating in secret under the noses of those trying to stop them.

Enslaved people generally practiced this mindset constantly: feigning ignorance to avoid work, using linguistic code (spirituals about "crossing the Jordan" meant escaping North), working slowly as subtle resistance, and maintaining secret spiritual practices while appearing to be Christian converts.

This wasn't "lying" in a moral sense. It was strategic survival in a system designed to destroy you. When you have no legitimate power, you use illegitimate power. When you can't win directly, you win indirectly.

Seeing How Practitioners Manifest the Hoodoo Mindset

Some people are born with quick, creative minds and a playful intelligence. They can see multiple solutions, naturally consider angles and leverage points in a situation, read people accurately, and feel comfortable with ambiguity and indirect approaches to clever solutions.

These people are natural rootworkers of the trickster variety. They think like Hoodoo practitioners without necessarily practicing the magical or spiritual aspects of Hoodoo. Put them in any challenging situation, and they'll find a way through it.

Other people develop their creative, flexible, Hoodoo-like mindset through necessity. For example, they may be enslaved, oppressed by systems designed to keep them powerless, marginalized and excluded from legitimate channels, poor and lacking resources, or facing prejudice that denies their humanity. In these situations, people learn to think creatively so that they can survive.

Oppression and misfortune help people develop the creative mindset of Hoodoo practitioners and teach them how to:

- **Read situations carefully** because their survival depends on accurately assessing threats
- **Find hidden opportunities** when the obvious paths are blocked
- **Work with what they have** since they may be unable to access what others have
- **Think several moves ahead** because they know that one wrong step can be catastrophic
- **Use indirect methods** when direct confrontation is too dangerous

Bringing trickster traits to the forefront

Not every effective Hoodoo practitioner's primary personal power involves what people conventionally think of as magic. Some people's primary gift is the trickster's strategic, clever mindset itself. A practitioner with this skill exercises the trickster mindset by using these methods:

- **Finding unique solutions.** Tricksters may not be the practitioners doing elaborate candle workings or making complex mojo bags. They might not have strong gifts in divination or spirit communication. But when confronted with an impossible problem, a blocked situation, or an oppressive circumstance, they'll find a way through it that no one else saw.

- **Becoming the embodiment of the trickster.** Their power is in seeing solutions others miss, strategic thinking that operates several moves ahead, psychological insight that reads people with uncanny accuracy, creative problem-solving that turns obstacles into opportunities, and the ability to make the impossible happen through cleverness, timing, and lateral thinking.

REMEMBER

Relying on the creative, problem-solving trickster mindset is legitimate Hoodoo power. The rootworker who can brew powerful formulas or the seer who receives clear visions isn't more Hoodoo-like than the creative problem solver. These two roles are different manifestations of the same tradition.

Recognizing practitioners who have the mindset

You might know someone who exhibits these traits:

- **Ingenuity:** They always seem to find a way no matter how blocked the situation appears. They see opportunities and connections others don't notice.
- **Flexibility:** They navigate complex social or institutional situations with apparent ease. They help people solve unsolvable problems through unconventional approaches.
- **Practical effectiveness:** They might not describe themselves as magical, but they're incredibly effective at making things happen. People come to them for advice because they always have ideas.

The people who have these traits may not even identify as practitioners. They may just believe that they're good at figuring things out or solving problems creatively. But they're operating with core Hoodoo consciousness, the same mindset that allowed enslaved Africans to survive, resist, and eventually overcome slavery.

TIP

If you recognize the traits of ingenuity, flexibility, and practical effectiveness in yourself, understand that this is your *Ashe*. This is your gift to the Hoodoo tradition. You don't need to force yourself to be a great diviner, herbalist, or spirit worker if that's not your natural strength. Your strength is strategic thinking, creative problem-solving, and trickster consciousness. Develop it. Refine it. Use it to help yourself and your community. That's your rootwork.

TECHNICAL STUFF

Ashe is a Yoruba term that represents divine energy, power, and the authority of the spoken word; see Chapter 10.

Cultivating the Hoodoo Mindset through Practice

Even if you're not naturally inclined to think with a Hoodoo mindset, you can develop it through practice. You can train yourself to overcome rigid thinking, look for multiple paths to solutions, recognize patterns, change your perspective, and build strong problem-solving habits. And if you already have some of these skills, you also have room for growth.

Table 6-1 offers a look at how you can build a Hoodoo mindset and gives you specific ideas for doing so.

TABLE 6-1 Building a Hoodoo Mindset

What to Do	How to Do It	How It Applies to Hoodoo
Break functional fixedness	Take a common object (for example, a paperclip) and generate 20 different uses for it. This forces you past the obvious and into creative thinking.	When you need an ingredient you don't have, look for something else that has similar properties. When you can't do traditional rootwork, look for other ordinary objects or activities that can help you accomplish the same goal.
Use constraint-based creativity	Give yourself a problem that has severe constraints. "How would I protect myself magically if I had only salt, water, and a candle?"	Constraints force creativity. When you can't use the obvious solution, you find clever alternatives.
Practice reverse thinking	Take a goal and think about achieving it through reverse means. Instead of "How do I attract this person?", ask "How do I make them pursue me?"	Employs the Br'er Rabbit trickster principle. Sometimes the best path is counterintuitive.
Analyze multiple paths	For any goal, generate at least five completely different paths to achieving it. Don't stop at the first solution. Force yourself to think of alternatives.	Never rely on one method. Have multiple approaches working simultaneously. If one path is blocked, others remain open.

(continued)

TABLE 6-1 ***(continued)***

What to Do	How to Do It	How It Applies to Hoodoo
Play devil's advocate	For any plan you make, deliberately try to find the flaws, weaknesses, and failure points. Then design backup plans or countermeasures.	This trains you to think like an opponent or see obstacles you'd otherwise miss. It's what good rootworkers do before working — they consider what could go wrong and plan accordingly.
Develop pattern recognition	Practice finding patterns in apparently random information. Look for connections between seemingly unrelated things. Ask "Why?" about everyday occurrences.	Good rootworkers see signs, connections, and patterns others miss. They notice when things aren't coincidental. This trained perception is a form of magical attentiveness — the same quality that allows rootworkers to read signs, recognize omens, and discern patterns others dismiss as coincidence.
Shift perspectives	For any situation, deliberately view it from multiple perspectives: yours, your opponent's, and a neutral third-party's. Try to think like someone who'd approach the problem differently, and consider the perspective of ancestors who faced similar challenges.	Shifting perspective reveals opportunities and solutions you can't see from your initial viewpoint.
Practice strategic ambiguity	Practice being strategically ambiguous or redirecting attention in harmless ways. When someone asks something you don't want to answer directly, practice redirecting to a related topic. In negotiations, practice not revealing your full position immediately.	This trains the trickster mindset. You're not lying or being malicious; you're learning to control information flow and use psychology strategically. ***Note:*** Practice on low-stakes situations, and never harmfully. The goal is developing the cognitive skill, not becoming manipulative.
Embrace resource scarcity	Deliberately constrain yourself for a while. "This week, I can only eat what I can make from ingredients I already have" or "This month, I can't buy anything new; I can only use, repurpose, or trade things I already own."	Scarcity breeds creativity. You learn to see potential in what you have rather than focusing on what you lack. This is core Hoodoo thinking.
Build daily problem-solving habits	Each day, identify one problem (yours or someone else's) and spend 10 minutes generating creative solutions. Don't censor yourself. Write down even impossible or ridiculous solutions. Then evaluate which might work.	Strengthens your Hoodoo mindset by making it a daily habit and not a crisis response.

Integrating Your Magical and Practical Lives

As you develop the Hoodoo mindset, you'll notice something interesting: The line between magical problem-solving and practical problem-solving blurs. The same thinking that helps you design effective rootwork also helps you navigate workplace politics, find creative solutions to financial problems, handle difficult people or situations, see opportunities others miss, turn apparent obstacles into advantages, and survive in systems not designed for your success.

This is why Hoodoo is more than just techniques you apply in specific magical contexts. It's a way of moving through the world — a mental orientation that makes you more effective at everything, from the magical to the mundane. Whether you're lighting a candle for money or figuring out how to advance your career with limited resources, you're using the same mindset.

When you think like a rootworker, you approach your life situations by:

- Assessing situations accurately rather than seeing what you want to see
- Working with what you have rather than waiting for ideal conditions
- Finding multiple paths rather than giving up when one route is blocked
- Using strategic thinking rather than just reacting emotionally
- Combining practical and spiritual approaches rather than separating them
- Staying flexible and adaptive rather than rigidly following plans that aren't working
- Thinking several moves ahead rather than just addressing immediate problems

Seeing the Hoodoo mindset in practice

The conventional approach to problem-solving can be linear and passive, and it gives up easily. The Hoodoo mindset approach is multi-dimensional, active, creative, strategic, and persistent. Consider this example of how the Hoodoo mindset approaches the problem of searching for a better job differently than conventional thinking.

The problem: You need a better-paying job, but you're in a field in which advancement is blocked by discrimination, you lack certain credentials, and the job market is tight.

The conventional approach:

- Apply to job postings.
- Hope someone calls.
- Feel defeated when they don't.
- Maybe update your resume and try again.
- Blame external circumstances (of course).

The Hoodoo mindset approach:

- *Assess the situation accurately.* If the standard path is blocked, identify multiple alternatives.
- *Identify leverage points.* Determine what you *do* offer as an advantage for this job and find out who needs what you can do.
- *Create multiple paths working simultaneously.* Network strategically, make yourself visible, create your own opportunity, do door-opening work, and improve your skills.
- *Use psychological insight.* What do employers actually want?
- *Be strategically patient.* Understand that getting the job might take months. Don't become desperate.
- *Adapt as circumstances change.* If one path shows promise, invest more time and effort there.
- *Combine practical and spiritual work.* Rootwork opens doors, but you still must walk through them.

Achieving integration as the ultimate goal

The goal for establishing the Hoodoo mindset isn't to think like a rootworker only when you're doing rootwork. The goal is to make this mindset your default way of perceiving and problem-solving. With this mindset Hoodoo becomes not just something you do, but who you are — a way of being in the world that's simultaneously practical and magical, strategic and spiritual, grounded and transcendent.

When you've truly integrated the Hoodoo mindset, you automatically see multiple solutions to problems. You naturally work with what you have rather than focusing on what you lack. You instinctively assess situations accurately rather than emotionally. You habitually think several steps ahead. You comfortably combine spiritual and practical approaches. You creatively turn obstacles into opportunities. You strategically use both direct and indirect methods. You persistently pursue goals through multiple paths simultaneously.

REMEMBER

The Hoodoo mindset is your most powerful tool, and after you develop it, no one can take it from you. You can have all the herbs, formulas, and techniques, but without the mindset, you're just going through the motions. With the mindset, you can make magic with anything, solve problems others think are unsolvable, and navigate circumstances that would defeat someone who thinks conventionally. The mindset is what makes a rootworker effective, and it's what made enslaved Africans survive and eventually overcome slavery despite unimaginable oppression.

IN THIS CHAPTER

» Understanding why spirit work defines Hoodoo

» Recognizing spirit work in its many forms

» Deciding to engage with spirits and spirit work

Chapter 7
Spirit Work: The Soul of Hoodoo

If I had to point to one foundational element that makes Hoodoo *Hoodoo* and distinguishes it from European folk magic or general American folk practices, I'd choose this spiritual basis: the ancestors who chose the sea. During the Middle Passage, millions of enslaved Africans died while crossing the Atlantic. Their bodies went into the water, but their spirits remained — powerful, watching, and connected to their descendants in the Americas.

The ancestors who chose the sea and became spirits rather than survive in bondage witnessed unspeakable suffering during their journey. Their experience and sacrifice somehow transformed into power, and these ancestors became the foundation of Hoodoo's spiritual dimension. Their existence is why Hoodoo is sometimes described as a magical inheritance.

Spirit work, also called *conjure* or *working*, is where Hoodoo's magical technology meets its spiritual depth. Within the spiritual depth, Hoodoo practice can become religion for some practitioners. The cultural heritage becomes lived experience, and the dead aren't gone but are present and powerful.

In this chapter, you explore what spirit work is and why it's the heart of Hoodoo identity. You find out which spirits practitioners work with and how the spirit work connects to familiar Black church experiences. And you discover the importance of careful preparation, self-protection, and seeking experienced guidance when you decide to incorporate spirit work into your Hoodoo practice.

Understanding Why Spirit Work Defines Hoodoo

You can perform changemaking magic without Hoodoo, and many traditions work with herbs, candles, and intention. You can divine without Hoodoo because methods that use card reading, pendulums, and scrying exist worldwide. And you can build personal power without Hoodoo; many spiritual systems teach this practice.

But Hoodoo's relationship with the ancestors — particularly the ancestors who died in the Middle Passage and those who survived slavery — is unique. This relationship makes the Hoodoo tradition what it is.

Spiritual ancestors aren't abstract historical figures. They're grandmothers, grandfathers, aunts, uncles, and cousins. They're specific people who had names that were often lost and stories that were often left untold. But they retain a continued presence in the lives of their descendants. When Hoodoo practitioners call on the ancestors, they're not invoking a general concept. They're connecting with actual people who lived, suffered, survived, and in some cases chose death over bondage.

The power in Hoodoo comes from this unbroken line of heritage that includes the knowledge, the spiritual technologies, and the survival strategies passed down across generations despite slavery, Jim Crow, and continued oppression. The ancestors maintained their Hoodoo practices under threat of death, encoded spiritual knowledge in songs and stories, and kept African spirituality alive by disguising it as Christianity when necessary.

The ancestral power still flows through the tradition, which is why Hoodoo without ancestor work feels incomplete to many practitioners. They can use the techniques, follow the formulas, and burn the candles, but if they're not connected to the ancestors who created and preserved this tradition, they're missing the heart of it.

REMEMBER

The importance of ancestral connection is why Hoodoo's relationship to non-ADOS practitioners is complex. The ancestors of Hoodoo are specifically African and African American. If you're not part of that lineage, you can certainly learn Hoodoo techniques, but the deep ancestral current that powers the tradition for Black practitioners isn't available to you in the same way. This doesn't mean you can't practice respectfully or effectively, but it means acknowledging that you're working with a tradition whose spiritual power flows through a lineage that may not be yours.

TECHNICAL STUFF

ADOS stands for American Descendants of Slavery.

Identifying Spirit Work and Its Many Facets

Spirit work in Hoodoo is the practice of actively engaging with spiritual beings such as ancestors, saints, angels, and sometimes other entities. Practitioners ask these beings for guidance, assistance, protection, and power. This engagement involves communication, relationship, and partnership with the spiritual realm.

You can find this idea of spiritual connection through other frameworks, including these similar practices that exist in different traditions:

- **In parapsychology,** calling on spirits is often called *mediumship* and is the practice of mediating communication between spirits or between spirits and living humans.
- **In some Western magical traditions,** conjuring spirits is called *theurgy*, and its purpose is to make earthly use of supernatural beings' powers.
- **In many religions,** including Christianity, contacting spirits is called mysticism or communion and involves seeking direct connection to the divine.
- **In African traditional religions,** spirit work takes many forms depending on the tradition. Practitioners may engage divine intermediaries such as the orishas in Yoruba tradition, propitiating, honoring, and serving these beings through offerings and ritual, or working with them as active partners in spiritual life.
- **In the Black church,** spiritual connections manifest as practices such as catching the spirit, being moved by the Holy Ghost, or receiving direct messages from God. I describe all of these in the next section.

All these traditions point to similar phenomena: humans connecting with and being influenced by spiritual forces or beings beyond the purely physical realm. Hoodoo's version is specifically rooted in African ancestor veneration combined with Christian theology and shaped by the unique historical experience of African Americans.

REMEMBER

When a Hoodoo practitioner works with spirits — calling on ancestors, feeling their presence, receiving their guidance, and being ridden or moved by spiritual force — they're engaging in something that's both deeply African and uniquely African American. This part of Hoodoo survived mostly intact from African spiritual technologies and was adapted and strengthened through the crucible of slavery and its aftermath.

Recognizing spirit work in Black church traditions

If you were raised in Black Baptist or Pentecostal churches, much of the content in this section will feel familiar because spirit work is already part of your religious experience, even if it wasn't called that. If you grew up in the Black church, you already know what spirit feels like, what it means to be moved, to receive messages, and to have spiritual presence be real and tangible. Hoodoo's spirit work is tapping into that same spiritual technology.

Here are specific examples of spirit work in church:

- **Catching the Holy Spirit:** When someone is moved by spiritual force during worship and begins to shout, dance, speak powerfully, or *falls out* (falls to the floor during intense worship), this is spirit work in action. The spirit has taken hold of the person and is working through them.
- **Waiting to hear from God before making major decisions:** Sitting in prayer until you receive clear guidance, feeling moved in a certain direction, and having a voice or a knowing come into your head are all manifestations of spirit work. You're opening yourself to receive spiritual communication.
- **Consulting the mothers and fathers of the church who have insight:** These individuals always seem to know what's happening, may have prophetic dreams, and can use prayer to make shifts in what's happening. They're doing spirit work, whether they use that terminology or not.
- **Engaging in ring shouts and ecstatic worship.** The old *ring shout* tradition of moving in a counterclockwise circle while singing and clapping, building spiritual energy collectively until people are caught up in the spirit is communal spirit work. The group creates a spiritual opening, and the Holy Spirit moves through those present.
- **Using gospel music and spirituals.** Musical worship that can move you to tears, shift the atmosphere in the room, and seemingly carry a force beyond just sound demonstrate the spirit working through music. Using music is one of the most powerful technologies for opening spiritual channels.

REMEMBER

Many Black Americans who would never identify as practitioners of Hoodoo have been doing spirit work their entire lives through church. Hoodoo's spirit work uses similar techniques and experiences but explicitly includes ancestor veneration alongside (or sometimes instead of) Christian framing. Consider these perspectives:

- **Church and Hoodoo aren't opposites.** Despite old stereotypes about Hoodoo being devil worship or anti-Christian, many traditional rootworkers were — and are — devout Christians who see no conflict between working roots and serving God.
- **The Bible itself is full of spiritual experiences.** In the Bible, you can find instances of dreams, visions, angels appearing, spirits moving people, and prophets receiving direct messages. Hoodoo's spirit work is simply another expression of the same spiritual reality that church people experience when they catch the Holy Spirit.

Understanding spirit work as religious practice

For some Hoodoo practitioners, spirit work is an aspect of magical practice, and they use it as a tool alongside candles, baths, and formulas. For others, spirit work becomes the center of their spiritual life, making Hoodoo less a magical practice and more a religion or spiritual path. Practitioners who have the spiritual path focus may orient their entire lives around spiritual service and connection. They may also have these experiences and characteristics:

- Spending more time at their altars in prayer and meditation than doing practical magic.
- Receiving direct messages, guidance, or commands from spirits.
- Feeling called to serve their communities as spiritual leaders, counselors, or healers.
- Viewing themselves as mediums, channels, prophets, or vessels for spiritual forces.

Under these conditions, Hoodoo becomes truly religious for some people. Spirit work isn't just a toolbox of techniques, but a lived spiritual practice centered on relationship with the divine through ancestors, saints, and direct spiritual experience. These practitioners don't separate their Hoodoo practice and their religious life; it's all one integrated spiritual reality. The rootwork, the church work, the divination, the prayer, and the spiritual counsel are all part of their calling to serve as a bridge between the physical and spiritual realms.

Distinguishing veneration from worship

Some Christians can be uncomfortable with Hoodoo's spirit work and ask these questions:

- » Aren't you worshipping the dead?
- » Isn't that forbidden?

I want to make this point clear: Ancestor veneration isn't ancestor worship. *Worship* in monotheistic religions means recognizing a divine entity that's ultimate in power and worthy of absolute devotion and submission. Christians worship God, and they reserve that worship for the Divine alone.

Ancestral veneration means honoring, respecting, remembering, and maintaining relationship with those humans who came before. It acknowledges that the dead are not gone, but instead, continue to exist spiritually and can be in relationship with the living. When you visit a grave and talk to your deceased grandmother, tell her your troubles, ask for her guidance, or feel her presence, are you worshipping her? No. You're maintaining relationship, honoring her, and asking for her help from wherever she is now. That's ancestral veneration.

Theologically, many Christians believe in the *communion of saints*, in which believers who've died are still part of the spiritual community, can pray for those still living, and remain connected across the veil of death. Ancestor veneration in Hoodoo is essentially this concept applied to your own family and lineage.

Seeing spirit work in cultural examples

Spirit work in Hoodoo is rarely portrayed accurately in media. Instances of spirit work in action may be sensationalized, demonized, or made spooky for entertainment. But the following sections offer a few examples in which spirit work is shown with respect and accuracy. And Chapter 17 has more details about the topic of Hoodoo in entertainment.

Nova Bordelon in Queen Sugar

The character of Nova in the Oprah Winfrey Network (OWN) series *Queen Sugar* offers one of the best mainstream representations of what spirit work in Hoodoo can look like when it's lived as spirituality and cultural practice, even though the show never gives her work an official name. Nova performs spirit work that portrays baby blessing ceremonies, cleansing rituals that use sage, serving as community herbalist, ancestor veneration ceremonies, spiritual presence at death, and connection to land and history.

Significantly, the show never explicitly names what tradition Nova practices. The script doesn't label her work as Hoodoo or Voodoo. Instead, her spirituality isn't presented as exotic or frightening; it's normalized and simply woven into the character.

The blues singer Sammie in Sinners (2025)

In the 2025 film *Sinners*, you find a scene in which the singer Sammie conjures spirits of the past and future through blues music practiced in a communal way. This scene presents a strong cinematic example of how spirit work as magic can appear:

- The use of music and rhythm to open spiritual channels
- Communal participation that creates collective spiritual energy
- The singer serving as medium for spiritual forces in which the called spirits manifest
- The line between past, present, and future becoming fluid in spiritual space

This portrayal reflects the historical reality of how music in African American tradition has always served as spiritual technology. From Ring Shouts to gospel and spirituals to blues and hip hop, music doesn't just express spirituality; it creates spiritual openings, calls spirits, and moves power.

Answering the Call to Develop Spirit Work

I encourage you to start simple with ancestor work. You don't need elaborate altars, expensive offerings, or complex rituals to begin connecting with your honored ancestors. Start with a glass of fresh water (changed weekly), a white candle (lit when you pray), and a photo or symbolic representation of your ancestors. Sit calmly and talk to them like you're talking and sharing your life with living elders. That's enough to begin building connections and relationships for the spirit work in your practice of Hoodoo.

WARNING

Spirit work isn't for everyone, and that's okay. Some practitioners are called to deep spirit work; it's their primary gift and focus. Others are called to change-making magic, healing, or divination, with only basic ancestor connection. And some have no calling to spirit work at all and work entirely with material and personal power. All of these approaches are valid Hoodoo practice. Don't force yourself into spirit work if it doesn't feel right or necessary for your practice.

Beginning with general guidance

If you feel called to develop spirit work within your practice, here are general guidelines for getting started:

- **Start with your own ancestors.** Don't reach out to random spirits or powerful entities you don't know. Begin with your own deceased family — people who loved you and have reason to want your well-being.
- **Use simple offerings and communication.** Water, light (candles), and conversation are the basics. Sit at your altar (or any quiet place), tell your ancestors about your life, ask for their guidance and protection, and thank them for their help.
- **Listen and observe.** Spirit communication often comes through dreams, intuition, signs, synchronicities, or sudden insights. Pay attention to what happens after you pray or ask questions, and keep records of your communication and experiences.
- **Protect yourself first.** Before opening yourself to spiritual communication, ensure you're protected. Pray for protection, use protective techniques (such as a white candle protection prayer or a cleansing bath with hyssop or salt before working), and only work with spirits you trust.
- **Seek guidance from experienced practitioners.** If you want to go deeper into spirit work, find a teacher who's practiced in the spirit work tradition and can guide you properly.
- **Go slowly.** Don't rush into heavy spirit work. Build gradually by incorporating simple prayers and offerings first. You can then go deeper with communication and more advanced practices after you're feeling more comfortable with the work.
- **Trust your instincts.** If some message or connection feels wrong, off, or frightening, stop what you're doing. If a spirit feels malevolent or demanding, disengage and seek help. Good spirits don't threaten, manipulate, or push you into things you're uncomfortable with.

» **Remember relationship.** Spirit work is about relationship, not control. You're not commanding spirits; you're building mutual relationships of respect and reciprocity.

Working with various types of spirits

Spirit work in Hoodoo can involve various types of spiritual beings, depending on the practitioner's beliefs, calling, and relationships. In this section, I include a brief discussion of identifying spirits and determining whether and how to work with them.

Connecting with ancestors: The foundation

Your own deceased family members and the broader lineage of African and African American ancestors form the foundation of spirit work. This includes personal family ancestors (grandparents, parents, and other relatives you knew), lineage ancestors (going back generations to those who survived slavery or died in the Middle Passage), elevated ancestors (particularly powerful spiritual leaders in your family line), and adopted or claimed ancestors (powerful historical figures like Harriet Tubman or unnamed ancestors of the tradition).

Distinguishing ghosts from ancestors

Ghosts aren't the same as ancestors, although people sometimes confuse the terms. A *ghost* is the spirit of a dead person who has some or all of these characteristics:

- They may or may not be related to you.
- They're often earthbound or stuck rather than properly transitioned to the afterlife.
- They may be haunting a location or seeking something unfinished with the goal of finishing it.
- They can be neutral, helpful, or harmful depending on who they were and what their current state is. Troubled ghosts are often called *haints* in Hoodoo.

Ghosts are spirits you might acknowledge, help to move on, protect yourself from, or (rarely) negotiate with if they're not hostile. But you don't typically invite them to guide your life or put them on your altar.

On the other hand, *ancestors* are honored spirits that you invite into regular communication, build relationship with, ask for guidance from, and make regular offerings to. This type of spirit work cultivates beneficial spiritual connection.

WARNING

Not every spirit deserves your attention or relationship. The fact that some entity is dead and spiritual doesn't make it wise, benevolent, or worthy of connection. Just like you wouldn't invite every living stranger into your home, don't invite every ghost or spirit into your spiritual life. Your honored ancestors are chosen relationships. Random ghosts are like random people on the street. And most of them should be politely ignored, some might need help from someone qualified, and a few might be dangerous. Stick with your honored ancestors and established spiritual allies unless you're trained in working with unknown spirits.

Petitioning saints and holy figures

If you're a practitioner who works within a Christian framework, you may petition Catholic saints who each have specialties. For example, you may ask St. Michael for protection or St. Expedite for help in urgent matters. You may also seek out biblical figures such as Moses, King David, Mary, Jesus, and various prophets. Guardian angels, archangels, and other celestial beings can also supply assistance and guidance.

Expanding beyond blood relatives

Honored ancestors aren't limited to direct genealogical relatives. Your honored ancestors can include chosen family and these types of relationships:

- **The uncle or auntie** who wasn't blood-related but nonetheless raised you
- **Community ancestors and elders** who served and blessed your community
- **Cultural and spiritual ancestors** such as Harriet Tubman
- **Ancestors of place** who are the spirits of those who came before and lived on land you now live on
- **Spiritual lineage ancestors,** which include rootworkers and healers who came before you in the Hoodoo tradition

The key to any spirit connection is relationship, honor, and mutual respect. Blood creates possibility for connection, but honored ancestor status is earned through the way the ancestors lived and granted through your choice to honor them.

Handling problematic ancestors

You must consider that not all of your ancestors were perfectly well-behaved or well-meaning people. What about the alcoholic grandfather who beat his children? The ancestor who betrayed the family? The relative who died bitter and causing harm? Most practitioners would tell you to acknowledge these people's existence, but don't invite them to your altar or ask for their guidance.

Traditional practitioners take several approaches to dealing with troublesome ancestors:

- » Acknowledge the ancestor but maintain your distance.
- » Pray for their elevation to find peace in the afterlife, but don't work with them directly.
- » Call on the generation beyond them by reaching over the problem generation to connect with ancestors further back.
- » Work with the elevated ancestors who were spiritually advanced and loving.
- » Cleanse your life of the problem ancestor's influence if you're carrying trauma or patterns stemming from them.

REMEMBER

You have agency for deciding which spiritual relationships to cultivate. Blood connection doesn't obligate you to give someone access to your spiritual life, especially if they were harmful while living their own physical life.

Living as a future honored ancestor

Considering how you live your life flips the perspective of spirit work: How are you living now so that your descendants will want to honor you?

When you think of yourself as a future honored ancestor, it changes how you move through the world. Your choices have legacy implications. Your character matters spiritually. Your struggles can become strength for future generations. Your focus on service compounds, and the heritage you build now serves descendants you'll never meet. Your spiritual development continues and affects the type of spirit you become after death.

Living as a future honored ancestor isn't about being perfect. It's about living with intention, integrity, and awareness that you're part of a chain. You receive from those who came before you and pass on to those who come after.

REMEMBER

You're building your own ancestor legacy right now. Every choice you make about how to treat people, handle difficulty, develop your character, and maintain your spiritual life is shaping what kind of ancestor you'll be. Your descendants will either reach past you to look for better ancestors, or they'll call on you gratefully because you lived in a way that makes you worthy of honor. This idea of living well isn't about perfection; it's about overall patterns of integrity, love, courage, and growth.

Setting up altars as spiritual signal boosters

Do you need an altar or dedicated space to do spirit work? The simple answer is no. Many Hoodoo practitioners believe they can connect with spiritual allies anywhere, anytime, even while walking down the street, sitting in their car, or lying in bed. Accessing the spiritual realm doesn't require physical props, but using an altar can make spirit work easier and stronger. Think of your altar as a signal booster for your spiritual cell phone. Can you make calls without it? Yes. Do calls come through clearer and stronger with it? Absolutely.

An altar serves multiple functions:

- Making a focus point that helps you shift into spiritual mode.
- Creating ongoing connection, like keeping a line connected rather than dialing fresh each time.
- Showing respect and honor for your spirits, while serving as a visual reminder for you to tend your spiritual relationships.
- Accumulating energy through prayers said at the altar, offerings made, and spiritual presence welcomed to the altar. The space itself becomes spiritually charged.

Not everyone has space for elaborate altars. But your altar can be a single white candle and small cup of water on a windowsill (as shown in Figure 7-1), a shoebox under your bed with photos and prayer cards, the top of your dresser with one meaningful object, or an altar app on your phone where you keep photos and prayers. You may need no physical space at all but just develop a practiced ability to connect spiritually wherever you are. What matters is the relationship and your intention for the spiritual practice, not how fancy your altar looks.

FIGURE 7-1: A simple altar for spiritual practice.

© John Wiley & Sons, Inc.

TIP

If you come from a Christian background, you may already have experience with the concept of spiritual space existing anywhere through *prayer closets*, which are dedicated spaces for private prayer and communion with God. In Hoodoo, these spaces function as altars by another name. The prayer closet *is* the altar. It's that quiet corner where you pray, that spot in your bedroom where you feel closest to the Divine, and that shelf where you keep your Bible and prayer journal. All these spaces represent altar work, even if you've never called it that.

RESPECTING ETHICAL BOUNDARIES IN LEARNING SPIRIT WORK

Spirit work is the heart of Hoodoo, yes, but it's also the most serious, potentially dangerous, and culturally sensitive aspect of the practice. Unlike lighting a candle or reading cards, working with spirits requires proper preparation, cultural context, and often direct teaching from experienced practitioners.

Done incorrectly, spirit work can result in spiritual attachment, possession by unwelcome entities, mental or emotional distress, or opening doors you don't know how to close. The ancestors of Hoodoo — particularly those who died in the Middle Passage — aren't spiritual tourist attractions.

(continued)

(continued)

This chapter explains what spirit work is, which spirits practitioners work with, why spirit work is central to Hoodoo, and how it connects to familiar experiences. The chapter purposefully doesn't provide specific invocation techniques, possession protocols, or detailed altar rituals for calling spirits.

Consider these guidelines for accepting spirit work teaching:

- Spirit work is traditionally taught person-to-person, with mentorship and gradual development.
- Unlike changemaking practical magic, spirit work is highly individual. Methods you use for calling your ancestors may not work for someone else's.
- Some knowledge is meant to be earned and not given freely. The process of learning spirit work properly is part of what prepares you to use the knowledge you gain wisely.

IN THIS CHAPTER

» Understanding why divination matters in rootwork

» Recognizing three types of practitioners: seers, readers, and those who are both

» Exploring traditional divination methods

» Developing your own divination abilities through practice

Chapter 8
Practicing Divination in Hoodoo

Before you fix a problem, you need to know what the problem is. Working your magic on a situation requires understanding what's really happening — not just what appears to be happening on the surface. Determine whether you're likely to succeed or face serious opposition prior to committing time, ingredients, and spiritual energy to a Hoodoo working.

This need-to-know is why divination is essential to Hoodoo practice. Assessing situations is so essential that some practitioners act primarily (or only) as diviners. Working blind is like gambling, but working with clear vision holds power.

In this chapter, you discover different approaches practitioners use for divining. Some diviners see naturally, some use devices to help their vision, and some do both. You also find out about the major divination methods in the tradition and how to develop your ability to see what can be hidden in a situation.

Understanding Why Divination Matters

Divination isn't fortune-telling entertainment; it's diagnostic Hoodoo work. Think of divination as a process by which a rootworker can see what's hidden, read what's coming, and understand the spiritual dimensions of a situation. Diviners gather intelligence, ask the right questions, and get clear answers before they act. The result of this diligence makes Hoodoo working far more effective than just throwing ingredients at problems and hoping something sticks.

Chapter 5 discusses the idea that Hoodoo is results-oriented. Specifically, if it doesn't get results, it's not Hoodoo. Divination helps ensure that practitioners get results through several means:

- **Accurate diagnosis:** You think your problem is bad luck, but divination reveals that someone's been working against you. You think you need a love spell, but divination shows that the relationship is fundamentally incompatible. Correct diagnosis leads to correct treatment.
- **Strategic planning:** Divination tells you the best timing for your work, which approach is most likely to succeed, what obstacles you'll face, and whether you should even attempt what you're considering. It's reconnaissance before battle.
- **Course correction:** Midway through a nine-day working, you divine to check progress. The cards or signs tell you something's off. Maybe you need to adjust your approach, add protection work, or abandon this method and try another. Without checking, you'd waste the full nine days.
- **Confirmation:** After completing work, you divine to see if it's taking hold, if you need to reinforce it, or if something went wrong that needs fixing. You're not just hoping. You're checking.
- **Spirit communication:** Many rootworkers divine to receive guidance from ancestors, guardian angels, or other helping spirits. The divination tool becomes a telephone line to the spiritual realm.
- **Warning system:** Regular divination helps you see trouble coming before it arrives, giving you time to protect yourself, avoid problems, or prepare your response.

TIP

Traditional rootworkers divine before major work, during work to check progress, and after work to confirm success. Divination isn't optional; it's integral to effective practice.

Recognizing Three Types of Practitioners

In traditional Hoodoo communities, divination ability showed up in various ways, and practitioners specialized accordingly. Divination illuminates your understanding of a situation; it doesn't make you all-knowing. Even the most gifted seers usually receive partial or incomplete information, and the most skilled readers interpret through their own experience and perception.

No practitioner — seer, reader, or one who does both — has access to the full picture of a client's situation, and any who claim otherwise are overstepping what the tradition itself teaches. Hoodoo divination is a tool for sharpening your perception and discernment, not replacing them. Receive what a practitioner offers as an informed perspective, weigh it honestly against what you already know, and trust your own judgment about what rings true.

REMEMBER

You don't need to be naturally psychic to divine effectively. Although seers exist and their gifts are regarded as real in Hoodoo, most accurate divination comes from people who learn solid techniques and practice them diligently. Card reading, pendulum work, and sign interpretation are skills that people can learn. Natural psychic ability is a gift, but learned divination is a craft. Both can work. Start with what you can learn, and if you have natural gifts, they'll develop alongside your technical skills.

Seers: Those who just know

Some people are born with "the sight." They see things others don't, know things they couldn't logically know, sense spiritual presences, or receive information through dreams, visions, or sudden knowing. In Hoodoo communities, these individuals might be called *two-headed* (someone with both physical sight and nonphysical sight), *seers* or *prophets* (those who see what's coming or what's hidden), or *dream-walkers* (individuals whose dreams consistently bring true information).

Seers generally don't need tools — the information comes to them directly. They are what parapsychologists would call psychics. They might have premonitions, see spirits, pick up on energy or feelings around people, or receive downloads of information seemingly from nowhere. Many practitioners describe this gift of sight as an ability that every person possesses to varying degrees. And they can also develop and refine it with practice.

Not everyone has this natural ability at a level high enough to be thought of as a seer. Most traditional rootworkers aren't seers; they're readers who use tools, and they do outstanding work. The next section covers those who use tools.

Readers: Those who use divination tools

Most divination in Hoodoo happens when practitioners use *divination tools* — physical objects that serve as interfaces between the practitioner and *numinous* (awe-inspiring and mysterious) information. The tools are nearly countless, but readers commonly learn systems such as choosing playing cards, throwing bones, working with a pendulum, *bibliomancy* (random Bible passages), examining tea leaves or coffee grounds, and interpreting oil in water patterns.

These systems involve learned skills, which I talk more about in the section "Using oracular devices: Tools of the reader" later in the chapter. You study the meanings, practice the techniques, and over time, become proficient. A good reader can be extraordinarily accurate without having natural psychic gifts because they grasp the language of their chosen tools.

REMEMBER

Many rootworkers prefer tools because they provide structure, can be taught to others, and offer a concrete object to focus on. The tools become extensions of the practitioner's intuition.

Those who are both: Seers who also use tools

Some practitioners have natural sight and use divination tools. The tools help them articulate what they're sensing, give clients something concrete to focus on, or provide a second opinion about what they're seeing intuitively.

A seer might *pull cards* not because they need the cards to show the answer, but because the cards help them explain what they're seeing to their client. In addition, combining natural sight with formal divination methods can provide more detailed information. For example, a card may serve to specify the timing of an event the seer is already perceiving.

TECHNICAL STUFF

Pulling cards is a method by which the reader draws cards at random from a shuffled deck and interprets their imagery and positions.

Natural sight and divination tools don't always agree with each other. Experienced practitioners who work with both regularly encounter moments in which *what they sense* and *what the cards say* point in different directions. Most develop a feel over time, built from years of practice, for when to trust the sight and when to trust the tools. Some approach the disagreement empirically, running multiple sessions on the same question and treating the majority of results as the working answer before committing to an interpretation. The disagreement itself isn't a failure of method. It's additional information.

The relationship between sight and tools also shifts as a practitioner develops and gains experience. Readers and seers often travel in these opposite directions but end up with the two trajectories converging:

- Readers who start out depending entirely on tools may find that, over time, meaning surfaces before they've finished laying the cards.
- Seers often adopt tools over time, not because their natural perception weakens, but because tools provide structure. Tools can catch what unassisted sight misses and make their work understandable to others.

In Hoodoo communities, practitioners aren't evaluated on whether they use sight, tools, or both. What matters is accuracy. Whether a practitioner works through cards, bones, natural perception, or some combination is largely beside the point. The tradition has always resisted the kind of methodological gatekeeping that other traditions use to establish hierarchy. You're either good at divination or you're not, and the community will tell you which.

TECHNICAL STUFF

The tradition has no single term for practitioners who combine natural sight with divination tools. Regional communities use different language: *two-headed* (carrying both physical and nonphysical sight) is one common descriptor; *prophet* or *prophetess* is used in some communities; *psychic* is increasingly common in contemporary practice. *Diviner* appears more in academic writing than in community usage. Most practitioners are simply described by what they can do rather than categorized by a label.

Uncovering Hoodoo's Divination Methods

Before tools, before decks of cards or pendulums, people read the world around them. Natural sign reading is the oldest form of divination, and it remains important in Hoodoo today. Although seers might receive information directly — psychically or perceived from the natural world — most Hoodoo divination uses tools. These objects help you focus spiritual information and translate it into readable form.

Dreams are also a primary way in which spiritual information comes through in Hoodoo. In Hoodoo, dreams aren't just random brain activity. They're messages, warnings, teachings, and sometimes direct communication with spirits or the divine. In this section, I cover all these divination methods.

Reading natural signs and omens

Signs are meaningful patterns in the natural or everyday world that carry spiritual messages. A bird's unusual behavior, a dream that feels significant, an unexpected encounter, and a series of coincidences that form a pattern aren't random. They're the universe, spirits, or God trying to communicate.

The divining skill that Hoodoo practitioners develop includes learning to distinguish between ordinary natural randomness and meaningful signs and then interpreting what the signs mean.

Identifying types of natural signs

When you look at the world around you to discover signs, you can focus on natural aspects of reality, as I outline in the following groupings.

Animal messengers usually involve creatures behaving unusually or appearing at significant moments:

- **A black cat crossing your path** can be a warning of danger ahead.
- **Birds flying into windows** may be an omen of death or a major life change.
- **Unusual animal behavior** around your property indicates that spiritual activity is ongoing.
- **Animals appearing repeatedly** may signify a spirit guide making contact.
- **Finding dead animals** often portends endings, transformations, or someone working against you.

Weather and natural phenomena also have meaning:

- **Sudden storms** can indicate a turbulent answer or opposition when you're asking a question.
- **Unexpected sunshine breaking through clouds** foretells a blessing, a clearing, or hope for a situation.
- **Wind directions and intensity** can show that spirits are moving or that change is on the way.
- **Lightning striking near you** can accompany a powerful spiritual event or give a warning about a significant crossroads or confrontation ahead.

Household signs occur in and around the home:

- **Objects falling or breaking without apparent cause** may denote spiritual disruption in your home or a warning about an unresolved conflict or spiritual threat that needs your attention.
- **Clocks stopping at significant times** can urge you to take note of the related situation or happening.
- **Pictures falling off walls** may signal a useful connection to the person in the photo.
- **Unexplained sounds in the home** often indicate the presence of a spirit, also in your home.
- **Candles and electric lights behaving strangely** (flickering dramatically, for example) may also suggest a spiritual presence.

Body sensations are real and have purpose:

- **Sudden chills or hot flashes** can mark the presence of a spirit.
- **Ringing in your ears** may mean that someone is talking about you or a spirit is trying to communicate with you.
- **Itching palms** have meaning related to money. In some traditions, itching in the right palm means you'll receive money, and itching in the left palm may mean spending money.
- **Eye twitching** indicates that someone is watching you or directing attention your way.
- **Unexplained exhaustion** can be the warning of a spiritual attack or distress from an *energy vampire*, which is someone who, knowingly or not, drains emotional and spiritual energy from those around them through negativity and exploitation.
- **A lie bump materializing on the tongue** can indicate that someone is lying. A *lie bump* is a small, temporary, and often painful red or white bump caused by inflammation.

Synchronicities and patterns that are outside of your usual experience may occur:

- **Seeing the same number repeated** involves *angel numbers*, which are sequences of the same number, such as 111. They have specific spiritual emphasis, depending on the digit repeated.

- **Running into the same person multiple times** can be a seemingly accidental occurrence, or it may mean that person carries spiritual significance for your current situation and warrants closer attention.
- **Books falling open to relevant passages** may offer the guidance you need to solve a problem.
- **Overhearing conversations that answer your unspoken questions** may signify that the universe is responding directly to something you've been holding in your mind.
- **Specific things happening in threes** can indicate that a pattern is fully confirmed and requires your attention, or in some traditions, that a death is coming.

Learning how to read signs

WARNING

Don't see signs in everything. You must develop a balance between awareness of possible natural signs and paranoia. Not every bird is a messenger, not every broken dish is a spiritual warning, and not every coincidence is meaningful. If you find yourself seeing ominous signs everywhere and living in constant anxiety, you've gone too far.

Real signs usually have a quality of emphasis. They're notable, repeated, or create a strong feeling. Random everyday events are just that: random and everyday. And here's how you can maintain awareness of your surroundings but also distinguish between random events and meaningful signs:

- **Pay attention.** Most people miss signs because they're not looking. Develop the habit of noticing unusual occurrences, patterns, and synchronicities.
- **Note the context; it matters.** A crow cawing is normal. A crow appearing on your doorstep repeatedly over three days while you're considering a major decision is a sign. Consider timing and circumstances.
- **Trust your gut reaction.** When something gives you a strong feeling — comfort, warning, excitement, or dread — that's often your intuition reading spiritual information. Don't dismiss it as just a feeling.
- **Look for patterns.** One coincidence is chance. Two is interesting. Three is a pattern, and you should pay attention.
- **Ask for clarification.** If you're unsure what a sign means, pray for clarity or use another divination method to get more information.
- **Keep a journal.** Recording signs and their outcomes teaches you your personal sign language and helps you recognize patterns over time.

When you put these practices to use over time, you develop your own vocabulary of signs. Traditional meanings of natural signs are guidelines, not rules. A black cat might traditionally signal a warning, but if you love cats and feel comforted when you see one, that's your personal sign language.

Using oracular devices: Tools of the reader

Hoodoo practitioners use several kinds of *oracular devices* to aid traditional divination. These devices mimic the working of ancient oracles, which gives them their name. Reading playing cards is probably Hoodoo's most common device-related divination method for the past 100 years, and using a 52-card poker deck is the traditional standard.

Some other items in a practitioner's toolbox include pendulums for yes or no questions, small objects thrown and interpreted by how they land, and passages read from sacred books that practitioners open randomly. This section covers these and other oracular tools.

Reading playing cards

A regular deck of playing cards — not tarot, though a growing number of modern practitioners use tarot in traditional Hoodoo card reading — becomes a sophisticated divination system. Why do practitioners rely on playing cards? They're widely available and inexpensive, don't draw undue attention (unlike tarot cards or occult-looking tools), can be used in plain sight without raising suspicion, and are simple enough to learn but complex enough for nuanced readings.

Basic card meanings are organized by suit:

- **Hearts** relate to emotions, relationships, and home.
- **Diamonds** relate to money, work, and the material world.
- **Clubs** relate to work, growth, and social matters.
- **Spades** relate to challenges, endings, and difficult truths.

Then each card within a suit has specific meanings. For instance, the ace of hearts represents new love or emotional beginning, while the nine of hearts is the wish card, which signifies what you desire most. The ten of diamonds represents a large sum of money or significant financial change. The ace of spades represents death, endings, or major transformation.

Learning to read playing cards involves memorizing the meanings of all 52 cards, practicing different spreads (three-card, five-card, full layout), and developing your ability to synthesize multiple cards into a coherent story. Figure 8-1 shows a full layout of a card deck as it may be used in Hoodoo.

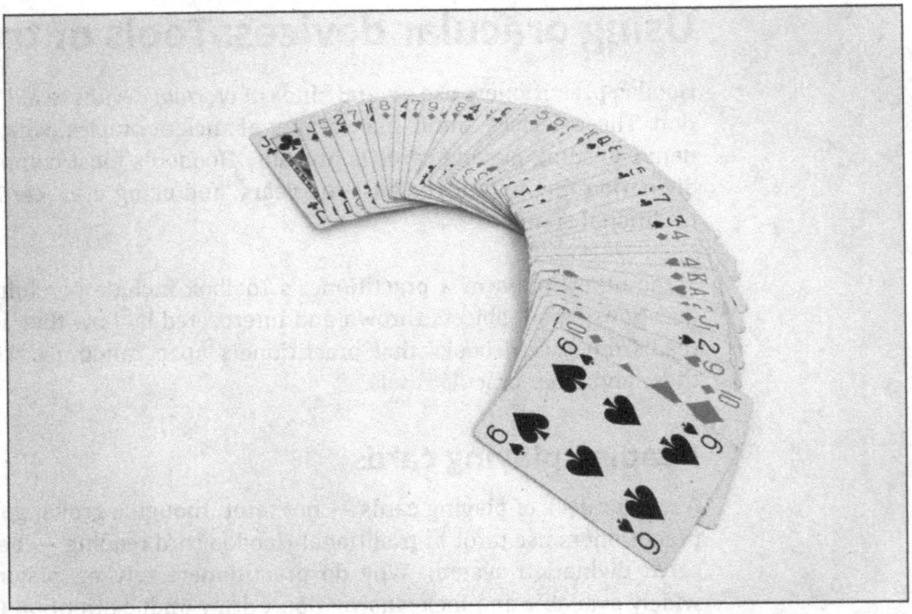

FIGURE 8-1: A standard poker deck in use for Hoodoo divination.

Nuno De Sá Teixeira/Adobe Stock Photos

Working with pendulums

A pendulum can be any weighted object on a chain or string. You hold it suspended and still and ask yes/no questions. The pendulum's movement gives answers. Back-and-forth or circular motions can indicate yes or no, depending on how you've established your system. Figure 8-2 shows a pendulum in use.

Before using a pendulum, you calibrate it by asking questions with known answers, such as "Is my name [*insert your actual name*]?" and establishing which movement means yes and which means no. Then you can ask unknown questions and trust the pendulum's response.

Pendulums work best for binary questions: Should I take this job? Is this person trustworthy? Will this approach work? They're less effective for complex situations that require nuanced answers.

FIGURE 8-2: A pendulum used in Hoodoo to answer binary questions.

Alex Pios/Adobe Stock Photos

Throwing bones for divination

Bone throwing and dream interpretation are the oldest divinatory tools used in Hoodoo. Bone throwing, also called *casting bones* or *throwing the bones*, uses small objects thrown onto a surface and read based on how they land. These objects may be actual bones, shells, stones, coins, keys, dominoes, or even buttons; their positions relative to each other and their individual orientation (whether they land face-up or touching) are important.

Each object in the set that you case has assigned meaning. For example: a key might represent solutions or opportunities, a coin represents money, a shell represents water or emotions, a white stone represents blessings, and a black stone represents obstacles.

REMEMBER

Bone throwing is a complex system that requires significant study and practice to operate effectively. The reader interprets the entire configuration of the thrown objects — not just individual pieces — and assesses the relative positions of pieces, clusters of pieces, and the overall pattern they create.

Practicing bibliomancy with sacred texts

Bibliomancy is divination by randomly opening a sacred book — traditionally, Hoodoo practitioners use the Bible — and reading the passage you land on as guidance or an answer to questions.

To use this divination technique, you hold your question clearly in mind, open the Bible at random (or let it fall open), and place your finger on the page. The verse or passage you've indicated is your answer. Sometimes it's direct and literal.

Sometimes it requires interpretation — metaphorical language, historical context, or understanding the passage's original meaning.

Some practitioners use other sacred texts in this way or extend it to meaningful books in their lives. The Bible remains most traditional in Hoodoo because of the practice's Christian roots.

Scrying with water and mirrors

Scrying involves gazing into a reflective surface until images, visions, or impressions arise. Traditional methods of scrying include using a bowl of water (sometimes adding oil, ink, or soot to darken it), a black mirror or regular mirror in dim light, a combined candle, and water. You gaze into water by candlelight.

Scrying requires patience and practice. Most people don't see dramatic visions. They only get subtle impressions, feelings, fleeting images, or sudden certainty about a relevant issue. This indirect messaging is both normal and valid.

Reading tea leaves and coffee grounds

Reading patterns in either tea leaves or coffee grounds follows similar principles. You drink either beverage from a light-colored cup, leaving some liquid and all residue. Then while thinking about your question, you swirl the cup three times in a clockwise direction, invert the cup onto a saucer and let the liquid drain, and then turn the cup upright to read the patterns formed inside. See Figure 8-3.

FIGURE 8-3: Reading patterns in tea leaves.

pixardi/Adobe Stock Photos

Symbols that may appear (such as hearts, letters, numbers, and shapes of objects or animals) are interpreted according to traditional meanings and the reader's intuition. Patterns near the rim relate to near future; patterns at the bottom relate to distant future or deep issues.

Working with dreams: The night school of Hoodoo

Regular dreams process daily life and help people work through stress with random imagery. These dreams feel vague upon waking and are hard to remember. Other types of dreams can be common to Hoodoo practitioners and include the following:

- **Medicine dreams** are teaching dreams in which you find out how to heal something, what herbs to use, or how to do a Hoodoo working. You might wake up knowing a formula you didn't know before.
- **Prophetic dreams** show you upcoming circumstances. These types of dreams have a different quality; they're vivid, memorable, and often associated with strong emotion. They may be either literal (showing an actual event) or symbolic (requiring interpretation).
- **Warning dreams** alert you to danger, betrayal, or problems. These dreams often recur until you pay attention. Nightmares that persist may be warnings rather than random fears.
- **Visitation dreams** occur when ancestors, other dead people, or spirits visit you directly to communicate. Visitation dreams often feel more real than regular dreams and have clear communication and strong presence in memory upon waking.
- **Spirit travel dreams** happen when you visit other places or realms in sleep. You might check on distant loved ones, scout out locations, or receive teaching in spiritual dimensions.

Interpreting dream symbols in Hoodoo

Some symbols and imagery have traditional meanings in African American dream interpretation. Here are a few examples:

- **Water** represents emotions, pregnancy, spiritual flow, or cleansing.
- **Snakes** represent enemies, betrayal, or hidden threats.
- **Teeth falling out** suggests death in the family or major loss.

» **Fish** indicate pregnancy, fertility, or abundance.

» **Birds** represent messages, spirits, or freedom.

» **Blood** relates to family matters, life force, or sacrifice.

» **Deceased loved ones** usually indicate actual contact with the dead.

TIP

Personal dream language matters more than universal symbols. If cats always mean comfort to you, then a cat in your dream carries that meaning regardless of traditional interpretations.

Requesting dreams for guidance

In the practice of Hoodoo, you can intentionally request dreams that answer questions or provide guidance by following these steps:

1. **Before bed, clearly state your question and write it down to lodge it in your mind.**
2. **Use dream herbs, such as mugwort tea or African dream root under your pillow, and do so carefully.**

   Remember the saying, "The difference between a medicine and a poison is dosage." The same principle applies to using dream herbs. Additionally, some people may be allergic to certain herbs or herbs in general. If so, use other oracular methods listed in the chapter.
3. **Pray for clear dreams that hold the information you need.**
4. **Keep paper nearby to write down dreams immediately upon waking.**

Following this process doesn't guarantee prophetic dreams every time, but it dramatically increases meaningful dream activity when done consistently.

REMEMBER

Not every dream is a message. Sometimes dreams are just dreams — your brain sorting through the day's events, processing anxieties, or replaying random memories. Prophetic or meaningful dreams usually have a distinctly different quality. They're more vivid, more coherent, more emotionally charged, and they stick with you after waking. If you're not sure whether a dream was meaningful, "sit with it," as many practitioners in the tradition would say. This phrase means to meditate on the dream for a while and let the information reveal its deeper layers to you on its own schedule. Significant dreams tend to keep coming back to your attention, while regular dreams fade quickly.

Developing Your Divination Ability

REMEMBER

Divination is intelligence gathering, not fate. When you divine, you're not learning your unchangeable fate — you're gathering strategic information about the spiritual and hidden aspects of a situation. Divination reveals the playing field so that you can play effectively. Most practitioners view the future not as completely fixed, but as influenced by your choices. Divination helps you make better choices because what you do with the information you gather is up to you. Consider these possible revelations and responses:

- A warning about problems ahead gives you time to protect yourself.
- Knowledge that someone is working against you lets you counter them.
- Seeing a positive outcome encourages you to persist.

Whether you're naturally gifted or learning from scratch, divination skills improve with practice and proper development. Use these approaches to help you build the foundation for divining in Hoodoo:

- **Quiet your mind regularly.** Divination requires you to perceive subtle information. A constantly chattering mind drowns out quiet spiritual messages. Practice meditation (even 5–10 minutes daily), prayer or contemplative silence, time in nature without devices, or any activity that calms mental chatter. If you don't experience the stillness from one of these exercises, try another. Calming mental chatter is the goal.
- **Pay attention to your body.** Your body often knows things before your conscious mind catches up. Learn your body's signals for gut feelings, heart racing or calming, chills or warmth, and tension in specific areas. These feelings and signals in your body are data you can use.
- **Practice with verifiable questions.** When learning to seek guidance from divination, ask questions that you can verify: "Will my friend call me today?" or "Will it rain this afternoon?" Getting answers to verifiable questions helps you build confidence and recognize what accurate information feels like versus wishful thinking.
- **Start simple.** Don't begin your search for guiding answers with complex life questions. Start with yes/no questions, this-or-that choices, near-future events, and straightforward situations. Build skill with simple questions before tackling deep mysteries.
- **Keep records.** Write down predictions, readings, and signs you've seen and interpreted. Note which foresights came true, which didn't, and those that you misinterpreted. Reviewing your records of success and failure with divining answers teaches you faster than anything else.

Overcoming common obstacles

Wanting a specific answer is the biggest threat to accuracy when divining. If you desperately want the cards to say that your ex-partner will return to you, you can easily misread neutral or negative cards as positive. Here's a solution to this problem: Have someone else read the cards for you on emotional issues, or wait to read the cards until you're calmer.

Here are some other obstacles to an effective divination practice:

- **Second-guessing** means changing your interpretation when the initial one seems scary or unwelcome. The first read is usually correct. The solution: Write down your first interpretation before you talk yourself out of it.
- **Reading when depleted** affects accuracy. Divination requires energy and focus. When you're exhausted, sick, or spiritually drained, accuracy suffers. The solution: Take care of yourself first, and divine when you're at 100 percent capacity.
- **Ignoring unwelcome information** means getting a clear warning but proceeding anyway because you don't like what you heard. The solution: Remember that divination is there to help you, not to tell you what you want to hear.

TIP

Over-relying on divination can involve checking cards obsessively, asking the same question repeatedly, or making no decisions without consulting oracles. Divination guides you; it doesn't replace your judgment. Use it strategically, not compulsively.

Following ethical and safety guidelines when reading for others

If you start using your Hoodoo practice to divine for other people, certain guidelines apply to protect both you and your clients:

- **Get consent from the person you're reading for** and don't inject yourself into someone's business without permission.
- **Be honest but kind**, and deliver hard information compassionately.
- **Don't make unwarranted medical or legal claims** unless you're a doctor or lawyer.
- **Empower your clients without creating a dependency** on your guidance. Help people make their own decisions.

» **Know your limits** and refer a client to someone more experienced when you're faced with a situation that seems too difficult to address.

» **Protect yourself** by cleansing and using protective rituals (such as a protective herb bath or a cleansing bath with hyssop) regularly if you read for others frequently.

Understanding divination as spiritual practice

The more you divine, the more you'll notice something interesting: Divination changes you. Gaining divining expertise doesn't just develop a skill. It becomes a spiritual practice that opens your perception, deepens intuition, and strengthens your connection to spiritual dimensions of reality.

REMEMBER

Regular divination practitioners often report increased sensitivity to energy and atmosphere, better intuition in everyday life, clearer dreams and better recall, more frequent awareness of synchronicities, greater connection to ancestors or spiritual allies, and enhanced discernment about people and situations.

Developing and practicing divination exercises your spiritual senses the way physical exercise develops muscles. The more you practice reading signs, consulting cards, or interpreting dreams, the more naturally your perception flows. This demonstrates an organic progression of abilities. Eventually, you may discover that you *just know things* more often and rely on tools less frequently. The tools that help train your intuition also help it to work more directly.

TIP

Divination tools remain valuable even for very skilled practitioners. They provide structure, can catch things intuition misses, and offer concrete depictions to show clients. Exercising insights without oracular devices isn't abandoning tools. It's using them with deep skill and knowing when you don't need them.

Working through a sample reading

In this section, I walk you through the steps of a practical card reading for someone who is feeling blocked in a situation:

1. **Begin by clearly stating the question under consideration.**

   In this case, the question is "Why do I feel so stuck in my career, and what should I do?"

2. **Prepare the deck and draw the cards.**

   Shuffle the deck while holding the question in your mind, cut the deck three times with your left hand, and draw three cards from the top.

3. **Lay the cards face up from left to right in the order you drew them: the first card on your left, the second in the center, and the third on your right.**

   You position the cards as noted in the following table.

Position	Significance	Card Drawn
First	Past/root cause	Seven of diamonds
Second	Present situation	Four of clubs
Third	Advice/outcome	Six of spades

4. **Read and interpret the three drawn and positioned cards.**

   Begin with the first position and read from your left to right:

   - *The seven of diamonds in the past/root cause position* indicates financial worry and uncertainty. The client's sense of being stuck in their career likely originated here because financial anxiety drove them to stay in an unsatisfying job for the sake of security. Fear about money is the root of the stagnation.
   - *The four of clubs in the present position* represents deceit, betrayal, and false friends. Currently, someone in the workplace isn't trustworthy. This person may be taking credit for the client's work, undermining them, or blocking their advancement. The stuck feeling isn't just internal; an actual obstruction exists through another's deception.
   - *The six of spades in the outcome/advice position* indicates improvement of the situation. This positive card suggests that while circumstances are currently difficult, improvement is coming or available. The idea of coming into a better situation exists, but you may need to act for the improvement to manifest.

5. **Synthesize your reading of the cards succinctly to give the client the whole picture of the situation.**

   In this situation, you could sum up by saying the following:

   - You're stuck because financial fear kept you from taking risks or speaking up.
   - Currently, someone is actively working against you or taking advantage. This person may be a false friend or colleague who's blocking your progress.

- But the situation can improve. You need to address the deceptive person and resulting situation, probably by speaking up, documenting your work, or finding allies who will support you.
- After you deal with that blockage, your career can start moving forward again. The cards suggest that your situation of feeling stuck in your career is solvable and not a permanent situation.

6. **Potentially suggest follow-up actions based on information received during this reading.**

   Divination revealed the hidden problem of a betrayal or deception from a colleague. The client can now address the situation specifically rather than just feeling stuck. They know that improvement is available if they take appropriate action.

   You also have these options for continuing to help your client:

   - Performing protection work against the false friend.
   - Devising road-opening work for the client's career path now that the obstacle has been identified.

In this case, divination by card reading serves Hoodoo practice by clarifying hidden dynamics so that you and your client can work strategically to solve problems, rather than stumble blindly.

3 Living Hoodoo

IN THIS PART . . .

Examine the nuanced relationship between Hoodoo and religious faith, and understand why the question of whether Hoodoo is a religion doesn't have a simple answer.

Build an understanding of personal spiritual authority, how it develops, how it's maintained, and why it forms the bedrock of effective Hoodoo work.

See how Hoodoo serves the full range of human needs, from protecting family to navigating community relationships and pursuing everyday justice.

Explore Hoodoo's two heads in practice: the balance between personal empowerment and collective liberation that gives the tradition its enduring social force.

IN THIS CHAPTER

» Finding out various viewpoints on Hoodoo versus religion

» Recognizing how Christianity and Hoodoo became intertwined

» Examining whether Hoodoo is compatible with Judaism, Christianity, or Islam

» Finding your level of practice based on your faith commitments

Chapter 9
Understanding Hoodoo and Faith

This chapter addresses one of the most common questions that people ask about a potentially confusing Hoodoo-related topic: Does it count as a religion? You can find out why a single right answer to this question doesn't exist, how history and power shape the debate, and how practitioners themselves understand Hoodoo today.

But this chapter goes even further. Many people also want to know whether practicing Hoodoo puts them at odds with their existing faith, especially Christianity, Judaism, or Islam. You discover where the real conflicts are, how practitioners have historically navigated them, and what choices you need to make if you want to maintain both Hoodoo practice and religious observance.

This chapter helps you talk about Hoodoo and faith with confidence, respect, and accuracy, without forcing Hoodoo into categories where it doesn't quite fit.

Defining Religion and How That Relates to Hoodoo

Before you can decide whether Hoodoo is a religion, you need to understand how most people think about religion. In the US, *religion* usually means an organized system of belief. It often includes churches, clergy, holy books, shared doctrines, and regular worship services. This model comes largely from Christianity.

Hoodoo doesn't fit that model. Hoodoo has no central church, no universal creed, no required beliefs, and no governing authority. It has no Hoodoo pope, council, or headquarters. And those mismatched traits can be a source of confusion.

REMEMBER

Whether Hoodoo qualifies as a religion depends on how narrowly or broadly you define religion.

Recognizing Hoodoo as practice

Many practitioners are clear in their classification: Hoodoo *isn't* a religion. They describe Hoodoo as something you actively do, not something you formally join. It's a body of practices passed through families and communities. It focuses on healing, protection, justice, and survival. People work Hoodoo alongside whatever faith they already hold. Historically, that faith was Christianity because it was the religion the slave owners most often claimed.

You don't have to believe a specific theology to practice Hoodoo. You don't have to worship a particular deity. You don't attend services to be in good standing with the rules of the faith. And because of this, many rootworkers resist the *religion* label. They worry that categorizing it this way adds rules, structures, and expectations that Hoodoo has never had.

WARNING

Calling Hoodoo a religion when speaking with practitioners who reject that label can feel dismissive. Always listen to their viewpoint first.

Seeing Hoodoo as religion through a broader lens

Other scholars and practitioners push back on the idea that Hoodoo is "not religious." They point out that Hoodoo deals with sacred power, spiritual forces, ancestors, and divine justice. It answers the same questions that religions attempt to answer:

- How do you survive in a difficult world?
- Who helps you when human systems fail?
- Where does real, powerful assistance come from?

If religion is defined as a community's way of relating to the sacred, Hoodoo fits that category. Hoodoo has rituals, sacred objects, and spoken prayers. It also includes some basic rules learned through experience as well as moral logic tied to balance, justice, and consequence.

TIP

From the perspective of rituals, sacred objects, prayers, and morality, People can view Hoodoo as a *folk religion* or *vernacular religion* — religion as lived, not organized. Scholars often call Hoodoo an organic religion, which simply means religion that's practiced in daily life rather than in institutions.

Understanding Hoodoo's Roots in Enslavement and Survival

Hoodoo formed under slavery in the US. It wasn't shaped by theology seminars, but by the survival efforts of the enslaved people. (See Chapters 2 and 3.)

Enslavers forbade enslaved Africans from openly practicing their traditional religions. They enforced Christianity as the religion of the land. Practicing African spiritual systems invited punishment. But Hoodoo survived because it adapted:

- **Hoodoo moved underground.** It hid inside Christian language. It lived in kitchens, gardens, crossroads, and whispered prayers.
- **Hoodoo became the religion for many enslaved people.** They just couldn't name or practice it openly.
- **Hoodoo offered protection when law failed.** It provided healing when doctors refused care and justice when courts were off-limits to the oppressed.

The history of resilience and adaptation matters when you decide how to label the practice of Hoodoo.

Noticing the deep entanglement with Christianity

Hoodoo and Christianity intertwined and grew together in Black communities. For example, many Hoodoo practices use the Bible (especially the Psalms), prayer is central to spiritual connection, and God is often invoked directly. These qualities of Hoodoo practice don't indicate that Hoodoo is just Christianity. They show how African spiritual logic and Christian language fuse under pressure.

People who practiced Hoodoo went to church on Sunday and worked roots on Monday. They found no contradiction in these activities. For some people, Hoodoo was the mechanism by which faith became practical. For others, Hoodoo preserved African spiritual memory inside a Christian shell. Both experiences are true reflections of the entanglement between Christian beliefs and Hoodoo practices.

Taking its shape from Colonial power

The question of whether Hoodoo is a religion isn't a neutral topic. Colonial systems that subjugated the enslaved Africans decided which beliefs counted as religion and which could be dismissed as superstition or devilry.

African-derived practices were labeled dangerous, ignorant, or sinful. And that framing justified suppression. Over time, even Black communities internalized those judgments, and Hoodoo lost any public religious status. It wasn't because belief disappeared, but because acknowledging it became unsafe or shameful.

Today, reclaiming Hoodoo as a religion can be an act of resistance, which is a typical Hoodoo approach. But rejecting the label can also be an act of resistance. Context matters to this distinction.

Comparing Hoodoo with other African traditions

Hoodoo is often confused with other African traditions, such as Voodoo or Santería, that *diasporic* (displaced) people practiced after their transport to the West. Those traditions developed formal priesthoods, ceremonies, and communal worship. They openly organized as religions.

Hoodoo didn't embrace this type of structure. It stayed decentralized, personalized, and quiet. That difference in approach explains why *Vodou*, commonly known as Voodoo, is widely called a religion and Hoodoo often isn't.

REMEMBER Not being classified as religion doesn't make Hoodoo less spiritual. Organization, a defining quality of religion, isn't the same thing as depth of belief and spiritual connection, which Hoodoo has.

Navigating Modern Identity and Reclamation

Today, many African Americans are reclaiming Hoodoo as ancestral heritage. In this capacity, some Black communities call it a religion. But others call Hoodoo *tradition* or simply a way of life.

The disagreements about classifying Hoodoo continue, but what matters in the discussion is respect for everyone's view. Consider these points:

- Hoodoo was never meant to fit neatly into Western categories. Its strength is flexibility.
- Hoodoo can be deeply sacred without being institutional. Its connection to spiritual guidance doesn't need to follow explicit doctrine.

Talking about Hoodoo and faith with care

The most honest answer to the dilemma of whether Hoodoo is a religion is this: Hoodoo can be religious in the sense that the practitioner may understand the work as a living relationship with God, ancestors, or spirits, where that relationship is both the source of the work's efficacy and its moral accountability. So, Hoodoo can be religious, but it also functions differently depending on who practices it and why. And this aspect makes Hoodoo more like a learned traditional practice.

TIP If you want to talk about Hoodoo, first listen to practitioners' self-definitions, acknowledge its history and power, and respect the tradition's complexity. When in doubt, say, "Hoodoo is a spiritual tradition with religious dimensions." That phrasing leaves room for truth without making an absolute statement.

Before examining each religion in the next sections, I want to highlight the deepest tension. Hoodoo places spiritual authority with the practitioner, not with any institution, clergy, or creed. Institutional religions, reasonably enough, tend to have reservations about that arrangement. The next sections on religion describe how practitioners have historically navigated that tension. But navigation isn't resolution, and the version of Hoodoo you're called to practice may look different from traditional Hoodoo precisely because Hoodoo has always adapted to context. That adaptability is the tradition's most consistent feature.

Exploring compatibility with Abrahamic faiths

Many people ask whether practicing Hoodoo puts them at odds with their faith — especially the three major Abrahamic religions. Before diving into specifics, I want to be clear about what this section covers:

- **The primary focus is on Judaism, Christianity, and Islam** because these are the religions most Hoodoo practitioners historically have practiced alongside, especially Christianity. These three religions also have the most documented theological concerns about folk magic. Also, they represent the traditions for which I've collected copious research materials about their intersection with Hoodoo.
- **If you practice a different religion, such as Hinduism, Buddhism, or Indigenous traditions,** the principles I talk about in this section still apply. You just need to examine your own tradition's teachings about healing, divination, and ancestor work.
- **If you're irreligious, agnostic, or atheist,** you can skip to other sections. Hoodoo doesn't require faith in any deity. But you might still find this section interesting if you want to understand the historical context better, need to explain your practice to religious family members, enjoy theological debates, or are curious about how people reconcile seemingly contradictory beliefs.

What this section doesn't do is tell you what to believe. That's between you and your conscience (or between you and God, if you believe in one).

What this section does is show you where the real conflicts between religion and Hoodoo are, how practitioners have historically navigated them, and what choices you need to make if you want to maintain both Hoodoo practice and strict religious observance.

Addressing Hoodoo's three core practices

Hoodoo isn't a single thing; it's a collection of survival technologies. To understand compatibility with any religion, you need to break Hoodoo down into its three core components: herbalism and rootwork, divination, and ancestor veneration.

Each component has levels of compatibility with the different religions:

» **Herbalism and rootwork is the least controversial component.** Most religious traditions accept using plants for healing.

» **Divination occupies the middle ground.** All three Abrahamic religions have complex relationships with seeking knowledge of the future or hidden things.

» **Ancestor veneration is the most controversial component.** This aspect of Hoodoo creates the most tension with strict monotheism.

REMEMBER

Practitioners across many faith traditions have found their own relationship to Hoodoo's different components. The tradition has always accommodated that range of practice

Working with herbalism and rootwork across faiths

At first glance, all three Abrahamic religions seem fine with herbalism. The Hebrew Bible mentions myrrh, hyssop, frankincense, cedar, mandrake, and balm of Gilead. Jesus is anointed with spikenard, and the Good Samaritan uses oil and wine as medicine. The Prophet Muhammad taught uses of black seed, honey, henna, and olive oil for healing.

So what's the problem with the herbalism in Hoodoo practice? The issue isn't the herbs themselves; it's what you believe gives them power.

Using herbs as natural medicine

Using herbs purely for their chemical and physical properties — the properties God created — is universally accepted in all three religions. This is called *Tibb* in Islamic tradition and is considered part of natural science. Jewish tradition includes *refuah*, healing, using God-given plants. Christian monasteries maintained extensive medicinal herb gardens for centuries.

Understanding where tension arises

Some Hoodoo practices portray roots as having power beyond use as simple medicine. These practices include talking to a High John root to wake it up, asking the plant spirit to help you, believing the root has intelligence or agency independent of God, and feeding roots or treating them as spirit allies.

This view of the roots crosses into *animism:* the belief that plants, objects, or natural phenomena have their own spirits or consciousness.

In Judaism, treating natural objects as having independent power can violate the prohibition against ways of the *Amorites*, or non-Jewish magical practices. In Islam, ascribing power to anything other than Allah is potentially *shirk*, or idolatry. In Christianity, opinions vary widely by denomination.

Finding historical precedent

Despite prohibitions regarding some uses of herbalism in Abrahamic religions (see the preceding section), folk traditions persisted in all three religions:

- **In Jewish communities,** *segulot* (remedy prayers) combined herbs with Biblical verses. Kabbalistic practices sometimes attributed mystical properties to plants. Folk healers existed in every *shtetl* (small town with a Yiddish-speaking population), using both prayer and plants.
- **In Muslim communities,** *ruqyah* (spiritual healing) combined herbs with Quranic recitation. Islamic medicine texts describe both physical and spiritual properties of plants. *Sufi* traditions, which focus on the mystical dimension of Islam, sometimes viewed nature as manifestations of divine attributes.
- **In Christian communities,** Catholic tradition blessed herbs on feast days, and this practice still happens. Christian *cunning folk* (practitioners of white magic) and healers throughout Europe used herb magic. Black churches in the Americas never fully separated spiritual and medicinal healing.

None of these religious traditions involved treating plants as independent spirits, but they recognized that God worked through creation in mysterious ways.

Navigating modern practice

You have several options for integrating herbalism into your rootwork religious practices:

- **Using herbs purely as God-given natural medicine:** This approach requires no modification of beliefs or practices. You can say, "God created this root with healing properties" or "I'm using what the Creator provided." Pray to God for the herbs to work, not to the herbs themselves.
- **Viewing the spirit of the plant as God's presence within it:** This approach requires theological interpretation. When you talk to High John, you're really talking to God through God's creation. The intelligence in the plant is God's wisdom manifested. This is similar to how some Christians pray to saints — not worshiping them, but asking them to carry prayers to God.

» **Treating roots as having their own consciousness or spirit helpers:** This approach requires accepting theological tension because it's incompatible with strict monotheism. Some Hoodoo practitioners are comfortable with this tension. Others modify the practice to fit their faith.

TIP

Your choice of whether and how to incorporate various Hoodoo herbal traditions depends on how literally you interpret your religion's monotheism, whether you believe *spirit* means independent entity or God's presence in creation, and how your religious community views these practices.

Navigating divination across religious traditions

Divination involves seeking hidden knowledge, future events, or guidance through supernatural, magical, or intuitive methods, as discussed in Chapter 8. And the topic of divination within religion can get complicated because all three religions seem to say "no divination" — except when they don't.

WARNING

If you need certainty regarding the use of divination, stick to prayer-only methods approved by your religious tradition. If you can live with some ambiguity, you can use divination tools while maintaining that God is the source of all knowledge and accepting that some religious authorities will disagree with you.

Examining surface prohibitions

Explicit prohibitions against divination exist in all three Abrahamic religious traditions. Deuteronomy 18:10–12, used in both Judaism and Christianity, states:

> "Let no one be found among you who practices divination or sorcery, interprets omens, engages in witchcraft."

Quran 5:90 (in Islam) states:

> "O you who have believed, indeed, intoxicants, gambling, sacrificing on stone altars, and divining arrows are but defilement from the work of Satan."

These prohibitions seem pretty clear but aren't the end of the story. See the next section.

Discovering approved forms of divination

All three religions contain accounts of approved forms of seeking divine guidance.

- **In Judaism, the High Priest used *Urim* and *Thummim*, sacred lots, to determine God's will.** Prophets interpreted dreams and signs; Daniel and Joseph were prime examples. Casting lots was used to divide land and choose leaders. *Gematria*, or Jewish numerology, is still practiced in the Kabbalah tradition.
- **In Christianity, the Magi, a.k.a. wise men, in Matthew were astrologers who followed a star.** The apostles cast lots to choose Matthias as the twelfth apostle (Acts 1:26). Paul interprets visions and signs throughout Acts. Medieval Christians used *sortes sanctorum*, which is Bible divination. Charismatics today practice words of knowledge and prophecy.
- **In Islam, *Istikhara prayer*, or supplication, asks Allah for signs about decisions; this is often through dreams.** Navigation by stars, a form of divination, was essential and accepted. Scholars practice dream interpretation. Some Sufi orders practice *firasat*, or spiritual insight.

Understanding what's actually forbidden

The key distinction between permitted and forbidden divination in all three religions involves where the power comes from for the insight. Asking God for guidance and reading the signs that God provides is permitted. Consulting spirits, demons, or forces independent of God is not. Believing that a divination tool itself has power is forbidden.

And here's a gray area for you to consider. Does using cards, bones, or shells mean you're consulting something other than God? Or can it be a method of focusing your God-given intuition?

Recognizing historical folk practice

Despite official prohibitions, folk practitioners in all three religious traditions used divination tools:

- **In Jewish communities, dream interpretation books existed in every community.** *Bibliomancy*, which involved opening Torah to a random page, was common. Folk healers used various methods that rabbis considered questionable. Kabbalah developed complex divination systems.
- **In Christian communities,** *sortes Biblicae*, or Bible divination, was practiced even by church fathers. Medieval Christians used sieve and shears, key and book, and other methods. Cunning folk throughout Europe read cards, tea leaves, and signs. Black Christian conjurers used playing cards and Bible divination.

» **In Muslim communities, reading coffee grounds was especially common in Turkish and Middle Eastern cultures.** Dream interpretation manuals were widely circulated. Some communities consulted *fal*, or fortune books. Sufi orders had methods for receiving divine guidance.

TECHNICAL STUFF

Religious authorities often condemned these folk practices while laypeople continued using them, sometimes with the quiet approval of local religious leaders who knew their communities needed practical guidance.

Choosing your approach to divination

For the strictest religious compliance, Jews should use only prayer and study of sacred texts. Christians should pray for discernment and wisdom, use Bibliomancy with prayer, and develop spiritual gifts of discernment within your church tradition. Muslims should use only Istikhara prayer, pay attention to dreams following the prayer, and consult scholars for interpretation of difficult decisions.

For a theological middle ground, reframe divination tools as focusing mechanisms for God-given intuition, not as having independent power. Instill the proper mindset.

"The cards don't tell me anything; God speaks through my intuition as I read them."

"These shells help me focus my mind to hear God's guidance."

"I'm not asking the bones; I'm asking God and using the bones as a prayer tool."

This mindset requires believing that you're not consulting the tool itself, you're not invoking spirits, any insight comes from God alone, and the tool is like prayer beads — a focus object, not a power source.

For traditional Hoodoo practice, you use cards, shells, bones, pendulums, and other tools. Some practitioners believe these work through spiritual energies. Others believe they tap into collective unconscious or ancestral wisdom. Still others just find them useful without worrying about the mechanism. These beliefs can create theological tension if you also claim strict monotheism.

Understanding ancestor veneration and religious boundaries

Ancestor veneration is the most controversial practice. It's also the one that requires the most honest confrontation with theological tensions.

Examining surface and specific prohibitions

All three Abrahamic religions appear to forbid ancestor worship in these passages.

In Judaism, Deuteronomy 26:14 states:

> "I have not eaten of it [the tithe] while in mourning, nor have I removed any of it while unclean, nor offered any of it to the dead."

In Christianity, Isaiah 8:19 asks:

> "When someone tells you to consult mediums and spiritists, who whisper and mutter, should not a people inquire of their God? Why consult the dead on behalf of the living?"

In Islam, Quran 35:14 states:

> "If you invoke them, they do not hear your supplication; and if they heard, they would not respond to you."

And all three religions forbid worship of the dead — treating ancestors as gods or as having independent divine power. But they don't forbid relationship with the dead. What's actually prohibited includes praying to ancestors as if they're gods, asking ancestors for supernatural power they don't possess, treating ancestors as intermediaries who can grant wishes independently, *necromancy* (summoning the dead to gain forbidden knowledge or power), and offering sacrifices to ancestors as if they were deities.

But the ideas of relationship with the dead, memories of them, and connection with them is where addressing ancestor veneration gets interesting.

Finding ancestor practices within each tradition

The pattern in all three Abrahamic religions involves an official theology prohibition — don't worship ancestors — along with actual practices that portray a deep relationship with the dead.

In Judaism, despite Deuteronomy 26:14, Jewish tradition is full of ancestor practices that are forms of ancestor connection, not worship:

- *Kaddish* is a ritual prayer said to elevate the merit of the deceased. *Yahrzeit* involves lighting a memorial candle on the anniversary of death to strengthen the soul.
- *Yizkor* offers memorial prayers asking God to remember the dead.

- Grave visits are common practice where people talk to ancestors, update them on family news, and ask them to intercede with God.
- Every Jewish prayer invokes "the God of Abraham, Isaac, and Jacob" — the ancestors by name.
- *Zekhut Avot*, or merit of the ancestors, involves asking God for blessings based on ancestors' righteousness.

In Christianity, Catholic and Orthodox traditions include veneration of saints — holy dead who can intercede with God. You also find these other traditions:

- All Saints' Day and All Souls' Day are dedicated to honoring and praying for the dead.
- The "Communion of Saints" is the belief that living and dead Christians are spiritually connected.
- Black church traditions invoke "the prayers of our ancestors" in sermons, and founders and elders are honored spiritually.
- Churches are named after dead saints and founders.
- Grave decoration traditions are especially strong in African American communities.

In Islam, Ziyarat involves visiting graves of righteous ancestors and scholars. And here are other traditions involving ancestors:

- Dua for the dead means praying that Allah grants them mercy.
- Honoring prophets and companions involves deep respect for Muhammad's companions and family.
- In many Muslim cultures, including West African, Indonesian, and Turkish, visiting ancestor graves and asking them to remember you before Allah is common.
- Some communities visit graves of Awliya, saints and close friends of Allah.

Confronting the feeding problem

The concept of feeding the dead is the core incompatibility between Hoodoo and religion because traditional Hoodoo doesn't just remember ancestors. It feeds them.

Traditional Hoodoo ancestor practices include maintaining an ancestor altar; offering water, coffee, liquor, and food; lighting candles for them; asking them for help, protection, and guidance; and including them in spiritual work.

In Hoodoo, feeding ancestors shows respect and maintains relationship. It keeps them strong in the spirit world. The practice is reciprocal — you care for them, and they care for you. The concept is based on African cosmology in which the living and dead are in an ongoing relationship.

In Judaism and Islam, offering food to the dead is explicitly forbidden in scripture. Doing so suggests that spirits need sustenance, which they don't. It implies that they have power to help you in exchange, which violates monotheism. And it resembles pagan practices that the Abrahamic religions structured themselves to avoid.

In Christianity, the attitude toward feeding the dead varies widely. Some Catholic cultures leave food at graves on All Souls' Day (though officially, this is symbolic, not feeding). Most Protestant denominations reject the practice, but some Black church communities quietly accept it as reminiscent of old ways. Fundamentalists condemn it as demonic.

Choosing modified approaches

For full religious compliance regarding the treatment of ancestors, you can light candles in their memory, visit graves and speak to them as a form of meditation or prayer, ask God to bless you for their sake, tell stories about them to keep their memory alive, name children after them, and honor their values through your actions. These actions honor your ancestors without worshiping them. You can't leave food or drink offerings, ask them for supernatural help, or treat them as having power independent of God.

For a theological middle ground, reframe Hoodoo ancestor work as talking to God about ancestors, not talking to ancestors. This keeps God as the sole source of power while maintaining emotional connection to ancestors. The following mini table offers some alternatives for reframing your work.

Instead of	Reframe as
"Grandmother, please protect me."	"God, please grant me protection as you protected my grandmother."
"Ancestors, I'm feeding you this whiskey."	"God, I'm pouring this out in memory of my ancestors and in gratitude for their lives."
"Ancestors, help me find a job."	"God, in the merit of my ancestors who worked hard, please help me find work."

For traditional Hoodoo practice, you may maintain a full ancestor altar with offerings, feeding, and direct relationship. This requires accepting that you're practicing something your religion's official authorities may condemn. Some practitioners resolve this by separating "religious practice" from "cultural practice," believing ancestors are intermediaries God allows, accepting they're outside orthodoxy and being at peace with it, or finding religious communities that accept *syncretism*, which is a blending that produces a new synthesis.

REMEMBER

Millions of people have practiced Hoodoo while attending church, synagogue, or mosque. This duality doesn't make every Hoodoo practice theologically correct, but it makes it historically real.

Fostering Acceptance between Hoodoo and Your Religion

The Hoodoo legacy of adaptation enables you to shape your Hoodoo practice to fit your faith, but you can't erase all the tensions. Some practitioners choose full religious orthodoxy and modify Hoodoo to fit. Others choose theological interpretation that allows middle-ground practices. Still others choose traditional Hoodoo and accept being outside strict orthodoxy. Many choose different levels of religious compliance for different practices.

TIP

You can practice various Hoodoo traditions at different levels of connection with theology. Many practitioners use herbs at the first level (following universally accepted practices), divination at the second level (applying interpretation to debated practices), and ancestor work at the third level (acknowledging prohibitions). Define and defend your faith, your practice, and your decisions.

Some universal Hoodoo practices align with all three Abrahamic religions and create no conflict. (See the descriptions in the section "Navigating Modern Identity and Reclamation" earlier in the chapter.)

- Using herbs as God-given natural medicine
- Honoring ancestor memory through stories and remembrance
- Asking God for signs and guidance
- Lighting candles in memory of the dead
- Praying for wisdom and discernment

If you stick to these practices, you can work Hoodoo with zero theological compromise.

Recognizing debated territory

Some Hoodoo practices require theological reasoning and depend on interpretation. This level of practice requires understanding your specific religious tradition's teaching, deciding which interpretation you accept, being able to articulate your reasoning, and accepting that other believers may disagree.

You will need to determine whether plants have spiritual properties beyond chemistry, whether ancestors can hear when you speak to them, whether divination tools are prayer aids or forbidden instruments, whether water on an altar is symbolic honor or problematic offering, and whether asking ancestors to intercede is the same as asking for help from saints.

Acknowledging clear prohibitions

Some Hoodoo practices directly conflict with strict religious law and require that you either modify the practice or accept the religious tension. If you practice at this level, you're choosing traditional Hoodoo over strict religious orthodoxy. You need to make peace with that tension. You may face judgment from religious authorities, but you're in the company of millions who've made the same choice.

- **For Judaism and Islam:** Leaving food or drink offerings to ancestors, treating divination tools as having independent power, and asking ancestors for help as if they possess supernatural power.
- **For some Christian denominations:** All forms of divination, ancestor work beyond simple memory, and practices that seem to invoke the dead.

Recognizing denominational differences

Your specific religious community matters more than the broad category of your faith. Work to understand your specific community's teaching, not just the broad category.

Understanding Christian diversity

Christianity has more than 45,000 denominations. A Black Baptist church in rural Alabama may have zero problem with rootwork, while a Midwestern fundamentalist evangelical church might condemn it completely.

Churches most accepting of Hoodoo-adjacent practices include some Black Baptist and Methodist churches with strong folk traditions, African diaspora churches (like Spiritual Baptist traditions), progressive and liberal denominations, and some Catholic cultural communities.

Churches in the middle ground include mainline Protestant (varies by congregation), many Catholic communities (officially no, culturally maybe), and Orthodox (depends on priest and culture).

Churches least accepting include fundamentalist and evangelical churches, some Pentecostal and Charismatic churches (though they accept their own version of spiritual gifts), and conservative Reformed traditions.

Understanding Jewish diversity

Judaism has Orthodox, Conservative, Reform, and Reconstructionist movements with vastly different approaches.

Orthodox communities hold the strictest interpretation of theology with least flexibility. Conservative communities are moderate and evaluate Hoodoo practices case by case. Reform and Reconstructionist communities often view prohibitions against Hoodoo working as cultural artifacts rather than binding law. Cultural and secular Jews may practice ancestor traditions without religious concern. Hasidic communities may consult *rebbes*, or charismatic spiritual leaders, for guidance in ways that blur traditional lines.

Understanding Islamic diversity

Islam has multiple *madhabs*, schools of jurisprudence, with varying interpretations.

Strict Salafi interpretation forbids nearly all forms of spiritual practice that go beyond Istikhara prayer. Traditional madhabs allow more interpretive flexibility. Sufi orders are often more accepting of spiritual practices. Cultural variations mean Turkish, West African, and Southeast Asian Muslims often maintain folk practices alongside official Islam.

IN THIS CHAPTER

» Understanding Ashe as the power that moves through you

» Recognizing how your personal power manifests uniquely

» Building your power through daily spiritual practice

» Protecting and maintaining your spiritual charge

Chapter 10 Personal Power: Your Spiritual Charge and Authority

You can have the finest herbs, the most traditional formulas, and the perfect timing but still produce weak results from your Hoodoo work if you lack personal power. Conversely, a skilled rootworker with strong spiritual authority can work effectively with simple, everyday materials because they're the primary source of power. Their ingredients are tools, and their techniques are methods. But their personal authority is the engine that provides the power for Hoodoo practice.

This chapter helps you with understanding, building, and maintaining your personal spiritual power — what West African traditions call *Ashe* (also spelled Ase or Axé). Modern Hoodoo practitioners may call this quality spiritual authority, personal force, or simply having the power within.

Without a foundation of personal authority, all the other facets of Hoodoo that I cover in the book — changemaking, divination, and spirit work — operate at a fraction of their potential. But with the Ashe foundation, even simple Hoodoo work becomes remarkably effective. Your personal power is the difference between going through motions and moving spiritual forces.

In this chapter, you explore what Ashe is, how it manifests uniquely in each practitioner, how to recognize your gifts, and, most importantly, how to build and maintain the spiritual charge that makes you effective.

Uncovering the Ashe That Moves through You

In Yoruba *cosmology*, one of the major West African traditions that influenced Hoodoo, Ashe is the power to make things happen, the force that allows change and transformation. It's not quite energy in the New Age sense, not exactly will in the Western magical sense, and not simply authority, though that's part of it. *Ashe* is closer to effective spiritual force. It's the capacity to affect reality through spiritual means.

Everything contains some degree of Ashe — plants, stones, words, actions, places, and especially people. But the amount and quality of Ashe varies dramatically. Some people naturally have strong Ashe. Others develop it through practice and right living. Some have Ashe that's blocked or depleted and needs restoration.

When you work Hoodoo magic, you direct the Ashe that exists inherently in your materials (the spiritual properties of roots and herbs) and, most crucially, your own personal Ashe. Your spiritual authority, clarity, will, and connection to divine power all feed into your personal Ashe. When personal Ashe is strong and clear, your work is effective. When it's weak or blocked, even perfect technique produces poor results.

Describing personal power in Hoodoo

While Hoodoo doesn't often use the word *Ashe* (the terminology was often lost or replaced during slavery), the concept represented pervades the tradition. When old rootworkers talked about someone "having the power," being "gifted," possessing "the touch," or being able to "really work," they were describing strong Ashe.

You see the descriptions in phrases such as these:

- **She's got power in her hands,** which means that her personal Ashe is strong, particularly for healing.
- **He works roots and they work,** which denotes that his Ashe flows effectively through his formulas.
- **You need to get yourself right before you do this work,** which is the call to clear and strengthen your Ashe before doing Hoodoo work.
- **She was born with it,** which identifies a natural, strong Ashe from birth.
- **That root doctor has the touch,** which means that their Ashe is particularly effective.

Modern African diaspora practitioners are reclaiming the term *Ashe*, connecting back to African roots. But whether you call it *Ashe*, *personal power*, *spiritual authority*, your *gift*, or your *mojo*, you're talking about the same thing: the force within you that makes magic work.

Confronting the mojo confusion

You may have heard someone say, "I need to get my mojo working" or "I lost my mojo" in an everyday conversation. These phrases usually mean that they've lost their confidence, their effectiveness, and their spark. This casual usage points back to something real (an object), but linguistic drift has modified the meaning:

- **In traditional Hoodoo,** a *mojo* is a specific object. It may be a flannel bag filled with roots, herbs, or curios that people carry for luck, love, money, or protection. A mojo is a charm bag in this sense.
- **In modern usage,** the word *mojo* entered wider American culture through blues music, particularly Muddy Waters's song "Got My Mojo Working." Mojo in this sense means personal power, sexual magnetism, effectiveness, and confidence, which is basically Ashe or personal power. Someone who has their mojo working has their personal power flowing strong.

REMEMBER

Modern usage of *mojo* as personal power is accurate. The term just drifted from the specific (a charm bag) to the general (the personal power the bag helps channel or represent). For clarity in this book, when I say *mojo bag*, I mean the physical charm. When I talk about *personal power* or *Ashe*, I mean the spiritual force that makes you effective.

TECHNICAL STUFF

From Hoodoo to the mainstream: The word *mojo* entered mainstream American English through blues and rock music in the mid-20th century. Blues musicians singing about their "mojo" are often being deliberately ambiguous. They could mean their charm bag, their sexual power, their musical talent, or their general effectiveness. White audiences who don't know Hoodoo traditions may assume that it's slang for confidence or sex appeal, and that broader meaning works. So when someone today talks about "getting their mojo back," they're unknowingly referencing Hoodoo's concept of personal spiritual power, even if they've never heard of rootwork.

Grasping why personal power matters

Consider the scenario of two Hoodoo practitioners who work the same money-drawing spell. They include the same ingredients, use the same timing, and speak the same words. One practitioner gets results quickly and strongly. The other gets minimal or no results. So what makes the difference?

Often, it's personal Ashe.

The person with strong, clear personal power pours that force into their work. Their intention is focused, their will is strong, and their spiritual authority backs up the working. The ingredients and technique are just vehicles for their power. The person with weak or blocked Ashe goes through the motions, but no real force is behind the work. The herbs are just herbs. The words are just sounds. Nothing moves because no power is moving it.

And so, some rootworkers have legendary effectiveness while others doing the same work experience mediocre results. Consider these points:

- A simple prayer from a spiritually powerful person manifests results, but an elaborate ritual from a spiritually depleted person fails. Experienced practitioners often use simpler techniques than beginners but find better results. "Having the gift" or "the touch" is recognized; people can sense when someone has genuine power.
- Materials and techniques are important because they're the technology of the work. But the practitioner's personal authority is the battery that powers that technology. A Formula 1 race car driven by someone who can barely see over the wheel is less effective than a regular car driven by a skilled, alert driver. The tool matters, but the person operating it matters more.

TIP

Seeking strong Ashe is responsible preparation, not ego inflation. Personal power isn't selfish or ego-driven; it's necessary infrastructure. Building and maintaining your Ashe isn't about boosting your ego. Instead, it involves being effective at the Hoodoo work you're called to do. If you're meant to heal, you need strong healing Ashe to do it. If you're meant to teach, you need clear teaching Ashe to truly reach students. If you're meant to protect your family, you need strong protective Ashe to keep them safe. Cultivating your power is how you become capable of doing the work that your Ashe has for you.

Manifesting Ashe for Different Callings

Not everyone's personal power looks the same. Understanding where your personal power manifests is crucial to success in Hoodoo practice. You're not meant to be good at everything, and trying to force your power in directions it doesn't naturally flow is likely exhausting and ineffective. So instead, recognize one or two areas of Hoodoo work for which your Ashe is strongest and develop those areas. You can always maintain basic competency in the other areas.

Identifying common manifestations of Ashe

Ashe manifests uniquely based on who you are and what you're called to do with Hoodoo in your own and your community's life. Some people are natural healers; they touch someone, and pain eases. Others can't heal a headache but can see future happenings with stunning accuracy. And some people have power in words; when they pray or speak declarations, things happen. Others work best through the physical craft of building, making, and fixing things that have spiritual potency.

Consider your Ashe as it relates to these common areas of manifestation:

- **Healing power:** Some practitioners are natural healers. When they make medicine, lay hands on someone, pray for health, or prescribe herbs, people feel better. Their Ashe flows through healing work. They might not be great at love spells or money work, but put them in front of a sick person, and their power activates. Examples of people with natural healing Ashe include granny midwives and root doctors who specialize in physical healing.
- **Seership and divination:** Some people see beyond the surface, know things, sense hidden information, have dreams that ring true, or read oracles with uncanny accuracy. This is Ashe manifesting as clear spiritual perception. These individuals become the seers, prophets, card readers, and dream interpreters of their communities.
- **Protection and defense:** Some practitioners have warrior energy. Their Ashe is particularly strong in protection work, breaking hexes, defending against spiritual attack, or confronting evil. When they set a protection, it holds. When they go to spiritual battle, they win. Their power is martial.

- **Fertility and sexuality:** Some people have Ashe that manifests as sexual magnetism, fertility blessings, or power over love and attraction. These practitioners excel at love work, reconciliation spells, or helping couples conceive. Their personal power flows through intimate and creative channels.
- **Communication and teaching:** Some practitioners have Ashe in their voice and words. When they teach, people listen and understand. When they pray out loud, their prayers have weight. When they counsel or advise, their words land with authority. These people become the preachers, teachers, and counselors of the spiritual community.
- **Music and rhythm:** Some practitioners have Ashe that best flows through song, drumming, or rhythm. Their music moves spirits, shifts energy, and opens channels. The old-time ring shouts (as described in Chapter 2) and work songs weren't just cultural expression; they were spiritual technology operated by people whose Ashe manifested musically.
- **Crafting and making things:** Some people's hands are blessed with creative Ashe. When they build, cook, sew, or craft, their work carries spiritual power. A meal they prepare nourishes body and spirit. A protection packet they sew holds together stronger than other packets. Their Ashe works through physical creation.
- **Leadership and gathering:** Some practitioners are natural community leaders, and their Ashe manifests as the ability to gather people, organize, inspire, lead, and direct collective spiritual work. These people are the elders who lead ceremonies, coordinate community protection work, or organize group efforts.
- **Justice and truth:** Some practitioners have Ashe that specifically operates in matters of justice, truth-telling, oaths, and setting things right. When they work justice spells or testify to truth, their words and work carry weight. Court dealings, legal matters, and righteous confrontation are areas in which their power flows.

Recognizing your unique gift

Unless you're naturally single minded and focused on specific areas of Hoodoo practice, you probably need to explore your talents and interests. To find out where your Ashe flows strongest, begin by asking and answering questions about yourself, areas of your life, and your interactions with others:

- **Identify activities and interests that come naturally.** What kind of work do you find easy when others struggle? What can you do with simple materials that lead to notably strong results?

- **List the subjects and activities that you're drawn to.** What aspect of spiritual work excites you most? What do you read about, think about, and want to practice?
- **Document the aspects of your work that others notice.** Do people consistently come to you for any particular kind of help? Do they say, "You should do readings," "You have healing hands," or "I always feel safe around you"?
- **Remember the talents you had inherently as a child.** Natural gifts often show up early. Were you the kid who always knew when someone was lying? Who made everyone feel better? Who had prophetic dreams? Who led the games? These childhood tendencies often indicate where your Ashe naturally flows.
- **Assess the challenges you face.** Sometimes your gifts are forged through difficulty. Someone who survived a spiritual attack might develop strong protection Ashe. Someone who experienced healing might develop healer gifts. Wounds can become doorways to power, though they're not the only pathway, and healing is its own outcome.
- **Revisit the gifts your ancestors possessed.** Spiritual gifts often run in families. If your grandmother was a seer, you might have inherited seership. If your grandfather was an herbalist healer, healing Ashe might be in your lineage.

TIP

You don't have to pick just one special area for your Hoodoo work. Many practitioners have multiple gifts, with one or two being primary. But trying to be equally good at all areas of Hoodoo working can dilute your power. Focus on developing your natural strengths while maintaining basic competence in other areas.

REMEMBER

Your flavor of Ashe has a purpose. Your gift may not be what you expected or wanted. You may wish that you were a powerful seer, but your actual Ashe flows through healing hands. You might want to be a dramatic spellcaster, but your real power is in protection work or quiet counseling. Honor what you have rather than trying to force what you think you *should* have. Your specific gift exists because someone, somewhere needs it.

Building Personal Power through Daily Work

Strong Ashe doesn't just happen, although some people are born with more personal power than others. But you can cultivate your Ashe through consistent spiritual practice and right living. Think of personal spiritual power like physical fitness; some people are naturally coordinated and athletic, but everyone can become stronger and more agile through regular training.

Practicing right living: Daily conduct that sustains power

This aspect of maintaining Ashe is perhaps the least glamorous but most important one. How you live every day affects your spiritual power. You can do all the baths, prayers, and altar work (see the next sections), but if your daily conduct is chaotic, harmful, or out of alignment, your power stays weak. Table 10-1 contains general guidelines for right living.

TABLE 10-1 Guidelines for Right Living to Maintain Ashe

Guideline	How It Works	How to Live It
Keep your word	Your word is power. When you say you'll do something and then don't, you leak Ashe. When you lie, you damage your spiritual authority.	When you speak truth and keep your commitments, even small ones, you build power.
Manage anger and reactivity	Uncontrolled anger burns through Ashe like fire through dry grass. Spiritual power requires some degree of emotional regulation — not suppressing feelings, but also not being ruled by them.	Actively work on managing reactivity, anger, and emotional chaos.
Treat people fairly	Practice basic fairness to avoid cheating people, taking advantage of them, or betraying their trust. Cruel treatment of others damages your Ashe.	You don't have to be a doormat, but you do need to be just and treat others with integrity.
Honor agreements and exchanges	Pay your debts. Return what you borrow. Breaking spiritual agreements severely weakens your power.	Keep your bargains — especially spiritual ones. If you promised an offering to a spirit, give it; if you said you'd light a candle, light it.
Avoid spiritual pollution	Certain activities weaken or dirty your Ashe. Excessive alcohol or drugs cloud your spiritual perception and deplete power. Compulsive lying creates spiritual confusion.	Refrain from exposure to toxic habits and actions that contaminate your spirit.
Rest and renew	Physical exhaustion affects spiritual power. You can't run on empty indefinitely.	Get adequate sleep, eat reasonably well, and take time for rest and enjoyment. Your body is the vessel for your Ashe. Maintain it.
Show gratitude	Gratitude is spiritually generative. It creates more of what you appreciate. Constant complaining and bitterness drain power.	Regularly acknowledge blessings by saying thank you to God, ancestors, spirits, and other people, and recognize the good in your life.
Study and learn	Stagnation weakens Ashe. Growth strengthens it.	Keep learning, reading, and practicing. Even small daily efforts to learn something new or deepen your understanding keep your power fresh and developing.

WARNING

Focus on overall patterns of behavior, not perfection. Right living isn't puritanical moralism. This aspect of sustaining personal spiritual power isn't about being a perfect person or never doing anything wrong. You don't lose your Ashe by having a drink, getting angry, or making mistakes. What weakens your personal power is patterns of harmful behavior. Chronic lying, constant anger, persistent cruelty, habitual breaking of your word, or complete disregard for your physical and spiritual well-being are all examples. Think of this spiritual health like physical health: One unhealthy meal doesn't destroy your fitness, but eating junk food constantly does. One moment of anger doesn't erase your power, but being constantly controlled by rage does.

Cleansing and uncrossing: Removing what blocks you

You can't operate at full power when you're spiritually dirty or compromised. The process of living and moving through the world encounters and accumulates spiritual grime. You may receive negative energy from toxic environments, crossed conditions from conflict, and residue that clings to you from other people's issues. This gunk blocks your Ashe and can make you less effective at your Hoodoo practices.

Regular spiritual cleansing isn't optional if you want to maintain strong personal power. You can get clean and remove the spiritual grime by embracing these activities:

- **Cleansing baths:** Weekly baths with cleansing herbs — hyssop, salt, lemon, sage — wash away accumulated negativity and keep your spiritual field clear. When you feel particularly heavy, gunked up, or blocked, do a three- or seven-day uncrossing bath series.
- **Smoke cleansing:** Regularly pass yourself through sage, frankincense, or other cleansing incense smoke. This clears your aura and removes attachments.
- **Salt scrubs:** When you feel particularly contaminated, a salt scrub in the shower (sea salt or Epsom salt) pulls negative energy off your skin and spirit.
- **Floor washing:** Keeping your living space clean isn't just physical; washing floors with spiritual cleansers (Chinese Wash, saltwater, Van Van) clears the energy of your environment, which affects your personal energy.

TIP

Cleanse yourself after interactions with draining or toxic people, and after you spend time in places where heavy energy accumulates: hospitals, correctional facilities, funerals, or anywhere influenced by prolonged fear, grief, or suffering. These two circumstances are different situations, but both can leave a spiritual residue. Don't bring that weight home.

Protecting and shielding: Defending your charge

Cleansing removes the spiritual grime that blocks your Ashe, and protection prevents new contamination and defends against attack. You can't maintain strong Ashe if you're constantly being drained or attacked.

Here are some helpful areas of protection to work on:

- **Daily protection:** Many practitioners have a morning protection routine. It might involve praying Psalm 91 or 23, anointing themselves with protection oil, visualizing white light around themselves, or putting on a protection mojo. This sets spiritual boundaries for the day.
- **Home protection:** Your home should be your sanctuary that's protected at doors, windows, and property boundaries. Red brick dust across thresholds, salt in corners, protection packets buried at property edges, and regular prayers of blessing create a defended space where you can safely rest and recharge.
- **Protection mojos:** Carry a protective mojo bag regularly. It creates a portable shield and makes you a harder target for spiritual interference or people who sap your energy.
- **Boundary setting:** Protection isn't just magical. It's also about setting clear boundaries with people. Say no to things that drain you. Limit time with toxic individuals. Don't let people dump their problems on you constantly. These practical boundaries are spiritual protection.
- **Shield visualization:** Many practitioners visualize a protective barrier around themselves. The barrier could be a white light, a mirrored sphere, a wall of fire, or whatever image works for you. Spend a few minutes daily reinforcing this mental spiritual shield.

Feeding your head: Maintaining your power center

In Hoodoo and many African diaspora traditions, the head is your spiritual control center; it's your connection point to the divine, your antenna for spiritual information, and the seat of your Ashe. Keeping your head strong and well fed maintains your overall power. Consider these methods for feeding and nurturing your spiritual control center:

- **Anointing your crown:** Regularly anoint the crown of your head (top-center) with blessing or crown-of-success oils. This feeds your power center and keeps your spiritual reception clear. Some practitioners do this daily; others do it weekly.

- **Head washing:** Special baths or washes for just the head (not full body) that use blessed water, herbs, or Florida Water can cleanse and charge your crown. Florida Water is a special formulation of citrus, floral, and spice botanicals in an alcohol base; it's associated with the fountain-of-youth concept and used in Hoodoo for cleansing, protection, and blessing. Head washing often happens before major work or when you need extra clarity and power.
- **Covering your head:** Some traditions emphasize keeping the head covered during certain activities such as praying, doing major work, or when you need extra protection. The covering isn't about modesty; it's about protecting your spiritual antenna from interference.
- **Protecting your crown:** The crown of the head is spiritually vulnerable. Don't let just anyone touch your head. Some practitioners never let their hair be cut without prayer or intention. This isn't superstition; it's protecting your power center.
- **Mental clarity:** Your physical head and mental state affect your spiritual head. Reduce mental clutter by limiting excessive media consumption, practicing some form of meditation or quiet reflection, and getting adequate rest. A scattered, exhausted mind weakens your spiritual power.

Maintaining your sacred space through altar work

A working altar or sacred space dedicated to your Hoodoo activities isn't decoration — it's a spiritual battery and workspace that holds and amplifies your Ashe. Maintaining it keeps your power strong and your spiritual connections active. Maintenance of altars includes keeping them clean by dusting, removing dead flowers, cleaning candle holders, and refreshing water offerings. You can also do periodic deep cleansing every few months by completely dismantling, cleaning, and resetting your altar.

REMEMBER

A neglected altar weakens your power. Make regular offerings at your altar by lighting candles, pouring libations, placing fresh flowers, or offering food. Pray there daily because even a brief prayer keeps the altar active.

You can have different types of altars:

- **An ancestor altar** is a dedicated space honoring your beloved dead, with photos, offerings of water or coffee, candles, and items they loved.

» **A working altar** is your space for doing magic. It's where you keep tools, burn candles, assemble formulas, and pray.

» **A deity or saint altar** is for specific divine figures you work with.

Combination spaces serve multiple purposes, and many practitioners have one altar for honoring ancestors, working magic, and venerating divine helpers all in one space.

TIP

Start small with altars; you don't need an elaborate setup. A small shelf with a white candle, a glass of water, and one photo of an ancestor or meaningful spiritual image is enough to start. The attention and intention you give the space matters far more than how fancy it looks. A simple altar you tend daily is infinitely better than an elaborate altar you ignore. Build your practice first; you can expand your space later as your practice deepens.

Managing Your Ashe

Managing your Ashe involves the constructive daily effort presented in the section "Building Personal Power through Daily Work" earlier in the chapter. But it also includes special efforts to recognize the influences that drain your personal spiritual power, shield yourself against these influences, and work to regain your strength when needed. This section offers targeted advice for your efforts.

Identifying factors that deplete your power

Understanding what strengthens Ashe is only half the picture. You also need to recognize what drains your personal power so that you can defend against or minimize these influences.

Defending against spiritual attack

According to Hoodoo thought, when someone works magic against you with hexes, curses, or malicious work, it doesn't just cause problems in your life; it actively drains your Ashe. When working against an attack, you use spiritual power to defend yourself, which leaves less available for other Hoodoo work. Prolonged spiritual attack can leave you feeling exhausted, unable to think clearly, emotionally volatile, or physically ill.

Your defense against spiritual attack includes doing regular protection work, divination to catch attacks early, and strong uncrossing/reversal work when needed.

(See the section "Protecting and shielding: Defending your charge" earlier in the chapter.) Don't ignore signs of spiritual attack; instead, address them quickly before they drain you seriously.

Protecting yourself from energy vampires

Some people (often unconsciously) drain energy from those around them. After spending time with them, you feel exhausted, depleted, irritable, or foggy. Their personalities may be dramatic, needy, or constantly in crisis. Or perhaps they simply have a way of pulling all attention and energy to themselves.

Limit contact with energy vampires when possible. Shield yourself before and after interactions, and cleanse yourself immediately after being around them. Learn to say no and set boundaries. Some people are simply too expensive energetically to maintain close relationship with.

Avoiding toxic environments

Places hold energy. Hospitals, prisons, sites of violence, or locations where terrible things happened can drain your Ashe just by being there. Even less dramatically, workplaces with constant conflict, homes with chronic dysfunction, or spaces that are physically dirty and chaotic can slowly erode your power.

Cleanse yourself immediately after visiting toxic places that can drain your spiritual power. Protect yourself before entering known toxic environments, and limit the time you spend in these places when possible. Keep your own personal space clean and blessed as a sanctuary to recover in.

Recognizing crossed conditions

Being crossed (under a hex or jinx), experiencing things that go wrong in patterns, and being blocked or stuck are all situations that consume Ashe. In these instances, you're constantly fighting against spiritual interference, which is exhausting.

To defend against these situations, seek regular divination aid to catch crossed conditions early. And when you identify the conditions, swiftly apply the uncrossing work. Of course, practice strong Hoodoo protection to prevent crossings in the first place.

Avoiding spiritual neglect

Ironically, not doing spiritual work can weaken your personal spiritual power over time. If you have gifts and don't use them, if you have altars and don't tend them, and if you have spiritual relationships (ancestors, saints) and don't maintain them, your Ashe weakens from lack of exercise.

Maintain consistent Hoodoo practices, even when you don't feel like it. Engage regularly with your spiritual work and spirit relationships. Think of these practices as you would muscles; if you don't use them, you lose them.

Addressing physical depletion

Chronic exhaustion, poor nutrition, illness, or substance abuse all affect spiritual power. Your body is the vessel for your Ashe, and if the vessel is compromised, your power weakens.

Attend to basic physical self-care. Not many people are perfectly healthy, but you do need to tend your body reasonably. Get enough sleep, eat mostly nutritious foods, address health issues that arise, and limit substances that cloud your mind or drain your body.

Managing chaos and disorder

Constant chaos in your life, such as financial instability, relationship drama, legal problems, or living-situation turmoil, creates spiritual static that interferes with clear Ashe. A certain amount of situational life challenge is normal, but constant, unrelenting chaos drains power.

Work to create some islands of stability and order where you can in your life. Even small areas of consistent peace and routine can help. Sometimes the spiritual work you need to do involves the mundane work of organizing, paying a debt, or having a difficult conversation to reduce chaos.

Recovering depleted power

What do you do when you realize your Ashe is weak, blocked, or nearly gone? Recovery is possible, but it requires conscious effort and time. Start with thorough spiritual cleaning: a nine- or thirteen-day uncrossing bath series, smoke cleansing, and possibly professional uncrossing work from an experienced practitioner. You need to clear the spiritual gunk before you can rebuild power.

TIP

Recovery doesn't happen overnight. Rebuilding strong Ashe after serious depletion might take weeks or months. Be patient with yourself. Small, consistent efforts compound over time.

After you cleanse thoroughly, move on to these activities that are significant in the Hoodoo tradition and can help you regain your spiritual strength:

- **Taking radical rest:** Sometimes depleted Ashe requires physical and mental rest with time away from spiritual work, drama, and personal demands. Give yourself permission to do nothing spiritually intense for a while except basic protection and altar maintenance. Let the well refill.
- **Reconnecting with ancestors:** Call on your ancestors for help. They have investment in your well-being and can restore your power. Set up or tend your ancestor altar, make offerings, or ask for their support in recovery.
- **Returning to basics:** Go back to simple, fundamental practices: daily prayer, basic cleansing, protection work, minimal magic. Build a solid foundation again before attempting complex work.
- **Addressing life issues:** Sometimes spiritual depletion is a symptom of life problems that need practical solutions. The spiritual work is important, but you might also need to have a difficult conversation, leave a toxic situation, address a health problem, ask for financial help, or make another practical change. Spirit and matter are connected, and sometimes fixing the material situation is the spiritual work.
- **Seeking help from experienced practitioners:** If you're seriously depleted and can't seem to recover on your own, seek help from a more experienced practitioner. They can do work for you, divine to identify hidden problems, or teach you techniques you're missing. There's no shame in needing help; every practitioner has experienced depletion at some point.

REMEMBER

Don't give up on yourself. You can recover from spiritual depletion. Even if you're completely exhausted, blocked, or feeling powerless, you can rebuild your Ashe. Doing so requires work, time, and often help, but it's possible. Many powerful practitioners went through periods of severe depletion that included illness, trauma, spiritual attack, or burnout and came back stronger. Depletion is a condition, not a permanent state.

IN THIS CHAPTER

» Transforming household cleaning into spiritual protection

» Protecting the most vulnerable: children and elders

» Securing employment and economic stability through rootwork

» Pursuing justice when legal systems fail

» Responding to collective crisis through spiritual technology

» Recognizing relevant changes in Hoodoo's form and focus

Chapter 11 Hoodoo for Everyday Life

Like any living tree, Hoodoo's branches have spread far beyond the roots of liberation magic that grew from the origin in bonds of slavery, as covered in Chapter 2. The same tradition that helped people escape bondage also helps modern practitioners maintain peaceful homes, protect their children, secure steady employment, and navigate a biased legal system. The same spiritual logic that sustained communities through racial terror now supports families through economic hardship, illness, and the ordinary stresses of daily life.

This chapter explores how Hoodoo functions as an applied tradition — a set of practical spiritual technologies designed to address the pressing needs of the living in real time. You can find out how Hoodoo serves as a decentralized social safety net that fortifies the home and protects the vulnerable. And you see how Hoodoo responds to collective crisis and pursues justice when formal systems fail. Also in this chapter, I describe the evolution of Hoodoo in the 20th and 21st centuries that affects the current state of the practice.

The power of Hoodoo has always been in its practicality. And its cultural roots shape the communal nature and traditional focus, as discussed in Chapter 3. Hoodoo isn't magic for magic's sake. This magic serves the elements of survival, stability, and care that are much needed in everyday life.

Fortifying Your Home through Spiritual Power

One of the most profound applications of Hoodoo is the spiritual fortification of the home. In the tradition, your household is viewed as a fortress that you must maintain through consistent spiritual hygiene.

Family-focused Hoodoo is rarely dramatic. It doesn't require elaborate rituals or expensive supplies. Instead, it integrates into the daily chores of cleaning, cooking, and laundry to transform mundane labor into ritual protection and peace.

This approach reflects a core Hoodoo principle: The sacred isn't separate from the ordinary. Every time you sweep your floor, you have an opportunity to sweep out negativity. Every time you wash your doorstep, you can wash away bad intentions. The home becomes a temple maintained through the simple acts of daily care.

Sweeping with intention

In Hoodoo, physical cleanliness is a prerequisite for spiritual clarity. The act of sweeping, for instance, is performed with specific directional intent:

- **Sweeping from the back of the house toward the front door pushes out bad luck, stagnant energy, and negative spirits.** You're literally showing unwanted influences the exit. Many practitioners do this sweep at sunset or when the household has experienced conflict.
- **Sweeping from the front door inward draws in blessings and financial prosperity.** You're inviting good fortune to enter and stay. This sweep is often done in the morning or when beginning a new venture.

You can prepare the broom for this cleansing work. Some practitioners sprinkle their broom with Florida Water or pass it through incense smoke before using it. Others keep a separate broom dedicated solely to spiritual cleansing, distinct from the everyday cleaning broom.

TECHNICAL STUFF

Florida water is a special combination of ingredients for cleansing and spiritual protection. You can find it available for purchase at numerous stores that are located in communities with dense Black and Latine populations.

WARNING

Never sweep at night if you can avoid it. Traditional belief holds that sweeping at night may sweep away your luck along with the dust.

Adding spiritual power to cleaning supplies

Practitioners often add herbs and minerals to their cleaning supplies to fix (imbue) the house with a particular intention. These additions aren't random; each substance carries specific spiritual properties that align with its physical characteristics.

This table shows common cleaning agents and their spiritual applications.

Cleaning Agent	What It Does	How to Use It
Ammonia	Neutralizes hexes and clears conflict energy	Add it to mop water or use it to wipe door handles and drains.
Vinegar	Banishes unwanted visitors and protects from *bad air* (sudden bad luck)	Use it in floor washes or apply it to windowsills.
Laundry bluing	Brings peace and tranquility and cools hot situations	Add bluing to rinse water for bedding.
Salt	Provides universal purification and absorbs negative energy	Sprinkle salt on carpets before vacuuming.
Pine-Sol or other pine cleaner	Opens roads and breaks through stagnation	Scrub floors with pine cleaner when the family feels stuck.

Notice how the physical properties align with the spiritual uses. Ammonia physically cuts through grease; spiritually, it cuts through the "grease" of hexes and crossed conditions. Vinegar is acidic and inhospitable to bacteria; spiritually, it makes your home inhospitable to negative influences. Laundry bluing enhances the whiteness and brightness of fabrics; spiritually, it drives out the dark, or negativity, that can disturb peace and tranquility. Salt physically dries things out; spiritually, it dries up the power of curses.

Defending your threshold

The doorstep is the most critical spiritual site in the Hoodoo home. Everything that enters your life, good or bad, must cross that threshold. Protecting it is fundamental to household security.

REMEMBER

The threshold isn't just a physical boundary. It's a spiritual one. What you allow to cross it, you allow into your life.

Laying red brick dust

The use of red brick dust, also called *redding*, to guard the home's doorway is a hallmark of Southern and Creole Hoodoo practice. Red brick dust carries the symbolic weight of strong walls and strong law.

By laying an unbroken line of red brick dust across your threshold, you create a spiritual boundary that unwanted guests, malicious spirits, and negative intentions can't easily cross. The line must be unbroken; any gap in the barrier is a gap in your protection.

Some practitioners refresh the red brick dust line weekly. Others lay it once and maintain it only as needed. If you notice an unusual number of problems arriving at your door — unwanted visitors, bad news, conflict following people into the house — check whether your threshold protection needs renewal.

Adding additional threshold protections

Red brick dust isn't the only option for threshold defense. Salt sprinkled across the doorway absorbs negative energy. Vinegar washed on the doorstep makes the entrance inhospitable to those who wish you harm. A protective symbol drawn in chalk or traced in oil adds another layer of defense.

Some practitioners hang protective objects near the door: a horseshoe (points up to hold luck in), a mirror (to reflect negativity back to its source), or a specific herb bundle (to block unwanted entries). Others bury protective items beneath the threshold itself, creating permanent guardianship.

Offering Personal Care and Protection

Hoodoo rituals for family stability prioritize the most vulnerable members of the kinship group: children and elders. These groups are the people who can't fully protect themselves, and the Hoodoo tradition provides specific tools for their care.

The ethical framework of traditional Hoodoo mandated that practitioners work for the vulnerable — elderly residents, orphaned children, and those facing racial violence — long before state-sponsored social services existed. This was the original social safety net: neighbors caring for neighbors, using whatever tools they had available.

TIP

Hoodoo emphasizes that the practitioner's spiritual hygiene is essential for maintaining internal peace and effective practice. You can't effectively protect your home or your family if you're spiritually depleted yourself. As I describe in Chapter 10, regular rituals such a cleansing baths and restorative habits such as reciting Psalm 23 enable you to maintain your spiritual energy and equilibrium. Self-care in Hoodoo isn't selfish; it's necessary. You maintain yourself so that you can maintain your responsibilities to others.

Shielding children

For children, practitioners use materials that instill protection while supporting healthy development. Here are some common protective practices:

- **High John the Conqueror root** is often given to children to instill enduring spirit and cleverness, qualities they'll need to navigate a world that may not always be kind to them. The root is given in a small bag and shouldn't be ingested.
- **Angelica root, often called Holy Ghost root,** provides a shield of spiritual defense against harm. Some parents place a small piece in a child's pillow or sew it into the lining of a coat. The protection travels with the child wherever they go.
- **Other simple protective measures** include hanging a small mojo bag near the child's bed, adding a few drops of Florida Water to their bath water, or placing a protective Psalm (like Psalm 91) under their mattress.

These protective practices don't require the child's conscious participation because the parent does the work on their behalf.

Supporting elders

Elder care in Hoodoo focuses on both physical support and spiritual transition. Many traditional tonics serve dual purposes: They support the body while providing spiritual fortification.

Daily tonics of honey, lemon, and garlic support immune function and carry protective properties. Blessed Thistle is used for general health and for breaking any lingering jinxes that might hinder recovery. These remedies acknowledge that physical and spiritual health are inseparable.

As elders approach the end of life, Hoodoo provides frameworks for easing that transition. Prayers for peaceful passing, preparations to ensure that the spirit finds its way, and rituals to protect the living from any unsettled spiritual business fall within the tradition's scope.

Maintaining peace in multi-generational homes

Many families live in multi-generational households where tensions can arise from different personalities, expectations, and life stages sharing close quarters. Hoodoo offers practical tools for maintaining harmony.

Sweetening jars are containers filled with honey or sugar along with the names of family members. The intention is to "sweeten" dispositions and minimize conflict. You might write each family member's name on a small slip of paper, fold the papers toward you, and place them in a jar of honey. As the honey surrounds the names, relationships are sweetened.

Peace Water is another household staple. Characterized by its distinctive blue and clear layers, Peace Water is sprinkled in the corners of every room to invite tranquility and silence turbulent energy. It's particularly useful after arguments or when external stresses threaten household stability.

REMEMBER

RECOGNIZING CARE AS POWER

The power of Hoodoo doesn't lie in the spectacular. It lies in the profound acts of care.

- Protecting a child
- Supporting an elder
- Stabilizing a household
- Helping a neighbor find work
- Seeking justice for someone wronged

These acts of care are the heaviest spiritual works you can perform. They may not look dramatic from the outside, but they carry more weight than any flashy spell.

This focus on care reflects Hoodoo's original purpose: keeping people whole in a world that consistently tried to break them. The tradition was never about gaining supernatural powers for the sake of power. It was about survival, dignity, and mutual support.

Hoodoo was never meant to replace the human community. It was meant to strengthen it. The tradition lives in kitchens, in conversations, in the quiet habits of intentional living. It lives wherever people care for each other and use whatever tools they have available to make that care effective. You don't need rare ingredients or dramatic rituals to practice this tradition authentically. You need attention, intention, and a willingness to do the work. You need to care — for yourself, for your family, and for your community — and to act on that caring.

Securing Employment and Economic Stability

For many African Americans throughout history, steady employment was the only barrier against total poverty. Hoodoo adapted to these needs through steady work and prosperity rituals that remain popular today. Hoodoo used in this way is liberation magic applied to economic survival. The same tradition that helped people escape bondage now helps their descendants secure and maintain the jobs that keep their families housed and fed.

Working with botanical allies for employment

Hoodoo utilizes specific botanical allies known for their ability to secure work, command respect, and ensure loyalty from employers. The following table shows some common employment-related materials and their uses. Chapters 13 and 16 offer information about finding botanical and other materials for Hoodoo rootworking.

Material	What It's Used For	How You Use It
Gravel Root	Securing a job and ensuring raises	Carried in pocket or added to floor washes
Calamus Root	Commanding respect and leadership energy	Added to *boss=fix* work or used in promotion spells
Five Finger Grass	Success in manual and skilled labor	Added to mojo bags; find out how to make a mojo bag in Chapter 14

Material	What It's Used For	How You Use It
Pyrite (fool's gold)	Attracting cash and business growth	Placed in cash registers or safes
Devil's Shoestring	Protection from workplace jinxes and legal trouble	Carried during interviews or kept in a desk

TIP

You might carry Gravel Root to a job interview, dress a candle with steady work oil before an important meeting with your boss, or keep Devil's Shoestring in your desk drawer to ward off workplace drama.

Protecting your income

After you have employment, Hoodoo provides tools for keeping it. Steady work rituals focus on job security, positive relationships with supervisors, and protection from office politics that might threaten your position.

Simple practices include adding a few drops of Steady Work oil to your hands before clocking in, keeping a small pyrite stone near where you handle money, or reciting Psalm 23 before difficult conversations with supervisors. These aren't substitutes for doing good work at your job, but they support and reinforce your professional efforts.

TIP

Crown of Success products such as powder, oil, bath crystals, and incense are traditional Hoodoo preparations for career advancement and recognition. Use them when seeking promotions or taking on new responsibilities.

Pursuing Justice When Systems Fail

A core tenet of community-based Hoodoo is the pursuit of justice, particularly when formal legal and social systems are corrupt or inaccessible. Historically, the American legal system was weaponized against Black citizens through slave codes, Black Codes, and Jim Crow laws. Hoodoo stepped into this vacuum to offer a supernatural failsafe.

Understanding court case work

Scholars who study Hoodoo argue that court case magic is a rational response to structural inequality. Rather than acting from unprovoked malice, justice work in Hoodoo aims to restrain harmful behavior and reveal truth.

Consider the *Twelve Disciples ritual*, recorded by field researchers in the 1930s. In this ritual, the practitioner writes the names of the twelve disciples on sage leaves and places them in their shoes before the disciples enter a courtroom. The intention isn't to cheat the law but to ensure the judge will go no further than God has given them power to go. The ritual petitions for divine fairness where human fairness may be lacking.

REMEMBER

The distinction involves fairness in legal matters. Court case work doesn't aim to help guilty people escape consequences. It aims to ensure that truth is heard, that prejudice doesn't determine outcomes, and that those with power are held accountable to higher standards.

Taking advice from Dr. Buzzard of the Lowcountry

One of the most celebrated examples of Hoodoo court case work comes from Stephan Robinson, better known as Dr. Buzzard, who practiced in the South Carolina Lowcountry from the early 1900s until his death in 1947. His reputation for helping clients win court cases became so legendary that his name is still synonymous with legal rootwork today.

Dr. Buzzard operated during the height of Jim Crow oppression, when Black defendants faced overwhelming bias in Southern courtrooms. Judges and all-white juries were often hostile regardless of what the evidence showed. In this environment, Dr. Buzzard provided something essential: hope, confidence, and practical spiritual strategy. Here are depictions of Dr. Buzzard's association with Hoodoo in his legal work:

- **His methods combined psychological insight with traditional rootwork.** He prepared clients with specific roots to carry, powders to deploy in the courtroom, and precise instructions for behavior before the judge.
- **He employed Hoodoo herbal work to aid clients.** Some accounts describe him as providing *chewing root* (usually High John root or Galangal) that clients kept in their mouths while testifying; he believed that the root would make their words persuasive and true-sounding.
- **Stories circulated of jurors suddenly changing their minds.** Because witnesses seemed to become confused and prosecutors stumbled over simple questions, Dr. Buzzard's reputation preceded him. His success rate was remarkable enough that local law enforcement and judges became genuinely wary of cases involving his clients.

These depictions illustrate a fundamental Hoodoo concept: The magic is meant to meet your effort halfway. Dr. Buzzard's preparations didn't replace good legal strategy or honest testimony. They gave his clients the spiritual armor to stand firm in hostile territory.

TIP

When doing justice work, remember that Hoodoo helps those who help themselves. The magic supports your action; it doesn't replace it.

Practicing the ethics of restraint

Traditional Hoodoo ethics are practical and relational. Harm without cause is strictly discouraged because it disrupts community balance. And character is central to these ethics. A practitioner who acts solely from anger or ego is believed to risk the long-term stability of their lineage. The work practiced in an inappropriate manner can come back on the practitioner who uses it carelessly or cruelly.

Instead, Hoodoo encourages restraint and careful consideration of social consequences. Justice work is about accountability: making the boss who harasses workers answerable, making the unjust judge face consequences, making the truth come to light. It's not about revenge for its own sake.

WARNING

Hoodoo traditions consistently warn against doing harm without just cause. The ethical framework exists for a reason. Work outside it at your own risk.

Responding to Collective Crisis and Everyday Needs

The historical efficacy of Hoodoo is most visible during periods of collective trauma. When institutional systems collapsed or deliberately excluded the Black community, Hoodoo provided a failsafe mechanism for survival.

Some modern portrayals often reduce Hoodoo to a set of emergency: spells you perform when things go wrong. But traditional Hoodoo emphasizes ongoing care of your spiritual space and the people in it. The idea of *maintenance magic*, or regular practices that keep your approach to life running smoothly, prevents problems before they start.

REMEMBER

The rootworkers who sustained their communities through the worst conditions in American history were not self-sacrificing martyrs who gave until nothing was left. They cared for and maintained themselves precisely because the community needed them to be functional. This is still true. The floor wash you do for your own home, the cleansing bath you take after a hard week, and the prayer you recite before you start your day aren't interruptions to the work of caring for others. They are part of the work. As I describe in Chapter 10, regular cleansing and restorative habits keep your spiritual energy and equilibrium intact. Self-care in Hoodoo isn't selfish; it's infrastructure. You maintain yourself so that you can maintain your responsibilities to others.

Surviving the 1918 influenza pandemic

During the 1918 influenza epidemic, African American communities faced the dual threat of a deadly pathogen and medical apartheid. Segregated hospitals turned away Black patients. Racist medical theories suggested Black people were biologically inferior. The official healthcare system offered nothing.

In response, communities turned to Hoodoo's healing traditions. One of the most common protective measures was the *asafoetida* bag (sometimes called the acifidity bag), containing the pungent resin of the Ferula asafoetida plant worn around the neck. The smell alone was thought to ward off disease and evil spirits, and the strong antimicrobial properties of asafoetida may have provided some actual protection.

The sour vinegar practice involved reciting a petition while applying vinegar to the face and palms, serving as both a spiritual and a practical disinfectant. These remedies created what scholars call a cooperative healing literacy — a shared understanding that allowed families to take agency over their health when the state had abandoned them.

Enduring the Red Summer of 1919

The "Red Summer" of 1919 was a period of intense white supremacist terrorism and racial riots in over three dozen US cities. Black communities faced mob violence, lynching, and the destruction of entire neighborhoods.

During these events, Hoodoo functioned as spiritual armor. Practitioners provided returning Black veterans and their families with protective amulets and High John roots to embolden their resistance against mob violence. In Washington, D.C., and Chicago, where Black communities organized to fight back, the psychological boost provided by these spiritual protections supported the community's determination to survive.

Hoodoo practitioners during this era were original abolitionists in spirit who created charms that symbolically and psychologically protected individuals from the violent punishments of the Jim Crow era. The magic didn't make bullets bounce off. But it provided the spiritual resolve necessary to stand firm.

REMEMBER

Hoodoo's crisis-response traditions weren't superstition; they were survival technology developed by people who had no other options.

Avoiding the crisis-only trap

If you only practice Hoodoo when you're in trouble, you're missing most of its benefit. The tradition encourages consistent attention to your spiritual environment: regular cleansings, ongoing protections, and daily maintenance practices that keep your life running smoothly.

Think of spiritual practices like you do your physical health. You don't wait until you're seriously ill to start taking care of your body. You eat well, exercise, get enough sleep, and see the doctor for checkups. Spiritual maintenance works the same way. Refer to the section "Fortifying Your Home through Spiritual Power" earlier in the chapter to find out about and use these maintenance methods:

- **Regular floor washes** that keep negativity from building up in your home.
- **Consistent threshold protection** to stop problems at the door.
- **Daily prayers or affirmations** that maintain your internal spiritual clarity.
- **Weekly attention to your altar** for keeping your spiritual relationships strong.

TIP

Establish a regular schedule for spiritual maintenance: weekly floor washes, monthly threshold renewal, and seasonal deep cleansing. Consistency matters more than complexity.

Installing passive protections

Some Hoodoo practices provide ongoing, passive protection without requiring daily attention. Bottle trees are a prime example. Cobalt blue bottles hung on trees trap wandering spirits and burn away negative energy through the sun's light. These bottles are permanent fixtures in many Southern yards, providing passive, continuous protection for the family. You install them once, and they work continuously.

Buried protections beneath the threshold or at the corners of your property work similarly. Once installed, they guard your home without ongoing effort. The goal of maintenance magic is a constant feeling of guarded peacefulness rather than frantic response to sudden conflict. Prevention is easier than cure.

Noting Recent Evolution of Hoodoo

While Hoodoo began as a communal practice, several historical and economic forces in the 20th century pushed the tradition toward a more individualized focus. Understanding this shift helps you recognize which elements of the tradition were lost or retained.

REMEMBER

The individualization of Hoodoo wasn't a natural evolution; instead, it was a response to migration, stigma, and commercialization. But the communal roots remain available to those who seek them.

In the 21st century, Hoodoo has migrated to digital platforms. Scholars have identified *CyberHoodoo* as a new technology of wellness where practitioners on social media, YouTube, and podcasts share healing knowledge and protective practices.

Navigating the Great Migration

As millions of Black Americans moved from the rural South to urban centers during the Great Migration (1910–1970), the traditional networks of the rural community fractured. Migrants often became separated from the land where they had gathered herbs and from the elders who held ancestral knowledge.

Simultaneously, Hoodoo faced intense stigma from within the Black community. The progressive Black elite and established Northern churches pressured migrants to prove they were civilized by abandoning religious superstitions like Hoodoo.

This stigma drove the tradition underground. In anonymous urban environments, Hoodoo transformed from a communal practice into a private technology of the individual. Practitioners secretly selected rituals and objects, like the mojo bag, to seek personal agency. Some of the public, community-oriented aspects of the tradition faded.

Recognizing commercialized Hoodoo

The 20th century also saw the rise of what scholars call *marketeered Hoodoo.* Commercial entrepreneurs capitalized on the tradition by standardizing products and selling them through urban supply shops and mail-order catalogs.

This commercialized version replaced personalized, hand-to-hand community exchanges with manufactured, generic products of questionable quality. The focus shifted from communal rituals toward individualistic desires — primarily luck, love, and fast money — that used methods frequently stripped of the original ethical framework.

Not all commercial Hoodoo is bad, and many modern suppliers are ethical practitioners themselves. But the shift toward individual consumption rather than communal practice represents a real change in how the tradition functions.

Expanding into the digital age

Expansion of Hoodoo into digital spaces allows for what researchers call the aggregation of individual rituals for collective social change. Practitioners have organized ring shouts via social media to honor victims of state violence, coordinated protection workings for communities in crisis, and shared freely the knowledge that once passed only through in-person apprenticeship.

This evolution demonstrates that Hoodoo's core logic remains intact: Use whatever tools are available to ensure the survival and flourishing of the community. The tools change — from whispered prayers in slave quarters to herbs gathered in forests to products ordered online to rituals coordinated across continents through social media — but the intention endures.

REMEMBER

The tradition lives wherever its practitioners take it. Digital Hoodoo is still Hoodoo when it serves the same purposes of protection, survival, and care. If your ancestors could see practitioners sharing protection workings on Instagram or teaching rootwork through YouTube tutorials, they would likely recognize the spirit even if the form surprised them. Hoodoo adapts and survives.

IN THIS CHAPTER

- » Understanding Hoodoo's dual purposes that have always existed
- » Exploring personal power work and its ethics
- » Discovering collective justice work and its challenges
- » Navigating the tension between individual gain and collective good
- » Practicing both purposes with honesty, balance, and integrity

Chapter 12 Personal Power and Collective Justice

Hoodoo has two heads — personal power and collective justice — and they're not always comfortable with each other. Sometimes the two purposes align beautifully. But other times they're in tension or may flat out contradict each other.

On one hand, individuals use Hoodoo to get what they need: a job, a lover, protection from an enemy, money to pay rent, healing from illness, or success in court. This is personal empowerment work: using spiritual techniques to improve your own life, your family's life, and your immediate circumstances.

On the other hand, Hoodoo has always been a tool of collective resistance and liberation: protecting communities from violence, thwarting oppressors, creating solidarity, seeking justice for wronged people, and healing collective trauma.

This chapter explores both faces of Hoodoo: the "get mine" and the "free us all" aspects. I explain how many practitioners navigate between individual gain and collective good by discerning when personal work *is* political work. I also show you how Hoodoo serves both survival and resistance without apologizing for either.

Recognizing that the Two Heads of Hoodoo Have Always Existed

From the beginning, enslaved Africans used conjure for two distinct, but overlapping, purposes. Both were necessary. Both were legitimate. An enslaved woman who worked a love spell to keep her partner close wasn't being frivolous. She was trying to maintain family bonds that the system tried to destroy. An enslaved man who poisoned the overseer who whipped him mercilessly wasn't being petty. He was seeking justice where no legal justice existed.

Hoodoo isn't just one thing ethically. It's not purely selfless liberation magic, and it's not purely selfish personal gain magic. It's both, and it's always been both. That complexity is part of its power. Consider these facets of Hoodoo practice:

- **Personal survival needs** included getting enough to eat, avoiding beatings, protecting children, finding or keeping a partner, healing illness, settling disputes within the enslaved community, and competing for limited resources or favor.
- **Collective resistance and protection** included hexing brutal overseers or owners, protecting escape attempts, creating solidarity among enslaved people, seeking justice for murdered or brutalized community members, using spiritual warfare against the slave system itself, and protecting *maroon communities*, which are independent groups of formerly enslaved Africans and their descendants who escaped to establish isolated working communities, particularly in the Americas and the Caribbean.

REMEMBER

The idea that Hoodoo should be used only for noble collective purposes is modern revisionism. The ancestors used it for everything they needed it for, from the mundane to the revolutionary.

TIP

Hoodoo's two heads — personal power (love, money, success, protection) and collective justice (resistance, fairness, community healing) — have always coexisted in the tradition. Both were necessary for survival. But don't let either head dominate entirely. Some seasons require more personal work; others more collective work.

Exploring Personal Power: The Selfish Work

I want to first examine the work that makes some people uncomfortable: using Hoodoo to get what you want. Check out this list to find out what personal empowerment work looks like:

- **Love and sex work** includes drawing a specific person to you, keeping a partner faithful, breaking up someone else's relationship to attract the person you're interested in, increasing sexual attraction, and healing from heartbreak.
- **Money and success work** includes being hired or promoted, winning at gambling, drawing customers to your business, convincing someone to lend you money, and achieving success in legal matters.
- **Protection and revenge work** includes protecting yourself from a specific person, putting a curse on someone who wronged you, stopping gossip or slander, getting someone fired or evicted, and returning hexes to the sender.
- **Personal power work** includes increasing confidence, dominating situations, commanding respect, winning arguments, and getting your way.

Recognizing that the ethics are complex

In the realm of Hoodoo's use for personal empowerment, people can start judging and asking questions. For example, is it okay to:

- Work a spell to take someone else's partner?
- Put a curse on your coworker so you get the promotion both of you want?
- Dominate your boss into giving you a raise?

Different practitioners have different answers. Some say that anything goes; Hoodoo is amoral. It's a tool, and you can use it any way you need to. Others say that you can use Hoodoo for personal gain but not to harm innocent people. Still others say that personal gain work is fine but justice work should be the priority.

Regardless of your viewpoint on these two aspects of Hoodoo, one principle runs consistently through traditional practice: A Hoodoo practitioner is accountable to their community. The tradition has no central authority, no licensing body, and no pope, but instead, it has community. A practitioner whose work harms, deceives, or exploits people in the community around them will lose standing, clients, and credibility. Community accountability is the tradition's ethical infrastructure. *Note:* By most traditional measures, A practitioner with no community to answer to is not practicing Hoodoo at all but is engaging with something else that borrows its name.

REMEMBER

The honest answer is that the tradition of Hoodoo itself doesn't have one unified ethic. Hoodoo developed as a survival tool in an unjust system. When your options are limited, when the legal system doesn't protect you, when playing by the rules means staying oppressed, you do what you need to do.

That said, most experienced practitioners will tell you this: Consequences are real. What you put out tends to come back, not because of cosmic karma but because actions have effects. Desperation leads to bad decisions about how to use Hoodoo. The most ethically questionable work usually comes from people who feel powerless.

TIP

Correctly targeting recipients of your Hoodoo practice matters. Working against someone who's actively harming you is different from working against an innocent person who just happens to be standing in your way.

Understanding when personal is political

Here's the key insight that relates to the practice of personal empowerment Hoodoo: In an oppressive system, taking care of yourself is inherently political. The line between selfish and liberatory use gets blurry fast in a society structured by racism, classism, sexism, inequity, and other oppressions.

Consider these examples:

- When a Black woman in Jim Crow South uses Hoodoo to protect her children from violence, that's personal and political. Her children's safety is both individual concern and resistance to a system designed to harm Black children.
- When someone uses Hoodoo to succeed in a job interview despite facing discrimination, that's personal gain and political resistance. Getting the job you deserve despite racism isn't selfish; it's reclaiming what the system tries to deny you.
- When you work protection spells against police harassment, predatory landlords, discriminatory employers, or abusive partners enabled by patriarchy, you're addressing personal needs that exist because of systemic oppression.

Discovering Collective Justice: The Noble Work

In this section, I describe the Hoodoo work that's celebrated: using Hoodoo for justice, resistance, and community healing. This use of Hoodoo is sometimes referred to as *liberation work*. Here's what it looks like:

- **Historical resistance** included hexing slave owners and overseers, protecting escape routes and maroon communities, disrupting slave patrols, creating solidarity and communication networks, and using spiritual warfare against the slave system.
- **Civil rights era work** included protection work for activists and protestors, cursing violent racists and police, creating spiritual shields around organizing spaces, healing trauma in communities, and justice work for murdered activists.
- **Modern social justice work** includes building altars for victims of police violence (candles, offerings, written names, community prayers), using protection spells for protestors (group baths before actions, distributing mojo bags to activists), cleansing the community after violence (washing doorsteps, burning cleansing herbs in neighborhoods), cursing white supremacists and fascists, healing collective trauma through ceremony, participating in solidarity work across marginalized communities, and disrupting oppressive systems.
- **Environmental justice work** includes protecting natural resources from exploitation; seeking justice for environmental harm to communities; honoring the spirits in land, water, and plants; and resisting ecological destruction that harms marginalized communities.

REMEMBER

This environmental work might seem tangential, but it's not. Hoodoo practitioners draw on natural resources like roots, herbs, minerals, and water from specific sources. They're sensitive to resource scarcity and ecological health because their practice depends on it. When mining companies poison water sources or deforestation destroys medicinal plants, that's not just environmental damage, but spiritual harm. Protecting the environment isn't separate from protecting communities; it's part of the same liberation work.

Recognizing the power of collective work

Hoodoo practitioners experience something different when working for "we" instead of "me." When multiple practitioners focus spiritual energy on collective goals — protecting a protest, seeking justice for a murdered person, healing community trauma — the work feels bigger, more grounded, more connected to ancestral resistance.

But here's what doesn't get said often enough: Liberation work is also harder, riskier, and often thankless.

Noting the risk of liberation work

Here's the real talk about modern risks of using Hoodoo for liberation work:

- A rootworker livestreaming hexes on white supremacists might get viral likes but could also get *doxxed* (have their private information revealed online), threatened, or targeted by the very people they're working against.
- Publicly protecting protestors might draw police attention and negative reactions.
- Doing justice work for high-profile legal cases might bring unwanted personal scrutiny.

WARNING

Unlike personal gain work in which you see direct results (you got the job or attracted the lover), liberation work often involves slow, incremental change you might never see fully realized. The payoff must come as connection to something larger and honoring ancestors who used these same techniques to survive and resist. But that doesn't pay bills or solve immediate problems.

Addressing the Tension and the Debates

The two purposes of Hoodoo — personal power and collective justice — don't always play nice together. Sometimes personal gain work actively undermines collective liberation. When individuals focus solely on climbing out of oppression themselves rather than dismantling the systems creating oppression, they might carelessly step on others who are also trying to climb out.

Contemporary Hoodoo exists in a weird cultural moment in which both personal and collective purposes are being loudly claimed. In this section, you find out about the tension between purposes and the arguments used to support them.

Understanding the "crabs in a bucket" problem

This section offers a critique of the hustle culture of manifestation work, which focuses on individual success within oppressive systems rather than collective liberation from those systems.

To be clear about the crabs-in-a-bucket metaphor: The bucket isn't the crabs' natural environment. It's an artificial container that humans put them in. The crabs fighting each other when they're in the bucket is a symptom of being trapped; it's not their natural state.

The community liberation aspect of Hoodoo is about destroying the bucket entirely — dismantling the systems and institutions designed to contain, limit, and pit marginalized people against each other. When you're focused only on climbing out yourself, you're accepting the bucket as inevitable rather than recognizing it as something that shouldn't exist.

Personal empowerment work that ignores the bucket just gets you to the top of an artificial hierarchy while leaving everyone else trapped. Liberation work smashes the whole structure. Here are two examples to illustrate the crabs-in-a-bucket problem:

- A Black business owner uses Hoodoo to succeed financially but then exploits Black workers with low wages and poor working conditions. The business owner achieves personal gain while perpetuating community harm. They get out of the bucket but leave it intact for others.
- Someone works constantly to make money while ignoring the unpaid community organizing work that could improve conditions for everyone. They're climbing toward success while others are still trapped.

Considering the counterargument

There's another side to the tension: Sometimes individual success provides resources for collective work.

A financially successful practitioner can fund community organizing, support other Hoodoo practitioners, provide resources for liberation work, and create opportunities for others. The personal stability you achieve from success gives you the energy and resources to devote to collective struggle. If you're constantly in survival mode, you can't sustain liberation work.

This is the "put on your own oxygen mask first" argument: Take care of yourself so that you can help others.

Examining manifestation culture versus liberation magic

That tension shows up most clearly in how contemporary practitioners talk about what Hoodoo is actually for.

Hearing from the manifestation crowd

Some practitioners frame Hoodoo to support a manifestation culture that's primarily about personal abundance. They may be influenced by movements and beliefs such as the following:

- **New Thought,** a 19th-century spiritual movement teaching that focused mental intention shapes material outcomes
- **Law of Attraction,** the popular principle that positive thought draws positive circumstances
- **Prosperity gospel,** a Christian theological tradition that believes having wealth is a sign of divine favor

These schools of thought address ideas of right-thinking, a focus on attracting positive outcomes, and prosperity as a divine right. Practitioners who embrace them use phrases like these:

- Manifest your dream life.
- Abundance is your birthright.
- Use Hoodoo to become your best self.

The critique of this approach says that it strips Hoodoo of its resistance roots, turns it into capitalist self-help, and ignores systemic oppression.

In defense of this approach are those who espouse that Black people deserve abundance. Personal prosperity is resistance in a system designed to keep you poor. Telling Black practitioners they can't seek personal gain is respectability politics.

Hearing from the liberation magic crowd

Focused on social justice, liberation magic practitioners emphasize Hoodoo's revolutionary potential and claim these beliefs:

- Hoodoo is resistance magic.
- Hex the patriarchy.
- Your ancestors fought for liberation.

The critique of this approach is that it can be *performative*, treating Hoodoo as political theater. It can guilt practitioners for having personal needs, as if wanting love or money makes you a bad activist.

In defense of liberation magic, remember that Hoodoo was born in resistance. Ignoring that history and turning it into personal gain magic erases its powerful tradition.

Finding the truth

Both sides of Hoodoo — manifestation culture and liberation magic — are correct under responsible circumstances. They're also incomplete. Hoodoo is big enough to hold both purposes without choosing between them.

Most practitioners who've been involved in the tradition for a while exploit both avenues for Hoodoo work. They work for personal needs when they have them, and they work for collective justice when they're called to. They don't feel guilty about either.

Practicing Both Hoodoos: A Practical Approach

So how do you practice Hoodoo ethically while honoring both personal empowerment and collective liberation?

REMEMBER

Hoodoo doesn't ask you to choose between personal empowerment and collective liberation. It never has. The tradition was built by people who needed both aspects — those who couldn't afford to sacrifice personal survival for abstract principles and couldn't achieve true well-being while their communities suffered.

These early practitioners used Hoodoo to accomplish the following:

- Get food for their children and protect escape routes.
- Draw love in brutal circumstances and curse brutal oppressors.
- Compete for limited resources and build solidarity.
- Survive as individuals and resist as communities.

Knowing your motivations

Ask yourself this question about motivation and answer honestly: Am I working from genuine need or from greed? There's a vast difference between the answers "I need money to eat" and "I want to be rich because I deserve luxury."

This question is especially significant because Hoodoo was forged from genuine need, not greed. The tradition developed among people who needed food, safety, family bonds, and justice, all of which are survival needs in brutal circumstances. That's the tradition's nature. Working from genuine need honors that origin. Working from pure greed while ignoring others' genuine needs betrays it.

Here are a couple of other questions to consider:

- **Who does my Hoodoo practice for personal gain harm?** Personal gain that doesn't harm others is different from personal gain that requires harming others.
- **What am I avoiding by using Hoodoo the way I do?** Sometimes focusing only on personal gain work is avoidance of the harder and not-so-well-defined collective work. Sometimes focusing only on liberation work is avoidance of personal healing needs.

Don't expect clean answers every time you question the use of Hoodoo. *Discernment*, knowing in a given moment whether your work is serving genuine need or slipping into something harmful, is a skill that develops over years of practice. It's not a checklist that you run through before lighting a candle. Most experienced practitioners describe discernment less as a decision and more as a felt sense — one that sharpens the more honest you're willing to be with yourself. The questions in this section aren't tests to pass. They're habits of attention to cultivate.

REMEMBER

Discernment regarding the motivation for your Hoodoo work is the internal check. Community accountability is the external check. Traditional Hoodoo practitioners answer to someone beyond themselves, whether that's clients, elders, peers, or the broader community they serve. Without that relational accountability, the practice loses its grounding in the tradition's social fabric.

Balancing your practice and adjusting for context

In plain language, balancing your practice means that you do personal work when you need it without guilt. And you do collective work when you're called to it without resentment. Don't let either completely dominate your practice. Recognize that some seasons of life require more personal work, and others require more collective work.

Personal work in the context of oppression often is also liberation work. Protecting yourself from a racist system, succeeding despite discrimination, and keeping your family safe in a hostile environment aren't separate from liberation. They're part of it.

But personal work that perpetuates oppression — cursing other marginalized people to get ahead, exploiting your own community for personal gain, and working only for yourself while ignoring collective harm — deserves criticism.

Holding tension without resolving it

Maybe the point isn't to resolve the tension between personal and collective work. Maybe the tension is productive.

Holding both purposes — staying aware that you need personal well-being and collective liberation, that individual survival and community resistance both matter — keeps you honest. It prevents both pure selfishness and pure self-sacrifice.

REMEMBER

The ancestors held this tension between the two heads of Hoodoo. They worked for personal needs while resisting collectively. They didn't choose just one or the other because they couldn't afford to.

Identifying when personal work undermines justice

All Hoodoo practitioners need to be honest about when personal empowerment work actually harms collective liberation. This harm can happen if you do any of these:

- **Exploit others within the community:** Using Hoodoo to exploit other marginalized people for personal gain is a no-no. For example, overcharging desperate clients, scamming people in your own community, bullying or scaring others with claims of spiritual power, or using power to harm rather than help are situations in which personal work becomes actively harmful.
- **Ignore systemic issues:** Focusing exclusively on personal success while ignoring (or even benefiting from) systems that harm your community is ethically questionable. Think about manifesting wealth through real estate investments that gentrify Black neighborhoods and displace community members.
- **Hoard resources:** Achieving personal abundance through Hoodoo but refusing to share resources or support collective work is a lopsided practice. Treating success as a purely individual achievement rather than recognizing community roots can be harmful.
- **Perpetuate harmful hierarchies:** Using spiritual power to dominate or control others in ways that replicate oppressive dynamics — maintaining patriarchal control or enforcing rigid hierarchies within spiritual communities — should be avoided.

Recognizing when liberation work becomes performative

On the flip side of the risks of overreaching on the personal side of Hoodoo, its liberation work can also be problematic in these areas:

- **Performative activism,** including posting about hexing the patriarchy while doing no actual organizing, community care, or sustained resistance work. Don't use liberation language for social media clout without backing it up with action.
- **Purity politics,** such as judging other practitioners for having personal needs, treating personal empowerment work as inherently selfish or apolitical, or imposing rigid standards about what counts as "legitimate" Hoodoo work.

- **Martyrdom** that involves sacrificing all personal well-being for the cause, burning out, and then being unable to sustain the work. This situation helps no one.

Honoring both/and, not either/or

The tension between the personal and collective purposes of Hoodoo isn't a flaw. It's a feature of practicing survival and resistance magic in an unjust world. You don't have to choose exclusively between the two. You can work for personal needs when you have them. You can work for collective justice when you're called to. And you can hold both purposes as legitimate without guilt or apology.

What matters are these aspects of your Hoodoo practice, which I address in the section "Practicing Both Hoodoos: A Practical Approach" earlier in the chapter:

- Honesty about your motivations and effects.
- Awareness of how your personal work affects others.
- Balance between personal and collective focus over time.
- Integrity in not harming your community for personal gain.
- Sustainability in not sacrificing personal well-being for abstract principles.

The ancestors modeled this dual practice, and current practitioners can honor that by practicing Hoodoo in all its complexity: personal and political, individual and collective, self-interested and community-minded.

Both sides matter. Both are legitimate. Both are Hoodoo.

Looking to Historical Examples

In this section, I offer you a look at historical examples in which both purposes of Hoodoo — personal and collective — appear.

Harriet Tubman

Harriet Tubman is celebrated as a liberator. She led hundreds of enslaved people to freedom through the *Underground Railroad*, a secret network of safe houses used by slaves to escape bondage and reach non-slave states in the northern US or Canada. That's collective resistance work at its finest.

Tubman also carried a pistol and used it when necessary. She practiced various forms of folk magic and spiritual protection for herself and those she led. She made sensible, self-protective decisions about who to help and when. She wasn't purely selfless. She was strategic about survival.

Her work shows both purposes of Hoodoo: personal survival skills (including spiritual protection for herself) that enabled collective liberation work.

19th-century root doctors

Root doctors during and after slavery in the US practiced both kinds of Hoodoo work:

- They protected individuals from specific threats, healed community members from illness, and helped people with love and money problems.
- They cursed brutal overseers and slave catchers, helped individuals compete for limited resources, and protected maroon communities and escape routes.

They didn't separate these personal and collective Hoodoo purposes. They served whatever need presented itself.

Civil rights era practitioners

During the civil rights movement in the US, practitioners protected individual activists from harm. They also cursed violent racists, healed trauma in individuals, created protective spiritual shields around activism organizing spaces, and helped individuals with daily survival needs.

Both purposes of Hoodoo served the larger movement toward civil rights.

4 Embracing the Craft of Hoodoo

IN THIS PART . . .

Get acquainted with the roots, curios, and everyday materials Hoodoo draws upon, and grasp the spiritual logic that makes an ordinary object a conjure ingredient.

Find out about the four primary modes of Hoodoo work, and learn how practitioners choose and combine them depending on the situation's circumstances.

IN THIS CHAPTER

» Understanding traits and purposes of rootworkers materials

» Meeting the major categories of the materia magica

» Building your knowledge and skill with rootworking materials

Chapter 13

Workin' Part 1: Materials and Methods

Walk into a traditional rootworker's workspace, and you'll see jars of roots and dried herbs lining shelves, bowls of minerals and powders, bottles of oils with handwritten labels, odd items such as rusty nails and animal bones, and maybe a lodestone fed with magnetic sand. To the uninitiated, the workspace looks like a curiosity shop or a witch's lair. To the rootworker, the space is a pharmacy, an arsenal, and a toolkit all in one.

This chapter teaches you about the materials that rootworkers use and how they use them. Through their work, Hoodoo theories become practice and spiritual principles become tangible techniques.

I start by introducing the materials: the roots, herbs, minerals, personal concerns, and curios that form the foundation of Hoodoo work. After you understand the substances you're working with and why they have power, you find out about skills and knowledge to develop for exploring rootwork.

Identifying Materials' Spiritual Properties and Correspondences

Physical substances contain and transmit spiritual force. A root that Hoodoo rootworkers use isn't just vegetable matter; it's a carrier of particular spiritual qualities that they can direct toward magical purposes. But how do practitioners know what spiritual properties a given plant or mineral has?

Here are several ways in which a rootworker's knowledge of material properties and uses develops:

- **Traditional knowledge passed down:** Much of Hoodoo's materia magica comes from generations of accumulated wisdom. Enslaved Africans brought knowledge of their homeland plants, experimented with American equivalents, and shared discoveries with each other. Native American herbalism contributed extensively, as discussed in Chapter 3.

  Hoodoo practitioners passed along this knowledge base through apprenticeship, family teaching, and community practice. The knowledge evolved along the way into different branches over time and place. However, the core principles — its roots, if you will — steadfastly remained unchanged. So when an elder tells you that Five Finger Grass draws what you need, that's the distilled experience of centuries.

  TECHNICAL STUFF

  Materia magica refers to the physical materials used in rootwork: roots, herbs, minerals, curios, powders, oils, and other substances believed to carry spiritual properties. Think of these materials as the rootworker's pharmacopeia, the working inventory of ingredients they draw from when constructing a fix, laying a trick, or preparing a condition.

- **The Doctrine of Signatures:** Originating in European herbalism and associated with the 16th-century physician Paracelsus, this idea held that God marked plants with visual clues pointing to their medicinal uses. As a formal medical theory it has long since been set aside, but the observational logic persisted in folk traditions worldwide, including Hoodoo. A plant's appearance, habitat, or behavior can suggest its spiritual use:

  - *Heart-shaped leaves* suggest a plant to use for love work
  - *Thorns* suggest a plant that's good for protection
  - *Red sap* portrays strength or vitality
  - *Deep-holding roots* indicate a plant to use for grounding or staying power

Not every correspondence is obvious, but the principle functions as a useful starting point. Rootworkers observe nature and draw conclusions about symbolic properties from physical characteristics.

- **Folk names as guides:** Many plants have common folk names that reveal their uses. These names aren't random. They encode the plant's traditional magical application:
  - *Money Plant* is used for drawing financial luck and prosperity.
  - *Love Vine* can draw and bind a romantic target.
  - *Devil's Shoestring* is used to trip up enemies or evil spirits.
  - *Job's Tears* helps when seeking patience during hardship.
  - *Master of the Woods* helps with rootwork aimed to achieve domination and control.
- **Direct spiritual revelation:** Some rootworkers state that they receive information directly from spirits, ancestors, or through dreams and visions. A practitioner might be told in a dream or by the Holy Spirit to use a particular plant for a specific condition. Or they might pray over their materials and feel guided to combine certain ingredients. This occurrence isn't superstition to them. It's an intuitive way in which many traditional practitioners develop their most effective formulas.
- **Trial and observation:** Ultimately, practitioners test materials and pay attention to results. If a particular root consistently produces good outcomes in money work, it's incorporated into standard formulas. If a formula stops working or produces unexpected effects, it's modified. This empirical approach — trying things and seeing what happens — has been part of Hoodoo since the beginning. See Chapter 4 for more information about the empirical approach in Hoodoo.

Understanding Materia Magica and Its Categories

Every substance in a rootworker's collection is there for a reason. And together, all these substances make up the materia magica used in the practice of Hoodoo. Each root, herb, oil, powder, or artifact has specific spiritual properties that make it useful for certain kinds of work. Some draw money. Others repel enemies. Some cleanse spiritual contamination. Others bind or command. A skilled rootworker knows hundreds of these correspondences: what each material does, how to combine them effectively, and when to use each one.

If you're just getting started with rootworking, you don't need to memorize all the materials and their uses immediately. Traditional rootworkers learned gradually, often over a lifetime. But you must understand the need to know why materials work, how to apply them, and how to build your knowledge systematically.

You can organize the materia magica of Hoodoo into several main categories, each with its own character and typical uses. The following sections describe each category.

Working with roots: Underground power

Roots grow in darkness, anchor plants, and draw nourishment from the earth. Spiritually, they represent hidden strength, deep power, foundation, and persistence. Rootwork — literally working with roots — is central enough to Hoodoo that *rootwork* became another name for the entire practice.

Roots are particularly valued for work that requires drawing and attraction because, by their nature, they pull nutrients and water toward themselves. They also work well for grounding and stability because they anchor a plant and hold firm. Other common uses include workings for hidden influence (they work beneath the surface) and personal power (especially roots carried in mojo bags).

Some roots are used whole, especially in mojo bags. Others are ground into powder. Some are made into tea or infused in oil. The rootworker chooses the form based on the intended use.

Common Roots	Uses in Hoodoo
High John the Conqueror	Mastery, luck, personal power, and success
Angelica	Protection
Calamus	Control
Little John to Chew	Legal matters and court case work
Devil's Shoestring	Protection and tripping up enemies
Licorice	Commanding

Using herbs and leaves: Growth and change

Herbs and leaves represent items that grow in sunlight. Their powers include expansion, change, influence, and visible results. Herbs are the most numerous category in the Hoodoo pharmacopoeia, and they're used for virtually every kind of work.

TECHNICAL STUFF

Pharmacopoeia refers to documentation describing rootwork materials.

Leaves and flowering herbs are associated with growth and increase because of their tendency to grow toward the light. Herbs represent quick action because they mature faster than trees. Other uses involve influence and spread (leaves release scent and cover area) and cleansing and freshness (especially aromatic herbs).

Rootworkers use herbs either fresh or dried, in baths, burned as incense, sewn into packets, scattered on doorsteps, made into teas, or infused in oils. Their versatility makes them indispensable.

Common Herbs and Leaves	Uses in Hoodoo
Basil	Money and love
Mint	Prosperity and cleansing
Sage	Wisdom and purification
Rue	Protection and hex-breaking
Hyssop	Spiritual cleansing
Rosemary	Remembrance and protection

Harnessing minerals and stones: Permanence and power

Minerals and stones represent solid, enduring forms of matter. They're associated with permanence, protection, attraction (especially magnetic stones), and grounding heavy energy.

Rootworkers use minerals for long-lasting effects because they don't decay or easily change. They're great for protection and barriers since their physical solidity equates to spiritual boundary. Other Hoodoo workings that use minerals and stones involve attraction and drawing — lodestones particularly — and grounding and stability because of their weight and density.

Minerals and Stones	Uses in Hoodoo
Salt	Cleansing, protection, and creating barriers
Sulfur	Driving away evil and breaking hexes
Iron (especially old nails)	Protecting and cutting through spiritual attacks
Lodestones (naturally magnetic iron ore fed with magnetic sand)	Drawing money, love, or other desires
Alum	Binding and tightening
Saltpeter	Causing strife or breaking things apart
Red brick dust	Protection when sprinkled across doorways

Understanding animal curios: Specific powers

Animal parts such as bones, fur, feathers, shells, and claws carry the essence of that creature's nature and abilities. This category is probably the most controversial for modern practitioners — many modern-day rootworkers are vegan — but it's historically significant in Hoodoo.

Modern practitioners often substitute or skip animal curios entirely, especially those requiring killing animals. But understanding their traditional role helps you understand old formulas and why certain substitutions might or might not work.

Traditional Animal Parts	Uses in Hoodoo
Rabbit's foot	Luck, quick movement, escaping danger
Black cat bone	Invisibility, protection, making oneself irresistible (which requires a specific ritual)
Snake skin	Shedding old conditions, renewal
Chicken bones	Various purposes depending on which bone
Turtle shell or bones	Slowing down enemies or situations
Raccoon penis bone	Male virility and attraction

WARNING

Modern sourcing matters. Historical Hoodoo used animal parts that were readily available in rural settings: farm animals, wild creatures, roadkill. Today, sourcing animal parts ethically is more complex. Never kill an animal solely for magical use. If you use animal curios, source them ethically by collecting naturally shed feathers or bones from animals that died naturally. You can also turn to responsibly sourced materials from ethical suppliers. Many practitioners substitute other materials for animal curios by using plant-based alternatives that carry similar energy. The spiritual principle represented can and should be honored without causing harm.

Obtaining personal concerns: The most powerful ingredient

Personal concerns, or items intimately connected to a specific person, are the most potent ingredients in targeted magic. These personal concerns include hair (head hair is strongest, but any hair can work), nail clippings, and worn clothing, especially underwear. In addition, Hoodoo makes use of bodily fluids (blood, sexual fluids, urine, saliva, tears, and sweat) and dirt from a person's footprint. Also useful are personal possessions or practices such as handwritten documents, photographs, or items the person regularly touches or carries.

Personal concerns create a direct spiritual link to the target of the rootworking. Work done on these items affects the person themselves. This is why practitioners guard their own personal concerns carefully and why obtaining someone's hair or photograph is so valued in targeted work.

In love work, domination work, healing at a distance, or enemy work, personal concerns aren't just helpful; they're often essential. Without them, you're working more generally, which can still be effective but isn't as precisely targeted.

Preparing condition oils and powders: Concentrated formulas

Condition oils and powders are prepared formulas; they're blends of multiple ingredients designed for specific purposes. The formulas represent generations of experimentation and refinement.

Condition oils are made by infusing herbs, roots, and sometimes minerals into a base oil, which is mineral oil historically, although olive, jojoba, or other oils work. The spiritual properties of the ingredients transfer to the oil, creating a concentrated formula. These oils are used to dress candles, anoint the body, feed mojo bags, or mark objects and locations.

Common Condition Oils	Uses in Hoodoo
Van Van	Clearing obstacles and bringing blessings
Fast Luck	Quick opportunities
Follow Me Boy/Girl	Attraction
Commanding Oil	Control and authority
Protection Oil (various formulas)	Defense
Money Drawing Oil	Prosperity

Powders and dusts are finely ground mixtures of herbs, roots, minerals, and sometimes other ingredients. They're used to dress candles, sprinkle in shoes, dust doorways, scatter where someone will walk, or add to mojo bags.

Common Powders	Uses in Hoodoo
Goofer Dust	Cause harm to enemies
Hot Foot Powder	Drive someone away
Crossing Powder	Cause trouble for a target
Uncrossing Powder	Remove hexes and bad conditions
Drawing Powder	Attract money, love, or opportunities

WARNING

Commercial condition oils and powders vary wildly in quality. Some are made by knowledgeable practitioners who use traditional formulas and quality ingredients. Others are basically scented oil with food coloring or cornstarch with fragrance. If you buy oils and powders commercially, conduct research on the supplier. Look for companies with roots in the tradition, not just mass-market occult suppliers. Better yet, learn to make your own oils and powders after you understand the ingredients. That way you know exactly what's in your formulas and can adjust them to your specific needs.

Building Your Rootworking Knowledge and Skills

People learning about rootworking today have more options than were available in the past. You can take formal herbalism courses, read detailed materia-medica guides, or watch video lessons that past generations never dreamed of.

Those resources are valuable, but seasoned rootworkers still say that real skill comes from handling the plants and other materials yourself, watching how they behave, and building a personal relationship with them.

Here are some general guidelines for building your knowledge of materials and your skill for working with them:

- **Gain direct experience.** Handle your herbs and roots. Smell them, taste them (when safe), and feel their texture. Notice what they look like, how they grow, and what conditions they prefer. Physical familiarity with your ingredients builds spiritual connection.
- **Start with common materials.** Become expert with using salt, sugar, and cinnamon before worrying about rare roots. (See the later section "Exploring key ingredients every rootworker should know" for a look at the most common materials.) Build a deep understanding of the materials you can access easily, rather than knowing many ingredients superficially.
- **Keep records that document your work.** In your records, make sure to include the ingredients you used and the results you achieved. And write down whether the work turned out as you expected. This record-keeping builds your personal knowledge base.
- **Ask the plants themselves.** Some practitioners develop the ability to sense or hear what a plant does. Hold a new root or herb, quiet your mind, and pay attention to any impressions. Note what holding the material feels like spiritually. And recognize when anything about its use comes to mind. This conscious connection with the plants takes practice but can be remarkably accurate.
- **Learn from multiple sources.** Books, experienced practitioners, online communities, and historical documents all offer knowledge. But carefully evaluate sources to determine whether the information comes from people practicing the tradition or from outsiders who are just speculating. Different sources may present different properties and correspondences, which may be right for their context.
- **Study regional and family variations.** Your grandmother's formula for a specific work may differ from the formula you find in a book. That variation doesn't mean either formula is wrong; it means the tradition has branches. Respect what works, where it works.
- **Practice trial use and observation.** Ultimately, you learn by doing. Try formulas, pay attention to results, and adjust as needed. Build your practice empirically, not just theoretically.

REMEMBER

Ingredients of the Hoodoo practice are tools, not magic bullets. Having the right root or herb helps, but materials alone don't create magical effects. They're carriers of spiritual force that you direct through your intention, knowledge, and power. A skilled practitioner makes materials work. Materials don't make an unskilled person into a practitioner. Focus on building your understanding and spiritual authority alongside acquiring ingredients, and you'll develop real competency.

Recognizing hot versus cool and warm ingredients

Not all spiritual work needs the same intensity. Sometimes you need gentle, gradual influence. Other times you need aggressive, fast action. Understanding the temperature of ingredients that affect the intensity of the work helps you match the formula to the situation.

Using hot or heating ingredients

Hot or heating ingredients have aggressive, fast-acting, sometimes harsh energy. They force change, dominate, attack, or aggressively protect. Hot ingredients include peppers (cayenne, black pepper, chili), sulfur, nettles, rue (hot for protection), ginger, cinnamon (which can be warm or hot depending on its use), and tobacco.

You use hot ingredients in rootwork when you need fast results, are doing aggressive work (enemy work, domination, forcing movement), or are defending against serious attack. Also, you may need hot ingredients when gentler methods have failed to achieve the results you need.

TIP

Use hot ingredients intentionally, not as your default. Working with hot ingredients requires caution. The intensity can backfire if you use the ingredients carelessly. The work may cause unintended consequences and can be spiritually loud by drawing attention when you might prefer to work quietly.

Using cool, cooling, or warm ingredients

Cool or cooling ingredients have gentle, gradual, peaceful energy. They heal, bless, attract through sweetness, protect through blessing, and work without force. Cool ingredients include sugar, honey, molasses, rose petals, chamomile, lavender, milk, and angelica. Many gentle herbs are also cool ingredients.

You use cool ingredients when you want lasting, stable results or when you're healing or blessing. Try cool ingredients when you're working to sweeten someone's disposition and want to build up to an outcome rather than force results. With cool ingredients, you have time to let work develop naturally.

REMEMBER

Cool work is often more sustainable than hot work. It doesn't burn itself out or provoke resistance. But it's also slower and may be inadequate for urgent situations or serious opposition.

Warm ingredients have energy and movement without being aggressive. Examples of warm ingredients include cinnamon (which can also be considered hot), clove, orange peel, and coffee. Many prosperity herbs (such as basil, bay laurel, and allspice) are also warm ingredients.

Balancing formulas: Temperature and structure

A balanced formula often combines temperatures. You can use hot ingredients for quick action, warm ingredients for sustained energy, and cool ingredients for stability and longevity.

TIP

Start cool and escalate if needed. When you're learning or addressing a new situation, start with cooler, gentler work. If that doesn't produce adequate results, you can always escalate to warmer or hotter formulas. But if you start with the hottest, most aggressive work and it creates problems, you can't easily back down. You may have to do extensive cleansing and cooling work to undo what you started. Think of starting cool like seasoning food: You can always add more heat, but you can't remove it once it's in.

Temperature isn't the only consideration you have when building effective formulas. Many traditional rootworkers also balance formulas by the type of material they choose and by creating geometric spiritual structures. Here are some commonly used balanced formulas:

- **The three-part (triangular balance) formula:** Combines a plant, a mineral, and a liquid or oil. This combination creates directional energy and mimics an arrow pointing toward your goal. The three points work together to move energy in a specific direction.

  For example, a simple money-drawing formula might include these elements:

  - *A plant ingredient such as cinnamon* for warming and drawing prosperity.
  - *A mineral material such as lodestone* that involves magnetic attraction.
  - *A liquid or oil* such as honey to add sweetness and attraction.

The triangle structure points toward the goal (money), and the three types of materials create momentum with plant energy for growth, mineral for grounding and attraction, and liquid for flow and movement.

- **The four-part (square balance) formula:** Combines a plant, a mineral, a liquid or oil, and another element, such as an animal curio, a personal concern, or a metal. This four-part structure creates stable, lasting energy, like a square foundation that offers balanced protection that won't tip or collapse.

  For example, a protection formula may include these elements:

  - A plant such as rue, which is a protective herb.
  - A mineral such as salt to provide a barrier and cleansing.
  - A metal such as an iron nail for cutting through an attack.
  - An oil such as Protection Oil that binds all ingredients together.

Understanding the geometric principles of formula design helps you create your own formulas rather than just following recipes. If you need fast movement toward a goal, consider using the triangle structure with three ingredients pointing the way. If you need lasting stability, think about a square structure with four ingredients that create an unshakeable foundation.

TECHNICAL STUFF

People don't usually discuss Hoodoo in terms of sacred geometry, but practitioners intuitively understand that the number and arrangement of elements matters. Three creates movement; think of a triangle pointing out the direction. Four creates stability, like a square's foundation. Seven offers powerful completion through seven-day rituals and seven-knob candles. A structure involving nine — nine days, nine washes, or nine prayers — is particularly strong for persistent work. When you see formulas with specific numbers of ingredients or repetitions, understand that they're not arbitrary; they're creating spiritual structures through number and form.

Sourcing and preparing your materials

Having the right materials matters, but so does knowing how you obtain and prepare them. Long before eco-consciousness was a trend, traditional rootworkers paid attention to sourcing their materials. They considered aspects such as when and where they gathered plants, how they treated them after gathering, and in what condition they appeared. These factors don't represent superstition; instead, they help maintain the spiritual potency of your materials.

Finding your ingredients

Here are the ways and means of respectfully finding materials for your rootwork:

- **Growing your own:** This method is ideal when possible. Plants you grow yourself and tend with intention carry your energy and respond to your needs. You know exactly what they've been exposed to, and you can harvest at optimal times. If you have space, consider growing key herbs: basil, mint, sage, rosemary, and rue.
- **Wildcrafting ethically:** Gathering wild plants requires knowledge and respect. Learn to identify plants correctly because misidentifying and collecting the wrong plants can be dangerous. Gather your plants only where doing so is legal and permitted. Take only what you need, and never deplete more than a third of the plant that's present. Thank the plant, and leave an offering such as water, cornmeal, or a coin.
- **Buying from reputable suppliers:** Most practitioners buy at least some materials, particularly roots and other items that they can't grow or gather. Buy from suppliers who specialize in magical herbs and roots, preferably those who have roots (pun intended) in African American folk magic traditions. Avoid cheap bulk herbs from random sources because quality varies widely and really does matter.
- **Gleaning grocery store ingredients:** Many Hoodoo materials are common kitchen items such as salt, sugar, cinnamon, coffee, and vinegar. Finding these items in a grocery store is perfectly acceptable. In fact, the accessibility of everyday ingredients is part of Hoodoo's genius. You don't need exotic imports for effective work.
- **Sourcing of animal materials respectfully:** If you use animal curios, please source these ethically. Look for items from natural molting such as snake skins and bird feathers. If you harvest roadkill bones, clean them respectfully. Using sea shells that wash up onto shore or materials from animals that died naturally is acceptable. Never kill an animal for magical use. Hoodoo has evolved away from ever needing to do so. Many modern practitioners skip animal materials entirely.

Cleansing newly acquired materials

When you acquire new materials, cleanse them before use. They may carry energy that carries over from where they were grown, how they were handled, or who touched them. You want to use clean, neutral materials that are ready for you to charge them with your intention. This practice doesn't need to be elaborate; the intention to cleanse is most important.

Here are some simple cleansing methods:

- Pass the material through incense smoke, such as frankincense or sage.
- Sprinkle the material with salt water, particularly sea salt in spring water or Florida Water, which I talk about in Chapter 11.
- Leave out materials where they can absorb sunlight or moonlight for a few hours or days.
- Breathe over the materials with the intention to cleanse.
- Pray over the materials and ask that any unwanted energy be removed.

Storing and maintaining the power of ingredients

Proper storage keeps your materials potent. Use glass jars with tight lids. Plastic jars can work, but glass is traditional and doesn't react with materials. Label all materials clearly with the botanical name, the common name, and the date acquired, as needed. Store the jars out of direct sunlight unless you're specifically cleansing or charging a material.

For the longer term, keep your stored materials in a cool, dry place. Check them periodically for degradation from moisture, insects, or for loss of scent. Refresh dried herbs every year or two; they lose potency over time.

TIP

Keep your working materials in a dedicated space such as a cabinet, closet, or working altar area. Keeping materials separate maintains their spiritual charge and keeps your rootworking tools apart from mundane items.

Timing the collection of materials

Traditional rootworkers paid attention to the timing of when they gathered plants. Gathering times usually involve some of the following elements:

- **Moon phases:** Collect material for starting or drawing work during a new moon, for power during a full moon, and for banishing and cleansing (usually herbs) during a waning moon.
- **Time of day:** Collect materials at dawn for new beginnings, at noon for power, at sunset for endings, and at midnight for serious work.
- **Day of the week:** Follow planetary correspondences (named for the seven known planets which, in antiquity, included the Sun and the Moon) to gather materials appropriate for each day of the week.

Day of the Week	Planet	Associated With
Sunday	Sun	Success, vitality, and blessings
Monday	Moon	Emotions, intuition, and nurturing
Tuesday	Mars	Energy, action, protection, conflict, and ambition
Wednesday	Mercury	Communication, intellect, commerce, and travel
Thursday	Jupiter	Prosperity, luck, and expansion
Friday	Venus	Love, beauty, and pleasure
Saturday	Saturn	Banishing, binding, and reversal

- **Season:** Gather plants when they're at their strongest during the year.

Do these guidelines mean that materials gathered at other times don't work? No. But optimal timing can enhance potency. If you're wildcrafting or growing your own, timing matters more. If you're buying, you work with what you purchase and charge it appropriately through your own power.

Making substitutions and adaptations

What do you do when you can't get a traditional ingredient? For example, suppose that High John root is unavailable or too expensive, a plant doesn't grow in your region, or you're morally opposed to using an animal curio called for in an old formula.

This situation calls for knowing why some ingredient works; this understanding becomes crucial. If you know that you use a certain root in a formula because it grabs and holds, you can potentially substitute another grabbing and holding plant. If you know that an ingredient provides hot, aggressive energy, you can use a different hot herb.

Following principles for substitution

When substituting materials in a Hoodoo working, you must match the spiritual property of the ingredient, not just the category. Don't replace an herb with just any other herb, but make sure that the substitute you use does similar work. If you need a drawing root and don't have High John, another root known for possessing attraction (such as Adam and Eve root) might work. But replacing High John with a protection root (such as black cohosh root) wouldn't make sense.

Also remember these guidelines when substituting ingredients in a formula:

- **Consider ingredient temperature and substitute accordingly.** If the original material is hot and forceful, use a hot, forceful substitute. (See the section "Recognizing hot versus cool and warm ingredients.") If the ingredients temperature is cool, use a cool replacement. Changing the temperature changes how the formula works.
- **Local plants have power and may make good substitutes for unavailable traditional plants.** You can substitute plants that are indigenous to your region after properly studying their traits and usage. They can be as effective as traditional Hoodoo herbs from other areas. Southern rootworkers had different plants than Appalachian rootworkers, and both traditions work effectively.
- **Essential oils can sometimes substitute for dried herbs.** If you need basil and don't have the leaf, a drop of basil essential oil may work in some applications. ***Note:*** Don't make this substitution in baths because essential oils can burn the skin. And always use pure essential oil, not fragrance oil.
- **Setting intention and charging materials can bridge gaps when substituting.** If you absolutely must substitute something quite different from the ingredient in the traditional formula, you can charge it with clear intention to perform the role you need. This practice isn't ideal, but using your focused will can make imperfect materials work.

Recognizing when substitution doesn't work well

You can't substitute other materials for personal concerns in formulas; you need an actual link to the person. Also, some traditional power items (High John, lodestone) are hard to replace because they're so associated with specific energy. In formulas with complex balance, substituting one ingredient might throw off the whole thing. Historical recipes passed down with specific ingredients probably work best as written.

REMEMBER

If you must substitute extensively in a formula, you're essentially creating a new formula. And that practice is how new formulas are born. But recognize that you must test the new creation. Don't expect it to work exactly like the traditional version.

Exploring key ingredients every rootworker should know

Although the full Hoodoo *pharmacopoeia* includes hundreds of materials, a core set of ingredients appears repeatedly across traditions and regions. Conquer the use of these, and you can do most common work effectively. Table 13-1 gives you the rundown on the core set of ingredients.

TABLE 13-1 Key Hoodoo Materials to Know

Category and Material	What It's Known For	How It's Used
Power Roots		
John the Conqueror (also High John or John)	Male power, success against obstacles and adversity, winning, domination, and sexual potency	Carried in mojo bags for luck and power, used in gambler's formulas, added to love work for men, and in any situation requiring victory
Angelica Root (Angelica archangelica or *A. atropurpurea*)	Angelic protection and blessing, cool or gentle work (not aggressive), and calling on spiritual help	In protection mojos, baths for spiritual cleansing, burned as incense for blessing, or placed around a home for ongoing protection, especially for children or creating safe space
Calamus Root (*Acorus calamus* or Sweet Flag)	Control, commanding (not gentle) domination work, success in court cases, commanding respect, or compelling someone to do what you want	Chewed before important meetings or court appearances, carried in mojos for control, or included in domination formulas
Devil's Shoestring (*Viburnum alnifolium* or *Tephrosia virginiana*)	Tripping up the devil or enemies (with tangled, stringy roots) before they can harm you, and personal/home defensive magic	Placed under door mats to prevent enemies from entering, in protection mojos, or when foiling someone working against you
Licorice Root (*Glycyrrhiza glabra*)	Commanding, controlling, and dominating (in an assertive but less harsh way), sweetening and bending someone to your will, attraction and control	In love work formulas, in commanding formulas, or for influencing someone's feelings or decisions
Essential Herbs		
Five Finger Grass (*Potentilla* species, Cinquefoil)	Grabbing what you need — attracting money, love, protection, wisdom, or general good fortune	In countless formulas because it's so versatile

(continued)

TABLE 13-1 *(continued)*

Category and Material	What It's Known For	How It's Used
Hyssop (*Hyssopus officinalis*)	Gentle and thorough spiritual cleansing, purification, and removing sin or negative conditions (as in Psalm 51)	In baths and floor washes for cleansing space, for blessing new homes, cleansing after illness, removing the spiritual residue of conflict, or preparing yourself for sacred work
Rue (*Ruta graveolens*)	Protecting and hex-breaking (somewhat hot and harsh), driving away evil, breaking curses, and protecting against the evil eye	In baths for removing hexes, in protection mojos, around property for defense, or in reversing work to send evil back to its source
Basil (*Ocimum basilicum*)	Bringing blessings, love, prosperity, and protection gently for money drawing, love work, blessing formulas, and protection work	Carried in a pocket or wallet for luck, added to love mojos, used in prosperity baths, or scattered around a business to draw customers
Mint (*Mentha* species, particularly spearmint and peppermint)	Prosperity, cleansing, healing, travel protection, clearing stagnation, and bringing fresh energy	In money-drawing formulas, cleansing baths, and healing work, to protect travelers, in wallets or cash registers to attract money and freshen energy
Sage (*Salvia officinalis* or *Artemisia ludoviciana*, multiple varieties)	Wisdom, purification, and protection (common garden sage); heavy-duty cleansing and blessing (white sage)	Burned to cleanse spaces, used in wisdom and clarity work, carried for protection, or put in baths for purification
Minerals and More		
Salt	Purification, creating barriers, absorbing negativity, and for protection	Alone or with other ingredients in baths, sprinkled in corners or across doorways, added floor washes, and to cleanse tools
Sulfur (also called brimstone)	Driving away evil, breaking hexes, and banishing negative spirits with harsh, hot energy	Burned for purification, sprinkled where needed to drive away evil, in protection mojos against serious spiritual attack, and in reversing work
Red Brick Dust (red brick ground into powder)	Protecting, creating boundaries, sealing against spiritual intrusion powder	Sprinkled across doorsteps, windowsills, and property lines to prevent evil from entering, sealing doorways against unwanted spirits
Lodestone (Magnetite, natural magnetic iron ore)	Attracting (specific people) and drawing work (particularly pulling money)	Fed regularly to maintain power, placed in the four corners of a business to draw customers, kept with money to attract more, in love work to draw a specific person, in work for pulling anything toward you
Iron (particularly old nails with historical energy)	Cutting through spiritual attacks, grounding excessive energy, protecting, and creating boundaries	Buried at property corners for protection, placed under the doormat to cut evil, carried in protection mojos, in binding work to "nail down" a situation or ground and stabilize scattered energy

TIP

Start with the classic materials used widely in the tradition. You may find hundreds of ingredients available, but you don't need all of them to do effective work. Start with the most common, well-tested materials — things like salt, sugar, cinnamon, and sage. Become expert at using those before expanding to more exotic items. A rootworker who really understands salt and knows 20 ways to use it is more effective than someone with 100 fancy ingredients they don't truly understand. Sticking with classic materials is also easier on your wallet.

TECHNICAL STUFF

Hoodoo practitioners treat lodestones as living spiritual tools. To keep them powerful, practitioners feed them weekly by sprinkling them with magnetic sand (fine iron filings) and sometimes anointing them with Magnetic Oil or Lodestone Oil. This habit isn't superstition because the magnetic sand is literally drawn to and clings to the lodestone, and practitioners believe this physical magnetism reflects and reinforces spiritual drawing power. A well-fed, well-tended lodestone can remain powerful for decades.

IN THIS CHAPTER

» Understanding foundational earth magic

» Immersing in water magic for spiritual cleansing, drawing, and protection

» Employing fire magic through candle work

» Discovering air magic in the power of petition and prayer

» Combining the four approaches for more powerful work

Chapter 14
Workin' Part 2: The Four Ways of Rootworking

Hoodoo contains countless specific techniques, but most changemaking magic falls into four primary approaches. Each approach corresponds roughly to a classical element of nature: earth, water, fire, and air.

All four approaches have their own character and strengths. Most rootworkers use all four methods by choosing the approach that best fits the situation. For example, you might combine methods by making a mojo bag (earth), bathing to prepare yourself (water), and burning a candle over the situation (fire) while praying (air).

In this chapter, you find out about how each approach individually helps you work with precision and intention. And you see how combining them adds power.

Note: The four-element framework in this chapter is a borrowed organizing tool, not a native Hoodoo category system. Practitioners don't generally sort their work into earth magic or fire magic, for example. Hoodoo's own logic is practical and results-focused, built around specific goals and ingredients. Think of the four groupings as a mnemonic, or a memory aid, for navigating this chapter, not a claim about how the tradition thinks about itself.

Rootwork: Earth Magic (The Foundation)

When most people think of Hoodoo, they picture mojo bags, gris-gris packets, and rootworkers assembling mysterious bundles of herbs and roots. This is rootwork in its most literal sense: working with roots and other physical materials to create tangible magical objects. But rootwork also includes consumables: teas, tonics, powders added to food or drink, and other preparations meant to be taken into the body. These consumables work from the inside out, changing the person who consumes them.

Forming physical materials into earth magic work

Earth magic operates on the principle that Hoodoo can bind spiritual force into physical form. When you assemble ingredients with intention, charge them with prayer and will, and create a contained object, you're making a battery that holds and radiates specific energy. For example, a mojo bag isn't just a collection of herbs in cloth. It's a concentrated spiritual tool that continuously works toward your goal. As long as you maintain your tools by feeding them with oil, praying over them, and keeping them hidden and safe, they radiate the intention you built into them.

But earth magic also works through consumption and incorporation. When you drink tea made from roots and herbs, you're not just experiencing the roots' and herbs' physical and chemical effects. Instead, you're taking their spiritual properties into yourself. The herbs become part of you, working from within to create change in who you are or what you're capable of.

Earth magic works in two main ways:

- **Internal transformation,** which includes works such as consuming herbs to change your nature, emotions, or condition from within. You can use calming herbs to reduce anxiety, love-drawing herbs to make yourself more attractive, and courage roots to strengthen your resolve.

* **Capability enhancement,** which involves consuming herbs to temporarily unlock or amplify specific abilities. You can use African dream root to induce prophetic dreams, certain herbs before divination work to sharpen psychic vision, or roots consumed before important confrontations to enhance your commanding presence or persuasive speech.

This giving of power from within is why fixing someone's food or drink — by adding magical ingredients without their knowledge — is such a powerful and controversial practice in Hoodoo. What goes into the body affects the spirit, both in terms of who people are and what they can do.

WARNING

Adding magical ingredients to someone's food or drink without their knowledge is controversial for good reason. It violates their consent and bodily autonomy. Historically, practitioners might fix someone's coffee to attract them, or they might feed an abuser something to make them sick or docile. Modern practitioners debate whether this type of earth magic is ever ethical. At minimum, you must understand that working on someone's body without their knowledge and permission carries serious ethical weight for you and potential spiritual consequences for both of you.

Table 14-1 looks at some common physical creations used in Hoodoo earth magic, including the materials incorporated and the objects' purposes.

TABLE 14-1 Common Earth Magic Creations

The Creation	Its Construction and Placement	Its Purpose(s)
Bottle spells	Ingredients placed in jars or bottles, sometimes with liquids, sealed and either kept, buried, or thrown into moving water depending on the purpose	Protection, love drawing, money drawing, or crossing/enemy work, depending on ingredients and placement
Gris-gris	Similar to mojo bags but often associated with New Orleans Hoodoo	Love drawing, money drawing, protection, or luck
Lodestone pairs	Two lodestones married (with magnetic attraction), kept together, and fed regularly	Drawing money or love or keeping a couple together
Magical cooking	Preparing food with specific intentions, adding herbs known for particular properties, praying over meals as you cook them	Infusing intention into nourishment
Mojo bags/hands	Small flannel or leather bags filled with roots, herbs, minerals, and curios — sewn or tied shut — and carried in a pocket, bra, or pinned inside clothing	Love drawing, money drawing, protection, or luck

(continued)

TABLE 14-1 ***(continued)***

The Creation	Its Construction and Placement	Its Purpose(s)
Nation sacks	Large protective packets buried at property corners or hidden in walls	Long-term protection of a location
Packets and bundles	Ingredients wrapped in paper or cloth — sometimes sewn, sometimes folded and tied — and carried, hidden in a home, or buried on property	Adaptable to nearly any goal: love drawing, money drawing, protection, crossing, or blessing, depending on ingredients
Powders in food or drink	Finely ground herbs, roots, or minerals added to someone's food or drink to influence them	Love powders to make someone desire you, confusion powders to cloud their judgment, or calming powders to reduce their anger
Teas and tonics	Herbal preparations ingested to bring about internal change on both physical and spiritual levels	Building courage, love-drawing power, success energy, cleansing, protection from within
Trick bags	Bundles with wrapped ingredients to be placed where a target will encounter them — under their doorstep, in their path, or near their home	For working on someone else, not yourself

Embracing the art of the process

Creating effective earth magic rootwork (especially mojo bags) involves several key skills you can learn and practice:

- **Selection:** Choosing ingredients that align with your goal and are balanced for temperature (see Chapter 13 for more about ingredient temperature) and *structural geometry* (the intentional use of space, direction, and arrangement — like a crossroad — as part of the work).
- **Preparation:** Cleaning and charging ingredients, as well as sometimes cutting or crushing them to release their properties.
- **Assembly:** Putting materials together in the right order, with intention at each step.
- **Charging:** After assembly, you must awaken the packet or bag to its purpose through prayer, breath, or anointing with oil.
- **Maintenance:** Most mojo bags need regular feeding and attention, including weekly oil, prayer, keeping it on your body, and talking to it.
- **Secrecy:** Traditional mojo bags are kept hidden because letting others see or touch your mojo can break its power.

Sample fixing: Building your own money magnet

In this section, I walk you through creating a traditional money-drawing mojo bag step by step. Creating this object is genuine rootwork, and it's simple enough for a beginner but effective when constructed with focus and maintained properly.

Here are the characteristics and ingredients of a money magnet mojo bag:

- **Its purpose:** To draw money and financial opportunities to you consistently over time.
- **Materials:** You need to gather these materials and ingredients:
  - *Green flannel cloth,* approximately 3 × 3 inches; green is for money and growth
  - Small piece or chip of *John the Conqueror root* for power and success
  - *Five Finger Grass* for drawing what you need
  - *Cinnamon chips or powder* for warming prosperity
  - *One or two whole cloves* for quick action
  - *Three dimes or three silver-colored coins* to represent money
  - *Lodestone* (small piece if you can get it) or magnetic sand/iron filings for drawing money and opportunity toward you
  - *Money-drawing oil or cinnamon oil* to attract wealth and financial opportunity
  - *Green thread or string* to tie the fabric closed
  - Optional: *A piece of your hair* and a small piece of paper with your name written nine times to anchor the bag's energy directly to you
- **Best timing:** Starting on a Thursday (prosperity day according to the tradition) during a waxing moon (associated with growth) is ideal. But you can start whenever you need money. Don't let imperfect timing stop you from working.

Follow these steps to prepare for working and put together your money-drawing mojo bag:

1. **Prepare yourself by cleansing if possible.**

   At the minimum, wash your hands with intention while thinking about clearing away any obstacles to prosperity. See the section "Taking a working bath" later in the chapter for how to cleanse in preparation to work.

2. **Set up your working space on a clear table or altar area where you won't be disturbed.**

   Have all materials assembled and close at hand.

3. **Light a green or gold candle if you have one available, take a few deep breaths, and focus your mind on your intention: drawing money.**

4. **Build the mojo bag by handling and placing each material ingredient on the cloth.**

   Perform these actions for proper bag construction:

   1. Lay the flannel cloth on your prepared work surface flat in front of you.
   2. Hold the John the Conqueror root and say the following, out loud or silently with conviction, before placing the root in the center of the cloth.

      "John the Conqueror, bring me power over poverty and success with money."

   3. Hold the Five Finger Grass and say the following before adding it to the cloth.

      "Five Finger Grass, grab and draw money to me from all directions."

   4. Hold the cinnamon and say the following before adding it to the cloth.

      "Cinnamon, warm my fortune and spice my prosperity."

   5. Hold the cloves and say the following before adding them to the cloth.

      "Cloves, bring quick opportunities and fast money." Add them.

   6. Hold the coins and say the following before adding them to the cloth.

      "Like calls to like. These coins draw more coins. This money draws more money."

   7. If using lodestone or magnetic sand, recite the following before adding it to the cloth.

      "Lodestone, magnetize money to me. Pull prosperity into my life."

   8. If adding your hair, say the following before adding it to the cloth.

      "This is me, [*insert your name here*]. This money comes to me, [*insert your name here*]."

   9. If using the paper that has your name, write your full name nine times, stacking the lines so they form a block. Turn the paper 90 degrees and write *MONEY* nine times across your name, so that the words cross, as shown in Figure 14-1.

      Fold the paper toward you (drawing it in) three times and place it in the cloth.

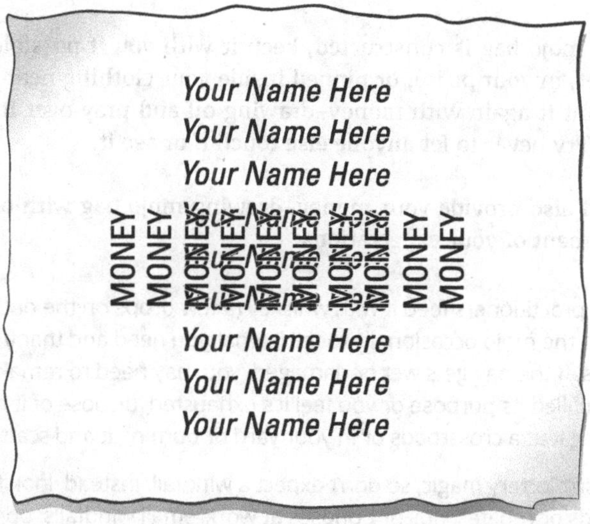

FIGURE 14-1: A paper with MONEY crossing your name.

5. **Complete the mojo bag by gathering up the corners of the cloth, bringing all the ingredients into the center, and tying it closed with the green thread.**

   For proper closure, wrap the thread around the corners of the cloth three times and tie three knots, saying the following with each knot.

   "As I tie this knot, I bind this magic. Money flows to me."

   Hold the completed bag in both hands.

6. **Charge and awaken the mojo by bring the bag close to your mouth and breathing on it forcefully three times.**

   With each breath say the following.

   "Wake up. You are alive. Your purpose is to draw money to me."

7. **Anoint the bag with money drawing oil by putting a drop of oil on your finger and touching it to the bag while turning it to anoint all sides.**

8. **Add intention by holding the bag to your heart and praying in your own words or with something like the following:**

   "By the power of the roots and herbs, by my will and intention, by [God's blessing/the ancestors' help/however you frame spiritual assistance], this mojo draws money to me. Money flows to me easily and continuously. Opportunities for prosperity come to me. Financial blessings are mine. This is done. Amen."

   Rather than Amen, you can say "So it is," or "Asé," or whatever closing feels right to you.

9. **If you burned a candle during the process (see Step 3), pass the completed mojo bag through the candle smoke three times.**

After your mojo bag is constructed, keep it with you if possible, whether it's in your pocket, in your purse, or pinned inside your clothing near your skin. Once a week, anoint it again with money-drawing oil and pray over it to recharge your intention. Try never to let anyone else touch it or see it.

You should also provide your money-drawing mojo bag with ongoing nurturing and adjustment of your expectations:

- Some practitioners feed it with whiskey (a few drops on the outside) or tobacco. Talk to the mojo occasionally to tell it what you need and thank it when money comes. If the bag gets wet or damaged, you may need to remake it. When it has fulfilled its purpose or you feel it's exhausted, dispose of it respectfully by burying it at a crossroads or in your yard or burning it and scattering the ashes.
- This isn't lottery magic, so don't expect a windfall. Instead, look for unexpected refunds or rebates, tips or bonuses at work, small windfalls, opportunities for overtime or side income, things you needed going on sale, finding money, debts being forgiven, or people repaying old loans. The mojo opens channels for money to flow to you through natural-seeming (but spiritually influenced) means. Keep your eyes open for opportunities, and act on them. The mojo draws opportunities, but you must take action when they appear.

TIP

A mojo involves a relationship: You're not creating a mechanical device. you're making a living, spiritual tool that needs attention and feeding to stay strong. Some practitioners talk to their mojos, thank them when things go well, and scold them if they seem to be slacking. This isn't crazy. It's treating your magical work as an ongoing relationship rather than a one-time spell. The more you tend it, the stronger it works.

Spiritual Baths: Water Magic (The Cleanser)

Water is viewed as spiritually powerful because it cleanses, transforms, carries, and renews. A spiritual bath isn't about getting physically clean; it's about washing away negative influences, absorbing beneficial properties, or preparing yourself for important work.

Understanding why water works magic

Water is a universal solvent and carrier. Physically, it dissolves substances and carries them away. Spiritually, it works the same way — by dissolving unwanted influences and washing them off your body and spirit. When you bathe in herb-infused water, you don't just get herb residue on your skin but also absorb the spiritual properties of the plants. When you pour water over yourself with intention, you're ritually washing away whatever you're ready to release.

REMEMBER

Water also holds intention and blessing. Praying over water charges it. The water then carries that prayer to everything it touches. This is why holy water works, why water blessed by spiritual workers is valued, and why even plain water poured with strong intention can be effective.

Table 14-2 gives you a look at common types of spiritual baths and how they involve water.

TABLE 14-2 Spiritual Baths and What They Do

Type of Bath	Ingredients Used	What It Does
Blessing and Prosperity	Blessed herbs and sometimes milk, honey, or other sweet substances	Brings general good fortune and divine favor
Cleansing and Uncrossing	Purifying herbs such as hyssop, rue, salt, and lemon	Removes negative influences, hexes, bad luck, or spiritual dirt accumulated from moving through the world
Drawing and Attraction	Sweet, attractive herbs and often honey or sugar	Pulls desired things (love, money, opportunities, or luck) toward you
Healing	Gentle herbs and sometimes combined with prayers for health	Supports physical or spiritual healing
Protection	Protective herbs such as angelica, basil, and salt	Creates a shield around you before going into difficult situations or to maintain ongoing protection
Road-Opening	Herbs associated with opening and clearing, such as abre camino or Five Finger Grass	Removes obstacles and clears the path for success

Taking a working bath

Spiritual baths follow specific protocols and go beyond simply adding herbs to your regular bath. Some spiritual baths are poured over you; others you sit in. Traditional Hoodoo usually uses poured baths. Properly preparing and taking a working bath includes the following processes:

- **Preparation:** Making your bath mixture usually involves steeping herbs in hot water (like making tea), straining out solids, and adding the strained herbal water to a bucket of plain water. You can also dissolve bath salts in plain water or add commercial bath crystals. The water should be a comfortable temperature: warm but not hot enough to burn.

» **Taking the bath:** First, take a regular shower or bath to get physically clean. Spiritual baths work on already-clean skin. Step into your bathtub or shower with your bucket of prepared spiritual bath water. Pray over the water, stating clearly what you want the water to do. For example, say something like

"This water cleanses me of all negativity and bad luck."

Or

"This water draws love and prosperity to me."

Then follow these steps:

1. Pour the water over yourself from the head down (most common) or from the feet up (for drawing baths — pulling things toward you). Use a cup to scoop and pour repeatedly, making sure to cover your whole body.
2. While pouring, pray and visualize the water doing its work. Envision negativity washing away, good things being drawn to you, or whatever your intention is.
3. Some practitioners say specific Psalms during bathing, such as Psalm 23 for protection or Psalm 51 for cleansing.
4. Don't rinse off with plain water after you finish covering your body with the bath water. Let the spiritual bath water dry on your skin or pat dry gently.

» **Disposing of bath water:** This part of the process is crucial because the water now contains what you've washed off or what you've charged it with. Follow these guidelines to dispose of the water:

- *For cleansing/uncrossing bath water,* throw it away at a crossroads (literally toss it into the intersection) or into running water flowing away from your home. You want that negativity carried far away.
- *For drawing bath water,* pour it in your yard near your front door or in a potted plant you keep near your entrance. You want what the water now contains to come to you.
- *For protection bath water*, pour this around your property line or near your doors and windows.

WARNING

Traditional practice advises disposing of spiritual bath water outside rather than down your bathtub drain. The concern is that energy can stagnate beneath your living space. If outdoor disposal isn't an option, some practitioners recommend a street-facing drain, a potted plant, or simply running the water with intention to release it fully.

Timing bath frequency

Some baths are one-time preparations, for example before a court date, job interview, or important meeting. Other spiritual baths are done in series to let the repetition build power and ensure thorough work:

- Three consecutive days for moderate issues such as a recent run of bad luck or low energy at work.
- Seven consecutive days for more serious cleansing or sustained drawing work such as breaking a persistent streak of financial hardship or clearing tension from a troubled relationship.
- Nine consecutive days for deep-rooted problems or major changes such as recovering from a significant betrayal, a legal matter, or a major life transition.
- Thirteen consecutive days for especially stubborn issues such as a long-standing curse, generational blockage, or a situation that has resisted all prior workings.

Sample fixing: Washing away what crosses you

In this section, I tell you how to prepare and take a spiritual bath that removes crossed conditions (such as hexes or jinxes), bad luck, and spiritual blocks that keep you from moving forward. Use this type of bath when you experience circumstances that have consistently gone wrong, when you feel spiritually heavy or blocked, or before starting major new work.

Here are preparations and conditions for the bath:

- **Gather your materials**, including Hyssop herb for cleansing and Biblical purification, rue plant for hex-breaking and protection, salt for purification and barrier-breaking, and lemon for cutting through and cleansing. Also have a white candle on hand; this is optional but recommended. And find a large pot for brewing, a bucket or basin for pouring, and a strainer or cheesecloth.
- **The best timing** for a spiritual bath starts on a Saturday during a waning moon. Saturday is considered a banishing day, according to Hoodoo tradition, and a waning moon is associated with removing and decreasing. This timing is ideal, but don't wait on these conditions if you need the bath now; work when you need to.

Now follow these steps to brew the bath water, take the bath, and dispose of the bath water properly:

1. **Brew the spiritual bath water by boiling about 2 quarts of water and adding the ingredients you gathered.**

   Quantities to use in the 2 quarts of water include:

   - A generous handful of hyssop (dried herb or fresh) and rue. Be careful with the rue because some people have skin sensitivity to it.
   - Three tablespoons of salt, whether sea salt or regular table salt.
   - The juice of one whole lemon: squeeze in the juice, and then add the lemon halves to the pot.

2. **Turn off the heat, cover the pot, and let the water mixture steep for at least 15 minutes while it cools to a comfortable temperature.**

   While the mixture steeps, light your white candle and pray over it, saying something like this:

   > "This light drives away all negativity and removes all blocks from my path."

3. **Strain the herbs out of the water, add enough cool water to make the temperature comfortable to pour on yourself, and pour the liquid into your bucket or basin.**

   You don't want plant matter stuck on you, so straining the water is essential. You'll probably have about a gallon of water in total.

4. **Take your regular shower or bath first to get physically clean; then stand in your bathtub with the drain closed so that the spiritual bath water stays in the tub. You're ready to take the spiritual bath.**

   Hold the bucket of bath water in both hands and pray over it. You can use your own words or something like this:

   > "Hyssop, wash me clean. Rue, break all crosses and hexes. Salt, purify me. Lemon, cut through all blocks. By the power of these herbs and by [God's will/my ancestors' blessing/divine authority], I am cleansed. All crossed conditions are broken. All bad luck is washed away. All obstacles are removed from my path. I am clean, clear, and free. All negativity flows away from me now and forever. Amen/So it is/Asé."

5. **Begin pouring the water over your head, letting it flow down your entire body while you continue praying or visualizing crossed, stagnant energy washing off and away from you.**

Use a cup to scoop and pour repeatedly until all the water has found its way to your body. Make sure to get every body part, from your arms and legs to your torso and back. As the last of the water flows off, say firmly:

"It is done. I am free."

6. **Step out of the tub and pat dry gently; then dress in clean clothes, ideally white or light colors during uncrossing work.**

   Don't rub vigorously to dry off because you'll rub off the blessing.

7. **Dispose of the used bath water properly by scooping up the water that's left in the tub and taking it away from your home.**

   As noted in the section "Taking a working bath" earlier in the chapter, throw the water at the nearest crossroads behind you without looking back (the traditional method), pour it into running water flowing away from your home, or pour it down a toilet in a public restroom.

You'll take the spiritual bath on consecutive days following the guidance you find in the section "Timing bath frequency" earlier in the chapter. To amplify the work of the baths, burn the white candle while bathing each day. Recite Psalm 51 ("Purge me with hyssop and I shall be clean") while pouring the water. After the final bath in your series, dress in all white for 24 hours if possible. Avoid negative people and situations during your bath series. After completing your uncrossing baths, follow with a blessing or drawing bath to fill the cleared space with positive energy.

REMEMBER

You may feel lighter, clearer, and more energized after spiritual bathing. During the bath series, you may have vivid dreams as your subconscious releases what you're clearing. Situations that were blocked may suddenly resolve or move forward. Negative people may distance themselves from you or lose interest in bothering you. You may feel drawn to clean your living space, organize, or declutter to match physical clearing with the spiritual clearing. By the end of a 7- or 9-day series, you should feel notably different, less weighed down, and more able to move forward.

WARNING

Uncrossing can stir up the situation temporarily. When you're clearing heavy spiritual gunk, some circumstances get messier before they get clearer, like stirring up sediment in a glass of water. You may feel emotionally volatile, physically tired, or have an increase in minor problems during the first few days of uncrossing work. This result is normal. Push through the full series of baths, and by the end, the stirred-up mess will have washed away and you'll feel clearer. If you stop halfway through, you've just stirred up problems without finishing the clearing.

Candle Work: Fire Magic (The Transformer)

Fire transforms everything it touches. Wax becomes liquid becomes smoke becomes light. Solid becomes gas. Matter becomes energy. This transformative power is why candle work is so central to Hoodoo magic — fire takes your intention and transforms it from prayer and will into reality.

Understanding candle work in fire magic

Fire has been spiritually significant across human cultures since people first learned to work with it. Fire is sacred, dangerous, transforming, and purifying. In Hoodoo specifically, candles work for several reasons:

- **They offer sustained focus:** A burning candle represents continuous prayer and intention. You can't pray actively for hours, but a dressed candle does that work for you, burning steadily while you do other things.
- **They represent visible transformation:** Watching wax melt and burn down shows your work manifesting. The physical transformation mirrors spiritual transformation.
- **They give off light and heat:** Fire generates light for illumination and revelation and heat for energy and activation. Your intention rides on that light and heat into the spiritual realm.
- **They emit smoke that carries prayer:** In many traditions, smoke carries prayers to heaven or to the spirits. A candle burning sends your petition upward continuously.
- **They signify completion:** A candle burned completely down signals work completed. The final flame seals your intention.

Table 14-3 gives you a look at the various types of candle work and their purposes.

TABLE 14-3 Types of Candle Work and Their Uses

Candle Work Type	What You Do	What You Get
Candle divination	Burn and read a candle for situational information	Discovery of how the situation is changing or how work is progressing
Color magic	Burn candles for their corresponding colors	Amplified intention: green for money, red for love, white for blessing, black for protection or banishing

Candle Work Type	What You Do	What You Get
Dressed/fixed candles	Prepare candles for your specific purpose	Candles anointed with condition oil and sometimes rolled in herbs
Image candles	Create human-shaped candles that represent a specific person	Candles burned to influence that person
Petition candles	Write your desire on paper, place it under a candle, and burn the candle over multiple days	A paper charged with intention
Seven-knob or seven-day candles	Mark tall candles in sections or contained in glass for sequential burning	Sustained work that burns a candle section per day over seven days

Understanding color correspondences

White candles can substitute for any color because white contains all colors and represents purity and blessing, but specific candle colors enhance specific work, as noted in this table.

Candle Color	How It's Used
White	Purity, blessing, peace, divine connection, and spiritual work. White can substitute for any color.
Green	Money, prosperity, growth, abundance, employment, fertility.
Red	Love, passion, sexual attraction, strength, power, vitality, courage.
Pink	Romance, gentle love, friendship, emotional healing, reconciliation.
Blue	Peace, healing, harmony, patience, understanding, calm.
Yellow	Communication, mental clarity, learning, joy, creativity, success in intellectual work, clearing the path forward.
Orange	Attraction, encouragement, stimulation, adaptability, legal matters, road opening, removing obstacles and blockages.
Purple	Power, spiritual elevation, mastery, psychic work, commanding, reversing.
Black	Protection, banishing, binding, absorbing negativity, breaking hexes, reversing curses.
Brown	Court cases, legal matters, indecision, locating lost items, grounding.
Gold	Success, wealth, confidence, fast luck, solar energy.
Silver	Intuition, moon work, psychic development, neutralizing.

Dressing and fixing candles

A rootworker prepares candles for magical work by dressing or fixing them rather than just lighting up and burning them as-is. Here are some methods practitioners use to prepare and use candles for magical fire work:

- **Basic candle dressing** involves starting with a clean, unused candle (either white or the appropriate color) and preparing it for the purpose of the work you intend.
  - Some practitioners baptize the candle first by holding it under running water while praying that any previous influences be washed away.
  - Choose an appropriate condition oil (or use olive oil in a pinch), put the oil on your fingers, and rub the candle from top to bottom for drawing work or bottom to top for banishing work. Some practitioners rub from the middle outward in both directions for general work. Optionally, you can roll the oiled candle in powdered herbs appropriate to your work. For example, you can roll a money-drawing candle in cinnamon powder or Five Finger Grass to reinforce your intention.
  - While oiling the candle, you can pray and focus your intention into the candle. Tell it the purpose you have for it: "You draw money to me" or "You open roads for me" or whatever your purpose is. Optionally, you can carve words or symbols into the candle, such as your name, your goal, or *sigils* (symbols used in magic work).
- **Petition under the candle** by writing your petition on clean paper and being specific about what you want in your working.
  - Some practitioners write their petition multiple times, or write their names crossed with the intention. That is, they write their name, stacked several times, turn the paper 90 degrees, and write the intention across their stacked names. See the example in the section "Sample fixing: Building your own money magnet" earlier in the chapter, and refer to Figure 14-1.
  - Place the paper under the candleholder before lighting. The burning candle charges and activates the petition.
- **Lighting and tending** by praying over the candle while lighting it and stating your intention clearly.
  - Some work requires the candle to burn continuously until you're finished; other work has you burn it in intervals (1 hour per day, for example).
  - Watch how the candle burns. A clean, steady burning is good, but sputtering, smoking, or extinguishing suggests obstacles or opposition.

WARNING

- Never leave burning candles unattended. This advice is both practical fire safety and spiritual responsibility because safety is part of responsible magic. A candle you're not watching can cause a house fire. If you can't sit with a candle until it burns out, use smaller candles, or burn it in intervals. Some practitioners use tea lights or chime candles (small, thin candles) that burn down in 1–2 hours.

Reading candle behavior

Choosing and preparing candles for fire magic work is important. But how a candle burns tells you the status of your work. If your candle burns poorly, it's telling you something. You may need to do cleansing work first, approach the situation differently, or acknowledge serious opposition to what you're trying to do.

Here are the good and not-so-good signs to look out for when burning your candles:

- **Good signs:** The candle burns cleanly and steadily with little or no smoke. The wax melts evenly, and the flame is bright and tall. The candle also burns down completely, leaving minimal residue. Any glass container you've placed the candle in stays clear.
- **Challenging signs:** The candle burns with excessive smoke, which indicates opposition or blockage. If the candle won't stay lit, you may be encountering strong opposition to your work. See the following table for other signs to watch for.

Candle Behavior	What It Means
Flame flickers wildly or dances	Turbulent energy or conflict
Wax melts unevenly or drips excessively	Obstacles or blockages present; the work may need repeating
Black smoke or soot on the candle's glass container	Heavy negativity or serious opposition
Wax forms shapes such as faces or hands	Symbolic of other influences
Candle breaks or explodes	Serious resistance or backlash to your work

Sample fixing: Clearing the road ahead

The work I describe in this section removes obstacles and opens the way for opportunities, success, and forward movement. Use it when you feel stuck, when opportunities keep falling through, or before major life changes. Here are the supplies and ideal conditions for this obstacle-clearing work:

» **Materials you need** include an orange or a yellow candle because the colors correspond to road opening and removing obstacles. (See the section "Understanding color correspondences" earlier in the chapter.) ***Note:*** You can always use a white candle for any situation.

  You also need the following:

  - Road Opener Oil, which is a commercial product, or an oil that you make with abre camino herb, cinnamon, and a drop of lemon essential oil in olive oil base
  - Small piece of paper and pen
  - Candle holder or fire-safe plate
  - Optionally, abre camino herb (road opener herb), Five-Finger Grass, and cinnamon powder to roll the candle in

» **The best timing** for the road-clearing work is Wednesday or Sunday. Wednesday is the day of Mercury, a planet of communication and removing blocks, and Sunday is success day. Doing this fire work during a waxing moon is ideal, but work when you need the obstacles cleared.

Gather your materials, choose your timing — preferably when you can sit with the candle for at least 30 minutes — and then follow these steps:

1. **Prepare your space by setting up your working space with the candle holder, oil, paper, and pen.**

   Take a few deep breaths, and center yourself on your intention: opening the roads before you.

2. **Fix the candle by holding it in both hands and speaking to it.**

   Say something like the following to your candle:

   "You are my road opener. Your work is to remove all obstacles from my path and open the way for success and opportunity."

3. **Put Road Opener Oil on your fingers and dress, or oil, the candle from the middle downward to draw success toward you, or the middle upward to push obstacles away.**

   While oiling the candle, pray something like this:

   "All blocks are removed. All roads open before me. Obstacles melt away. Opportunities come clearly. My path is clear and open."

If you're using herbs, immediately roll the oiled candle in the herb mixture so it sticks, and set the candle in its holder.

4. **Write your petition on the paper, and be specific but flexible.**

Here are some examples of specific but flexible language:

"All obstacles are removed from my path. Roads open easily before me."

"The way is clear for me to find the right job that uses my skills and pays well."

"My path to [specific goal] is opened and made smooth."

TIP

If you want to get more elaborate, write your full name in the center of the paper and then write "ALL ROADS OPEN" around your name, with the words going out from your name in all four directions (north, east, south, and west). See Figure 14-2 for an example. Fold the paper toward you and place it under the candle holder.

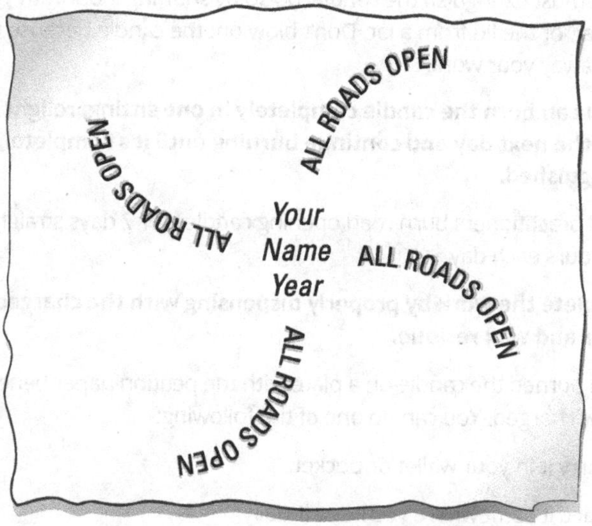

FIGURE 14-2: Your name as written for road opening candle work.

5. **Light and burn the candle while watching its behavior.**

Light the candle while saying:

"As this candle burns, my roads open. As this wax melts, obstacles melt away. As this flame shines, my path becomes clear. It is done."

Sit with the candle for at least 15–30 minutes, watching it burn and visualizing doors opening, paths clearing, and opportunities appearing. Pray over it. You can repeat your petition, say Psalm 23, or speak from your heart about what you want to open up.

6. **Read the signs that appear as your candle burns, using the following table as a guide.**

Burn Characteristic	What It Means
Clean, fast burn	Roads are opening easily
Slow, smoky burn	Significant obstacles are clearing, but they require work
Flame pointing in a direction	Opportunity is coming from that direction
Wax melting all to one side	An imbalance needs to be addressed
Candle burns completely clean	Your roads are now open

7. **If you can, let the candle burn completely down in one sitting, which is safest when the candle is small.**

   If you must extinguish the candle, do so by snuffing it out with your fingers, a snuffer, or the lid from a jar. Don't blow out the candle because that action can blow away your work.

8. **If you can burn the candle completely in one sitting, relight it at the same time the next day and continue burning until it's completely extinguished.**

   Some practitioners burn road opening candles for 7 days straight, lighting for 1–2 hours each day.

9. **Complete the work by properly dispensing with the charged petition paper and wax residue.**

   If you burned the candle on a plate with the petition paper beneath, the paper is now charged. You can do one of the following:

   - Carry it in your wallet or pocket.
   - Place it somewhere you'll see it daily.
   - Bury it at a crossroads.
   - Burn it separately and scatter the ashes at a crossroads.

   You can also bury any remaining wax at a crossroads or keep it as a talisman.

TIP

Be alert for opportunities over the next week after you complete your candle work; doors and roads should start opening. But after they open, you must walk through them. Pay attention to opportunities, invitations, ideas, and offers, and act on them. The candle opens the way; you still must move.

Prayer and Song: Air Magic (The Voice)

The spoken word has power. "In the beginning was the Word," says the Gospel of John, and Hoodoo practitioners take this seriously. Your voice, your breath, and your words aren't just methods for communication. They're creative, spiritual force.

Consider these aspects of your voice, breath, and words as forces in nature:

- **Sound as vibration:** Words create actual vibrations in the physical world. Those vibrations move air, move matter at microscopic levels, and, practitioners believe, move spiritual forces as well. The tone, volume, and conviction with which you speak affects the power of your words.
- **Breath as life force:** Your breath animates you. When you speak, you're putting your life force behind your words. Speaking over water charges it. Speaking over herbs awakens them. Speaking over a person or situation directly affects them or it.
- **Divine authority:** In Christian Hoodoo, which is the majority tradition, prayers invoke divine power. You're not working alone. You're asking God to act, commanding in God's name, or aligning yourself with divine will. This channels power beyond your own.
- **The creative power of declaration:** Speaking something makes it more real than just thinking it. When you declare, "I'm protected," you're not hoping; you're making it so through the authority of your word.

Table 14-4 lists the types of spoken air magic work and how they're used.

TABLE 14-4 Types of Spoken Air Magic Work

Spoken Work Type	What You Do	Your Focus
Prayer	Petition God, saints, or spirits for help, blessing, or intervention.	Asking humbly and respectfully, acknowledging that higher powers have authority.
Commanding prayer	State what will be, using divine authority.	Declaring as one with authority, "In the name of [Jesus/the Father/the Holy Spirit], all obstacles are removed from my path."
Psalms	Choose Psalms from the Bible that are suited to specific situations.	Praying the Psalms with intention as spiritual weapons and tools.

(continued)

TABLE 14-4 ***(continued)***

Spoken Work Type	What You Do	Your Focus
Incantations	Repeat phrases or words to build power through repetition.	Simply repeating something such as "Money comes to me" 100 times, or repeating more complex, traditional verses.
Naming and declaring	Speak the name of what you want to make real. (For example, "I name you *Success*; you are *Success*; *Success* is yours.")	Employing the ancient magic in which naming gives form to reality.
Breath work	Blow on things to activate them, breathe on water to charge it, exhale forcefully to send energy outward.	Carrying your intention physically through your breath.

Singing your power: Music as spiritual work

Singing may be the most overlooked form of air magic in contemporary practice, but historically it was central to Hoodoo tradition. When enslaved Africans couldn't openly practice their spiritual traditions, they sang. When they couldn't speak freely, they encoded messages in music. When they needed to build collective power, they raised their voices together. Song is prayer sustained, amplified, and made communal.

Here are genres of singing and music involved in the Hoodoo tradition:

- **Ring shouts:** These circular, counterclockwise dancing ceremonies combined movement, rhythm, and call-and-response singing to induce spiritual states and invite divine presence. Participants would shuffle in a ring (never crossing their feet because that would make it "dancing," which was forbidden), clapping and singing, building energy until the Spirit descended. The ring shout is African sacred circle practice adapted to American conditions; it's communal magic disguised as worship. The rhythm, the repetition, and the collective movement generates and directs spiritual force.
- **Spirituals:** These weren't just songs about heaven. They were coded communications, collective prayers, and spiritual weapons. "Wade in the Water" told freedom seekers to travel through streams to throw off dogs. "Follow the Drinking Gourd" encoded directions north using the Big Dipper. "Steal Away to Jesus" announced secret meetings.

  But beyond the codes, spirituals carried genuine spiritual power. Singing "Go Down, Moses" wasn't just remembering Biblical liberation. It was calling that same liberating power into the present moment. The emotional intensity, the repetition, and the collective voice transformed songs into sustained prayers that worked on both the singers and their circumstances.

» **Work songs:** Rhythm made unbearable labor survivable, but work songs did more than pass time. They synchronized collective effort, turning individual workers into a unified force. They carried complaints and resistance in ways that couldn't be directly punished. And they infused the work itself with intention. A song sung while planting could bless the crop. A song sung while building could strengthen the structure. The rhythm of the work became the rhythm of the magic, each stroke or step reinforcing the intention carried in the lyrics.

» **The blues:** Born from field hollers, spirituals, and work songs, the blues became its own form of spiritual technology. Blues lyrics are often spells in disguise: declarations of intention, complaints to the universe, negotiations with fate. When Robert Johnson sang about crossroads, hellhounds, and deals with the devil, he was working with the same spiritual vocabulary root-workers used.

REMEMBER

The blues moan — that distinctive vocal quality — carries something beyond words. It's a sound that moves energy, that reaches into places language can't touch. Many blues songs are essentially spoken-word spells set to music: "I'm gonna put you down" is a hex. "Come back, baby" is a drawing spell. "Hellhound on my trail" is describing a spiritual attack. The blues gave Hoodoo a public voice when direct practice had to stay hidden.

Engaging with magic through singing

Singing combines several magical principles at once. It uses breath (life force) to carry words (creative power) on sustained tones (vibration) with rhythm (repetition that builds force) and often in community (collective amplification). A prayer spoken once has power. But a prayer sung repeatedly, with emotional intensity, while others join in, is exponentially stronger. Singing also bypasses the rational mind in ways that speaking doesn't. You can sing something you're not sure you believe and still have it affect you. The melody carries the intention past your doubts.

You don't need a trained voice to use singing as spiritual work in your practice. Hum over your mojo while you feed it. Sing a Psalm instead of reciting it. Make up simple chants, and repeat them while bathing or working candles. Learn traditional spirituals, and sing them with intention. Even humming a sustained tone while visualizing your goal moves energy.

TIP

If singing feels awkward to you, practice singing when you're alone in the shower or in your car, where you won't feel self-conscious. Your voice wants to be used this way. For some practitioners, singing becomes their primary method of changemaking. It's more effective for them than any other approach. Pay attention to whether music moves something in you that speech alone doesn't reach.

Using Psalms in Hoodoo

The Book of Psalms is essentially the Hoodoo spellbook. Practitioners memorize the Psalms most relevant to their needs and pray them in specific situations. Some carry Psalm cards or small Psalms books to have them readily available. Each Psalm has traditional uses; the following table highlights a few of these.

Psalm	Its Use	First Line
Psalm 23	Protection, blessing, provision, calming fear	"The Lord is my shepherd . . ."
Psalm 37	Against enemies and for justice	"Fret not thyself because of evildoers . . ."
Psalm 51	Cleansing, forgiveness, purification	"Purge me with hyssop and I shall be clean . . ."
Psalm 91	Powerful protection, especially physical safety	"He that dwelleth in the secret place . . ."
Psalm 109	Particularly strong curse/enemy work	"Hold not thy peace, O God of my praise . . ."
Psalm 35	Defense against false accusations and enemies	"Plead my cause, O Lord . . ."
Psalm 27	Courage, protection, divine light	"The Lord is my light and my salvation . . ."

Praying powerfully

Effective prayer in Hoodoo isn't just reciting words. It's speaking with authority and intention. Here are some essential aspects of powerful praying:

- **Belief:** You must believe your words have power. Doubt undermines magic like nothing else. Even if you're not 100% certain, speak as if you are.
- **Clarity:** Be specific. Vague prayers get vague results. Don't just ask for "things to get better." Name exactly what you want.
- **Authority:** Speak as one who has the right to ask or command. You're not groveling You're claiming what's yours by divine right or petitioning with confidence.
- **Repetition:** Sometimes prayers need to be repeated nine times, daily for nine days, or continuously until you know it's done. Repetition builds power.
- **Combination with action:** Words are most powerful when combined with action. Pray while bathing, pray while dressing candles, pray while making a mojo. The physical action grounds the words.
- **Proper tone:** Match your tone to your purpose. Protection prayers might be firm and commanding. Healing prayers might be gentle and soothing. Justice prayers might be strong and declaring.

Sample fixing: Speaking protection into being

Psalm 23 is probably the most widely known and used Psalm in Hoodoo. It offers protection, blessing, provision, and peace. This working uses it for comprehensive protection and blessing by creating a spiritual shield and inviting divine favor. Here's how to begin your Psalm-speaking work:

» **Gather the materials and tools you need.** Your voice and breath are the primary tools. You can also use the following:

- A cup of water to charge with the prayer (optional but recommended)
- A white candle to light for extra blessing
- Protection Oil or olive oil to anoint yourself
- The text of Psalm 23 to read until you have it memorized

  The King James version of Psalm 23, which is the most used version in traditional Hoodoo:

  "The Lord is my shepherd; I shall not want. He maketh me to lie down in green pastures: he leadeth me beside the still waters. He restoreth my soul: he leadeth me in the paths of righteousness for his name's sake. Yea, though I walk through the valley of the shadow of death, I will fear no evil: for thou art with me; thy rod and thy staff they comfort me. Thou preparest a table before me in the presence of mine enemies: thou anointest my head with oil; my cup runneth over. Surely goodness and mercy shall follow me all the days of my life: and I will dwell in the house of the Lord forever."

» **Choose the best timing for your spoken work.** You can do this work anytime, but it's particularly powerful at sunrise (offering new protection for the new day) or before bed (giving protection through the night). And daily repetition builds strong, lasting protection.

After gathering your tools and choosing a time for your spoken air work, follow these steps:

1. **Prepare yourself by standing or sitting in a quiet place where you won't be interrupted, and have your tools and materials with you.**

   Light your white candle if you're using one. Have your cup of water in front of you. Take several deep breaths, centering yourself. Put a small amount of oil on your finger if you're using it.

2. **Speak out loud with confidence to declare and open your spoken work.**

   Declare your intention by speaking something like this:

   > "I call upon the protection and blessing of the Almighty. As it is written in the Holy Scriptures, so it is spoken. As it is spoken, so it is done. I claim the promises of Psalm 23 for myself this day."

3. **Speak your first prayer to charge the cup of water.**

   Hold your hands over the cup of water, or hold the cup in your hands. Recite Psalm 23 slowly and clearly, setting intention to every word. As you speak, visualize the words entering the water, charging it with protective and blessed energy. The water is receiving the power of the Psalm.

4. **Speak your second prayer while anointing yourself.**

   If you're using oil, anoint yourself on your forehead (the location of your third eye), heart, and wrists while praying the Psalm a second time. If you're not using oil, simply hold your hands over your head and heart while praying. This time, visualize divine protection surrounding you like a shield of light. See yourself walking through any danger unharmed, provided for, and blessed.

5. **Speak your third Prayer to seal your protection.**

   This time, as you pray, emphasize certain phrases that speak to your current needs: If you're afraid: "I will fear no evil." If you need provision: "My cup runneth over." If you have enemies: "Thou preparest a table before me in the presence of mine enemies." If you need guidance: "He leadeth me in the paths of righteousness."

   Speak with absolute conviction. You're not hoping these things are true; you're declaring that they are true.

6. **After the third recitation of Psalm 23, close and seal your spoken work with a firm declaration.**

   Say something like this:

   > "By the power of this Holy Psalm, I am protected. I am blessed. I am provided for. No weapon formed against me shall prosper. Goodness and mercy follow me all the days of my life. This is my truth. This is my reality. This is done. Amen."

7. **Embody your spoken work so that it becomes part of you.**

   If you prayed over water, drink it. You're taking that protection and blessing into yourself. Feel it entering your body and becoming part of you.

8. **Reinforce the protection of your spoken work by repetition and memorization.**

   This step is optional and can include these practices:

   Recite the Psalm while in the shower, letting water flow over you.

   Speak it over your doorways, one Psalm per door, sealing your home.

   Repeat the Psalm throughout the day whenever you feel fear or need reassurance.

   Memorize it so you always have it available.

Many practitioners recite Psalm 23 every morning as protection for the day, or every night before bed. Some recite it three, seven, or nine times for extra strength. Consistency builds a powerful protective shield that becomes stronger each time you reinforce it.

You may experience an immediate sense of peace or calmness and increased confidence when facing difficult situations. Things that would normally bother you seeming less threatening. Close calls or near-misses where you're protected from harm. A sense of being watched over or guided. Antagonistic people losing interest in bothering you. General sense of being blessed and provided for.

To expand your practice and protection, write Psalm 23 on a piece of paper, fold it small, and carry it in your wallet or shoe for mobile protection. Frame a beautiful copy and hang it over your doorway. Teach it to your children, for the Psalm protects all who know and speak it. Recite it over a protection mojo or candle to add extra power. Use it as part of larger protection workings; it combines beautifully with baths, mojos, and candles.

REMEMBER

The power is in the speaking, not just the reading: You can read Psalm 23 silently and find comfort in it. But in Hoodoo practice, you speak it out loud. Your voice vibrating the air and your breath carrying the words activate the power. Silent reading is fine for meditation, but magical work requires you to speak. Even if you're whispering, you're using your voice. The word must be spoken to have full force.

Combining the Four Approaches

In this chapter, I present the four approaches to rootwork separately so you can focus each one. But most experienced rootworkers combine approaches to create more powerful work. For example, a comprehensive money-drawing working might include these elements of the approaches, which reinforce each other:

- **Earth:** Creating and carrying a money-drawing mojo bag can create continuous drawing power.
- **Water:** Taking prosperity baths can clear obstacles and open channels for money.
- **Fire:** Burning a green money candle dressed with prosperity oil can transform your situation.
- **Air:** Praying specific Psalms can align you with divine provision daily, and speaking money affirmations can bring you money you need.

Here's another example of the four approaches involved in protection work:

- **Earth:** Burying protection packets at property corners or carrying a protection mojo.
- **Water:** Taking protective baths before important events.
- **Fire:** Burning black candles to absorb negativity.
- **Air:** Praying Psalm 91 daily for divine protection.

TIP

The key to effectively combining approaches in your rootworking is to choose methods that make sense for your situation, that you can commit to doing properly, and that you believe in. Three methods done with full commitment and intention are better than five methods done half-heartedly.

REMEMBER

Although traditional Hoodoo was practiced in private, many contemporary practitioners now share their work in closed online groups and communities by posting photos of candle burns for interpretation, sharing bath recipes that worked, or asking for guidance on challenging situations. The traditional principles remain the same, but the isolation of the practice has decreased. Technology enables practitioners to learn from each other across distances in ways that mirror the old tradition of rootworkers consulting with each other, but the consultation now happens in real time and across distances.

You have many aspects to consider when you're deciding which approaches and methods to use for fixing a particular situation. Think about these aspects and ask yourself relevant questions:

» **Consider your goal, as outlined in this table.**

If You Need	Try This Approach or Approaches
Quick, emergency protection?	Air (immediate prayer) + earth (existing mojo)
Deep cleansing?	Water (bath series)
Sustained drawing work?	Earth (mojo) + fire (candle series)
Opening a blocked situation?	Fire (road opener candle) + air (commanding prayer)

» **Consider your circumstances, as noted in this table.**

If Your Situation Is	Try This Approach or Approaches
Living with others who'd object to visible magical work?	Air (silent prayer) or portable earth (mojo)
Having time for daily practice?	Water (bath series) or fire (candle work)
Needing something quick and simple?	Air — just pray
Wanting something that continues working after initial setup?	Earth (mojo, bottle spell)

» **Consider your strengths, such as those listed in this table.**

If You're	You May Like This Approach
Drawn to physical crafts?	Earth work
In love ritual and ceremony?	Fire work
Very verbal or musical?	Air work (prayer, singing)
Good with cleansing and renewal practices?	Water work

Most practitioners develop a primary approach to working that they're particularly good at, while remaining fluent in all four. Versatility makes you more effective.

REMEMBER

Start in the approach where you're comfortable, and expand as you learn. If praying comes naturally to you, start with air work and add other methods gradually. If you already take regular baths, beginning with water magic makes sense. If you love candles or have craft skills, fire or earth work, respectively, might be your entry point. Don't try to master everything at once. Build competency in one approach, then expand. A rootworker skilled in one method is more effective than someone doing all four methods poorly.

5 Checking Out Hoodoo Now and Next

IN THIS PART . . .

Navigate the relationship between Hoodoo's centuries-long healing tradition and contemporary medicine, understanding where they complement each other and where they diverge.

Survey how Hoodoo thrives in the modern world, from digital communities to urban practice, as a living tradition that keeps evolving on its own terms.

Recognize Hoodoo's presence across film, music, and popular culture, and distinguish authentic representation from the distortions that flatten it.

Look ahead at the forces shaping Hoodoo's next chapter, and consider the questions that will define where the tradition goes from here.

IN THIS CHAPTER

» Tracing the roots of Hoodoo as folk medicine

» Documenting the systematic, racist destruction of Black folk medicine and granny midwifery

» Addressing the cost of destroying Hoodoo's role in healthcare

» Reconnecting to folk medicine to tackle healthcare disparities

Chapter 15

Hoodoo between Folk and Modern Medicine

Hoodoo as folk medicine and folk psychiatry has a curious relationship with modern forms of medicine and psychiatry in the Western world. On one hand, Hoodoo practices have been routinely dismissed as superstition, primitive belief, or dangerous quackery by mainstream medical establishments. On the other hand, those same establishments have quietly borrowed its remedies, absorbed its most effective practices, and studied its therapeutic success, often without acknowledgment. This double movement — simultaneous rejection and appropriation — has defined Hoodoo's place in American medical history from the beginning. The tradition that was too backward to be respected was somehow sophisticated enough to copy.

What makes this relationship even more curious is that, for much of American history, Hoodoo practitioners were the primary healthcare system for millions of people, Black and white alike. They weren't operating in opposition to medicine. They *were* the medicine, long before hospitals, pharmacies, and psychiatric institutions became widely accessible.

In this chapter, you can find out about the pillars of Hoodoo practice that serve as medical support to communities and how those pillars came about. You also discover how a campaign of misinformation by the professional medical community was designed to eliminate the influences of Hoodoo folk medicine specifically in the area of midwifery. This chapter can help you understand the revelations in modern medicine that advocate re-embracing Hoodoo folk medicine practices.

Finding the Foundation of Hoodoo as Folk Medicine

Understanding Hoodoo's medical and psychiatric dimensions means recognizing it not as a relic of the past or an alternative to real medicine, but as a parallel medical tradition. It has always existed alongside, intersected with, and in many cases, preceded the Western practices that society now takes for granted. In this section, you can discover the roots of the Hoodoo tradition that became an essential piece of America's development of medical practices.

Tracing the African roots of the medicine bag

Enslaved Africans arrived with an extraordinary pharmacopoeia. The Africans came from the Rice and Grain Coasts (Senegal, Sierra Leone, Liberia), the Gold Coast (Ghana), the Bight of Benin (Yorùbáland), and Kongo-Angola. And they carried with them not only seeds and formulas, but also a holistic view of the relationship of illness and spirit.

TECHNICAL STUFF

Pharmacopoeia refers to the official documentation of standards and formulas that describe finding and preparing medicines.

Specific medicinal plants brought over from Africa include the following:

- **Kola nut (*Cola acuminata/nitida*):** This was a stimulant and heart tonic that contributed to what would eventually become commercial cola drinks.
- **Grains of paradise (*Aframomum melegueta*):** This warming digestive and anti-inflammatory is still studied for COX-2 inhibition, which are medicines that reduce digestive distress while limiting side effects.
- **Dietary plants:** Okra, black-eyed peas, and sesame (benniseed) became daily food and quiet medicine.

These plants and others with African origins entered not only Hoodoo but also colonial and modern pharmacology. The 1721 Boston smallpox inoculation campaign, sparked by an Akan man named Onesimus, is a famous example of African medical knowledge reshaping Western science.

Learning from Native nations and European botanicals

In the Carolinas, Georgia, and the Gulf Coast, Black healers exchanged knowledge with Cherokee, Creek/Muskogee, Choctaw, Seminole, and Catawba neighbors. They learned to work with goldenseal (antimicrobial), boneset (fever), black and blue cohosh (women's health), and countless other plants. At the same time they incorporated European settler plants like plantain (white man's footprint), which made first-aid poultices for cuts and stings.

The result was a genuinely eclectic American medicine: African seedstock, Native herbs, and Old-World botanicals tested in the same garden. Long before white physicians adopted the label *eclectic medicine*, Black rootworkers were living it.

TECHNICAL STUFF

Eclectic medicine refers to a 19th and 20th century movement that prioritized botanical remedies and avoided invasive treatments such as bloodletting.

TIP

When reading old herb lists, think ecology. Many African plants had close American cousins; knowing substitutions was part of the art and often meant the difference between effective treatment and no treatment in rural areas.

Creating the village clinic before there were clinics

For centuries, the work of Black rootworkers, conjure doctors, and granny midwives continued the diverse West and Central African medicinal traditions of their ancestors' homeland. Many of these practitioners didn't distinguish between a physiological treatment and a spiritual one. They applied these treatments to the new land they found themselves transplanted to. These practitioners served as the medical backbone of rural America, providing care across racial lines and treating Black, white, and Native neighbors alike. Their practice wasn't a secondary or marginalized choice, but the accessible, trusted, and often sole source of healthcare.

Long before country doctors or county health departments were common, Black practitioners set broken bones, delivered babies, lanced infections, and treated the everyday fevers and stomach bugs of poor communities. In the South and along the Atlantic coast, a single rootworker might quietly care for an entire county.

Exploring the granny midwife tradition

The role of granny midwife exemplifies the Hoodoo tradition of providing community care. Consider the work described by one retired Halifax County, North Carolina, midwife in the early 20th century, as documented by anthropologist Holly F. Matthews:

> "You teach them how to take care of themselves, to keep the house clean and proper for a baby, 'bout good food to eat so they'll have good milk and how to make their old clothes. Then you get ready for the birthin' so they won't be scared and you be there with them any time of day or night. Lord, I've been called at some strange times. But when that baby's comin' there ain't nothin' for it to do it. And stay — stayin' after, that's the thing. That's when they really need you more than in the catchin' 'cause that's when the tiredness sets in and they're weak and that's when the baby prone to sickness, too. My ways been one to stay as long as they needed me; to help clean, cook, and sometimes show 'em what to do with that little baby. And I never lost but one baby in all my days of work."

Dismissing this essential support as merely birth attendance doesn't accurately describe all that granny midwives did. Their practice included prenatal care, nutritional counseling, postnatal support, newborn care instruction, and household management during the vulnerable postpartum period — often for one to two weeks after delivery.

The midwife monitored both mother and infant, taught hygiene and feeding practices, provided herbal remedies when needed, and served as the family's medical advisor during a critical transition. And she did this across racial lines. As Katherine Myers noted in 1921, Black midwives in North Carolina "attended births for white, Indian, and Black women and mothers and were respected by all for their dedication and ability."

Acknowledging the authority of granny midwives

Granny midwives were women who carried spiritual authority as well as medical knowledge. The role of midwife was often understood as a calling, passed down through family lines or received through spiritual revelation. Many granny midwives were also rootworkers, and their practice seamlessly integrated prayer, herbal medicine, protective rituals, and clinical skill. Because the tradition involved both physical and spiritual dimensions of care, the knowledge was tightly controlled in rural communities. Midwifery skills and lore were passed mother to daughter, aunt to niece, or elder to apprentice through years of observation and hands-on training.

By 1917, North Carolina alone had 9,000 practicing midwives. They delivered one-third of all babies born that year. And of midwife-assisted births, 80 percent were attended by Black midwives serving both Black and white families. In the eastern counties where Black populations were concentrated, midwives outnumbered physicians three to one for birth attendance.

Recognizing a psychiatric system hiding in plain sight

Hoodoo practice grew as a hybrid medical system, not just a magical one. In "Hoodoo: The Indigenous Medicine and Psychiatry of the Black American" (an article from the *Mankind Quarterly*. Vol. 18, Iss. 2, 1977), author Ralph R. Kuna calls the Hoodoo doctor "a system of native Black American folk psychotherapy and psychiatry" that flexed to meet real needs: diagnosing, treating, and even managing the social consequences of illness.

In this article, Kuna documents Hoodoo as a full-fledged mental-health system. Far from unsophisticated, it offered diagnosis, counseling, and ritual action that worked because it fit the patients' symbolic worlds.

A client who believed they'd been fixed or tricked might show what modern medicine would label psychosomatic pain or hallucinations. The Hoodoo doctor addressed the spirit of the affliction directly — sometimes with nine-day rainwater washes, sometimes with herbs or charms — so the cure matched the way the illness was experienced.

Dr. Yvonne P. Chireau adds a dramatic dimension in her 2012 paper published by Swarthmore College, "Invasion as Affliction: Worms and Bodily Infestation in African American Hoodoo Practices." The author documents bodily infestation narratives such as frogs croaking inside a belly, worms crawling under skin, lizards darting up a throat. These stories were offered with absolute conviction, encoded real suffering, and often came when "the medical doctors ain't no good for nothing like that."

Whether the underlying causes were, in the eyes of *allopathic medicine*, infection, trauma, or conversion disorder, folk psychiatry often succeeded where biomedical care failed.

TECHNICAL STUFF

Allopathic medicine refers to conventional, modern Western medicine in which doctors treat symptoms and diseases using evidence-based methods.

Documenting How Folk Medicine Was Systematically Destroyed

By the early 20th century, Black folk medicine — and granny midwifery in particular — had become too successful to ignore and too threatening to medical professionalization efforts to tolerate. The attack on Hoodoo as folk medicine was systematic, deliberate, and explicitly racist. In the next sections, I use an example from the efforts in North Carolina to eliminate midwifery to demonstrate how the attack against folk medicine took place and what its results were.

TECHNICAL STUFF

Although this chapter focuses on historical granny midwives who were women, people of all genders practice modern midwifery. Certified nurse-midwives and certified professional midwives today include men, women, and nonbinary practitioners. The historical gender association reflects the era's social structures, not an inherent limitation of the practice.

Exposing the campaign against ignorance

White physicians and public health officials launching campaigns against midwives framed them as backward, superstitious, and dangerous, despite evidence showing their outcomes were often better than physician-attended births. Here are examples of this depiction:

- In 1925, a North Carolina physician wrote that midwives like those in his home county of Robeson were "far below the European midwife in intelligence and no training under the sun could make her a competent obstetric attendant."
- Another obstetrician, writing in a state medical journal, described the typical Black midwife as "the logical, old, gin-fingering, guzzling midwife with her pockets full of forcing drops, her mouth full of snuff, her fingers full of dirt and her brains full of arrogance and superstition."
- A physician from Alabama doubled down, describing Black midwives as among "the most ignorant" practitioners, arguing their "disadvantaged status" kept them from establishing proper training institutions.

Notice what's happening with the content of these descriptions: The critique isn't actually about outcomes or safety. Instead, it's about race, class, and who gets to control the essential practice of childbirth.

REMEMBER

The medical establishment wanted birth moved into hospitals, attended by (predominantly white, male) physicians, and controlled through the emerging specialty of obstetrics. This move would monopolize an area of medical care that had been considered women's work, and it would generate significant income.

Understanding the licensing trap

Starting in 1912, North Carolina began requiring midwives to register with county health boards and eventually pass examinations in the elementary principles of midwifery. By 1924, the majority of registered midwives were over age 40, 15 percent were over 70, and the median age of registered midwives was 66. This situation wasn't accidental. The system was designed to phase out midwife practitioners while appearing to regulate them.

Counties began passing increasingly strict regulations:

- Mandatory retirement at age 70.
- Required attendance at training sessions, often far from rural areas.
- Permits that had to be renewed annually.
- Rules so detailed with specifications about bag contents, clothing cleanliness, when to refuse cases, and mandatory reporting that violations became nearly inevitable.
- Restrictions regarding practicing midwifery during pregnancy complications that required physician oversight — and rural areas had few physicians.

  In Durham County, for example, midwives were told they had to refuse cases when the patient "had fits or convulsions; when she was a dwarf or deformed, had syphilis, or was vomiting badly; when there was bleeding before labor or swelling in the hands or feet; or when the patient had dizzy spells."

The public health nurse would approve which pregnant women could use a midwife. The midwife's activities in attending the woman and the outcome of the birth could be monitored. *Translation:* Every birth became surveillance, and every midwife operated under the threat of having their license revoked.

Revealing the propaganda campaign

The 1920s saw physicians and public health officials circulating stories portraying midwives as the cause of infant mortality, despite midwives uniformly attending poorer women who had less access to prenatal care and nutrition, making outcome comparisons inherently unfair.

Dr. J. S. Brewer, a physician in Roseboro, North Carolina, wrote in 1928:

> "Child bearing has for so long a time been looked upon as an entirely normal and physiological affair that the idea that it borders closely on the pathologic and in an appallingly large and increasing number of cases is actually pathologic seems hard to get across to the lay mind."

In this statement, Brewer redefined childbirth as a medical emergency that only physicians could handle. And if women and the public persisted in seeing it as normal, they were simply too ignorant to understand.

The attack against midwives had two prongs:

- **Portraying rural Black midwives as ignorant and untrainable,** repeating that the granny midwife was "responsible for inhibiting rural North Carolinians from seeking proper medical care"
- **Proposing rural Black midwives as a temporary measure** while hospitals expanded and nurse-midwives were trained to serve as a professional bridge between old and new

According to Debra Anne Susie's 1988 article, "In the Way of Our Grandmothers: A Cultural View of Twentieth-Century Midwifery in Florida," published by University of Georgia Press, physicians portrayed these midwives as ignorant, backward, and superstitious. They argued that midwives spread disease with their filthy customs and practices in attending birth and thus contributed to high levels of maternal and child mortality.

Yet when examined honestly, midwives' records spoke for themselves. The 1932 White House Conference on Child Health and Protection found that, in the South, "the Negro midwives have shown themselves eager and willing to avail themselves of such educational advantages as have been offered to them . . . by state boards of health" and produced "very favorable maternal mortality rates . . . and remarkably low rates for the mothers attended by trained and supervised midwives."

But better outcomes didn't matter. The goal was elimination, not improvement.

Tracing the slow strangulation

By 1936, North Carolina had 117 prenatal medical centers staffed by physicians, and in 40 counties, they had one or more public health nurses. The infrastructure was being built to replace midwives, with these results:

- Midwife-attended births declined steadily to 24.6 percent in 1940 and 10.9 percent by 1950. Registered midwives had dropped to 915 by 1970.
- By 1980, only 50 registered midwives survived, and the General Assembly was considering prohibiting lay midwifery entirely. In 1971, Dr. Theodore Scurletis, director of the state Board of Health's personal health division, articulated the position voiced in public hearings: "The granny midwife has no place in the care of people today. She was ignorant and often dangerous. What was a logical solution for health care in the 1950s is an anachronism today."
- The North Carolina Health Bulletin in 1972 declared: "The demise of the practice of the granny-type midwife signals a victory for modern health care in the state. After centuries of her practice and generations of battling her existence, the granny is gone — hopefully, never to return."

Counting what was actually lost

When the last granny midwives were eliminated, rural communities, especially poor Black communities, lost beneficial access to women's and children's health services:

- **Accessible healthcare:** By 1989, only 26 certified nurse-midwives practiced in North Carolina, almost all in urban areas. Rural women had to travel hours for prenatal care or deliver in distant hospitals.
- **Culturally competent care:** Black midwives understood the social, economic, and cultural realities of the families they served. They worked within communities, not as outsiders.
- **Affordable care:** Midwives often accepted payment in food, goods, or services. Hospitals required cash.
- **Holistic support:** The postpartum care, household help, and extended family education that midwives provided disappeared entirely from the medical model.
- **Community-based knowledge:** Centuries of empirical observation about herbs, birth positioning, complication management, and postpartum care were dismissed as worthless superstition.
- **Women's autonomy:** Birth moved from the home (woman's domain) to the hospital (physician's domain). It also moved from being a normal life event to a medical procedure requiring expert management.

Ironically, infant mortality didn't improve as promised. By 1988, North Carolina's infant mortality rate of 12.6 per thousand live births was the worst in the nation, with nonwhite rates at 18.7 versus white rates at 8.8. The very problem midwife elimination was supposed to solve had worsened, especially for Black babies. The solution to infant mortality had created a crisis.

REMEMBER

This crisis of the significantly higher Black infant mortality rate would persist for decades. What the physicians who eliminated granny midwives didn't understand or chose to ignore was that they weren't just removing ignorant practitioners. They were dismantling a system in which cultural concordance, community trust, and holistic care created better outcomes for Black patients than professionalized medicine ever would.

Examining How Modern Medicine Confronts the Folk Practice It Destroyed

By the late 20th century, patterns emerged that should have troubled the medical establishment. But only in the 21st century did research quantify the facts that Hoodoo practitioners had always known: Who delivers healthcare matters as much as what care they deliver.

Discovering the psychiatric dimension: Houston and beyond

In 1977, emergency psychiatric staff at Houston's Ben Taub Hospital made a quiet acknowledgment. Some patients diagnosed as psychotic were experiencing culturally specific spiritual distress. In these cases, traditional healers — root doctors and *curanderos* — sometimes provided more effective care than conventional psychiatric treatment. As one psychiatric supervisor noted, folk healers were being considered "folk psychiatrists more effective in treating culturally predisposed blacks and Chicanos than is the established medical system."

TECHNICAL STUFF

Curanderos refers to traditional, community-based folk healers.

Instead of capitulation to superstition, this realization was recognition that cultural framework matters in mental health treatment. A patient who experiences illness through a spiritual lens needs intervention that addresses the spiritual dimension, which is exactly what Hoodoo psychiatric practice had provided for centuries.

The pattern of recognizing the importance of culture and spirituality repeats internationally. A widely read 2015 *Washington Post* essay described how a West African shaman helped a man's schizophrenic son after years of stalled Western treatment by using family-centered ritual and holistic care. Mental-health research consistently shows persistent misdiagnosis of schizophrenia in Black Americans and better engagement when care is culturally grounded.

What Hoodoo once provided — culturally competent, stigma-reducing, family-based mental health care — remains the frontier that modern psychiatry is trying to reach.

REMEMBER

While traditional healing practices demonstrate real value, especially for culturally specific concerns and when integrated with conventional care, serious medical and psychiatric conditions always warrant professional medical evaluation. The most effective approaches often combine cultural competency with evidence-based treatment.

Revealing the concordance breakthrough

Data arrived that should have vindicated the granny midwives against the medical community's campaign to discredit them. (See the section "Documenting How Folk Medicine Was Systematically Destroyed" earlier in the chapter.) However, the data arrived too late to save the midwives and their practice.

In 2020, researchers analyzed 1.8 million hospital births in Florida between 1992 and 2015, examining whether physician-patient racial concordance affected outcomes. You can find this research by Greenwood et al. under "Physician–Patient Racial Concordance and Disparities in Birthing Mortality for Newborns" at `https://doi.org/10.1073/pnas.1913405117`. The results seemed stark:

- **Black newborns:** Under white physicians, the study found significantly higher mortality. Under Black physicians, mortality was substantially lower, suggesting that concordance between patient and provider could be a meaningful factor in whether a baby lives or dies.
- **White newborns:** Under white or Black physicians, outcomes showed no meaningful difference, demonstrating that Black physicians aren't inferior caregivers. They're equivalent for White patients and, the study argued, beneficial for Black ones.
- **Latine newborns** showed no concordance effect. The mortality gap was specific to Black babies, and it was massive.

GREENWOOD AND OTHER CONCORDANCE STUDIES

TECHNICAL STUFF

The science involved in studies similar to the Greenwood study ("Physician–Patient Racial Concordance and Disparities in Birthing Mortality for Newborns") is still being actively worked out. A 2024 replication study (published in the same PNAS journal, a part of the National Academy of Sciences) found that when very low birth weight, a critical mortality predictor the original analysis hadn't isolated, was factored in, the concordance effect was substantially reduced and sometimes fell below statistical significance.

The original study hasn't been retracted, and the scholarly debate continues. What's not in dispute is the broader pattern: Decades of concordance research consistently show that Black patients experience better communication, higher trust, greater engagement with preventive care, and stronger satisfaction when treated by physicians who share their racial background. Whether concordance directly drives mortality or affects the quality of care that shapes mortality, the accumulated evidence points in the same direction.

The Greenwood study also found an uncomfortable truth about patient perceptions versus reality. White patients with Black physicians showed slightly lower satisfaction scores and, in experimental settings, even had blunted placebo responses when providers were Black or female. Their bodies responded less well simply because of provider race or sex. Yet their clinical outcomes remained unchanged.

Black patients with white physicians experienced both worse perceptions (lower trust, lower satisfaction) and worse outcomes (58% higher newborn mortality).

Evaluating the statistics

When North Carolina eliminated 9,000 Black midwives between 1917 and 1980, claiming to protect Black mothers and babies, they were removing practitioners whose racial concordance with patients likely produced better outcomes. Consider these points:

- They replaced Black midwives, who shared cultural background, understood community realities, earned generational trust, and provided comprehensive, culturally competent care, with predominantly white male physicians who had no cultural connection to Black communities, viewed Black patients through racist medical frameworks, and produced demonstrably worse outcomes for Black newborns.

» They pushed a jarring timeline.

- *1917:* 9,000 midwives, 80% Black, delivering one-third of all babies.
- *1931:* Midwives still delivering 31% of births with favorable mortality rates.
- *1950:* Midwife deliveries down to 10.9% of births.
- *1980:* Only 50 registered midwives remain.
- *1989:* Black infant mortality rate is nearly double that of white rate.

» The "professionalization" that promised to save Black babies may have killed them instead.

And the pattern continues; the lesson of the granny midwives appears to go unlearned. Research increasingly shows that Black patients have better outcomes with Black healthcare providers across cardiovascular disease management, diabetes control, preventive care utilization, patient adherence, communication quality, and trust. But Black physicians remain severely underrepresented (5% of physicians versus 13% of population), and healthcare systems prioritize cultural competency training for white providers over hiring and empowering Black practitioners.

Connecting this confrontation to Hoodoo

The concordance research provides empirical validation for what Hoodoo practitioners always knew: Shared cultural background, spiritual framework, and community trust aren't just comfort; they're clinically significant.

When a rootworker treats a Black patient, they share assumptions about how illness works (spiritual and physical causes intertwined), understand the social context (poverty, racism, medical mistrust), speak the same cultural language (metaphors and stories that resonate), allow patients to describe experience without translation into biomedical terms, and start with trust rather than requiring proof.

This approach may be thought of as superstition or placebo effect, but it can also be viewed as concordance. And modern research shows it saves lives.

The granny midwives were providing concordance-based care before the term existed. They were eliminated anyway. The cost is still being paid in Black infant mortality rates that remain twice as high as white rates nationwide — 134 years after the campaign against them began.

Recognizing that "If it doesn't get results, it's not Hoodoo"

A classic saying in the tradition insists that results define authenticity. If a practice doesn't work, it isn't Hoodoo.

Ironically, this success creates a double-edged sword. Remedies that prove too effective are often absorbed into mainstream medicine and renamed. *Variolation*, or deliberate infection, against smallpox, the use of certain laxative or antiseptic plants, and even aspects of talk therapy began as conjure or one of its African precursors and ended as science. What remains publicly labeled as *Hoodoo* is whatever hasn't yet been recognized by academic or commercial medicine. But many modern rootworkers don't bother to make that distinction. A homemade laxative that works for them is as much Hoodoo as a mojo bag for luck.

This pattern of effective folk remedies being absorbed into mainstream medicine without credit to their origins reveals something profound about how medical knowledge moves from margin to mainstream. When folk remedies prove effective, they're often stripped of their cultural context, rebranded with scientific terminology, and credited to the researchers who discovered them. This process erases the generations of practitioners who refined these treatments. The herbs become active compounds, the spiritual framework becomes placebo effect, and the rootworker's expertise becomes ethnobotanical data. Meanwhile, practices that remain labeled as folk medicine are often those that haven't yet been studied, can't be easily patented, or don't fit neatly into biomedical models, regardless of whether they work.

The granny midwives suffered this fate in the hardest way. Their decades of successful practice didn't protect them from systematic elimination. Their favorable outcomes didn't matter. Modern research now shows that Black birth attendants likely produced better outcomes for Black patients through racial concordance, but by the time the evidence arrived, the practitioners were gone. Their cultural knowledge was dismissed as ignorance, their spiritual authority reframed as superstition, and their community role erased in favor of professionalized, medicalized, expensive care that left Black babies dying at higher rates than when midwives practiced freely.

Seeing Why Folk Medicine Acceptance Matters Now

REMEMBER

Hoodoo has always lived between worlds: folk and scientific, spiritual and clinical, African and American. It is arguably America's first truly integrative medicine, and its record in both physical and mental healing is too strong to ignore. See the section "Discovering the psychiatric dimension: Houston and beyond" earlier in this chapter.

When a conjure practitioner said, "If it doesn't get results, it's not Hoodoo," that wasn't a boast. It was a clinical standard — the same standard that made granny midwives successful enough to threaten medical professionalization. The systematic destruction of Black folk medicine wasn't about safety or science; it was about control, profit, and the elimination of autonomous Black expertise.

Modern research shows that this elimination likely cost Black lives. Racial concordance research suggests that when North Carolina eliminated 9,000 Black midwives, they removed practitioners who, like modern Black physicians, would have produced better outcomes for Black patients.

Here are other areas of medical practice that probably should rely on influence from Hoodoo:

- **Health equity:** Hoodoo shows how community-based, culturally attuned care can reduce misdiagnosis and reach people that mainstream systems miss. Modern research on racial concordance validates what the granny midwives knew: Shared cultural background isn't just comfort, it's clinical effectiveness. The destruction of Black folk medicine created healthcare deserts and disparities that persist today.

  REMEMBER

  For Black patients, racial concordance improves both outcomes and experience. For white patients, outcomes stay the same regardless of physician race, but bias can distort how they feel about the care. This mismatch between perception and reality is exactly what Hoodoo midwives lived through: dismissed as "superstition" while delivering results that science now confirms were lifesaving.

- **Medical innovation:** Centuries of successful plant and ritual therapies argue for deeper ethnobotanical and ethno-psychiatric research. Rather than dismissing folk medicine as primitive, the modern medical community should be studying what made it effective enough to sustain communities for generations, and examining whether racial concordance in folk medicine contexts produces even stronger effects than in hospital settings.

TECHNICAL STUFF

Hoodoo doctors, regardless of the name they went by, weren't just charm makers. They were the Emergency Department, therapist, and pharmacist rolled into one. The granny midwife who delivered your grandmother probably also treated your great-grandfather's pneumonia, counseled your great-aunt through depression, and set your uncle's broken arm. The African medical traditions that would later shape Hoodoo healing practices gave America its first successful mass inoculation in 1721, when enslaved African Onesimus taught Bostonians variolation against smallpox, reducing death rates from 1 in 7 to 1 in 40. This pattern of Black medical innovation being appropriated without credit or compensation repeats throughout American history.

- **Cultural respect:** Recognizing Hoodoo's role in American medical history challenges the habit of dismissing Black folk knowledge as mere superstition. The granny midwives weren't ignorant; they were systematically disenfranchised by a medical establishment that prioritized profit, professional control, and white supremacy over patient outcomes.

WARNING

The success of Hoodoo remedies means that what worked best often lost the label Hoodoo, leaving outsiders to simplistically dismiss the tradition as superstition. Meanwhile, the practitioners who could have taught why their methods worked were systematically eliminated. Their knowledge was dismissed, their expertise was erased, and their communities were left with nothing.

- **Systemic patterns:** Understanding how folk medicine was eliminated reveals ongoing dynamics in healthcare: who gets to define legitimate medicine, whose knowledge counts as expertise, and what happens when care systems prioritize credentials over results. Research on racial concordance between patients and providers suggests that the cultural proximity granny midwives offered wasn't incidental to their effectiveness. In fact, it may have been central to it. Eliminating them didn't just remove practitioners. It removed a relational framework that mainstream medicine still struggles to replicate.
- **Evidence-based humility:** You could argue that the research I present in the section "Revealing the concordance breakthrough" earlier in the chapter should humble modern medicine. For decades, physicians claimed professionalization would improve outcomes for everyone. A growing body of concordance research complicates that confidence: It suggests that, for Black patients, shared cultural background between provider and patient shapes trust, communication, and care quality in ways that clinical credentials alone don't capture. Sometimes primitive folk medicine was superior, not despite its cultural specificity, but because of it.

IN THIS CHAPTER

» Understanding the modern Hoodoo revival from the 1970s to today

» Finding quality supplies and space to practice

» Finding teachers and community in a changing landscape

Chapter 16

Living with Hoodoo Tradition in the Modern World

From slave plantations to the global digital age, Hoodoo has traveled an incredible journey. The tradition that once passed quietly from hand to hand in Southern kitchens now spreads through YouTube tutorials and Instagram posts. The practices that families once hid from outsiders are now being proudly reclaimed by descendants and debated in online forums.

As a living tradition, Hoodoo continues growing and adapting while maintaining the same purpose at its heart: empowering and healing Black people facing adversity. Whether that purpose can or should extend beyond that community is a question the community itself is actively working through.

This chapter explores where Hoodoo stands today: how it's being revived, adapted, contested, and carried forward. In the chapter, you can find out about the modern renaissance that brought Hoodoo back into the light, the practical challenges of practicing in urban apartments, where to locate supplies and teachers you can trust, and the ongoing conversations about who this tradition belongs to.

Understanding the Modern Revival

After the civil rights era's social upheaval, African Americans began reclaiming pride in all aspects of their heritage, including spiritual practices that had been marginalized, hidden, or stigmatized. The result was a Hoodoo renaissance that continues today.

Starting around the 1970s and intensifying through the 1990s and 2000s, more Black Americans explored Hoodoo and other African diaspora traditions as sources of cultural identity and empowerment. This paralleled the Black Arts Movement and the broader Afrocentric turn in Black culture. People wanted to know: What did my great-grandmothers practice? What knowledge did my family carry that got lost or hidden?

An earlier generation kept practices quiet. Sometimes that was out of shame, sometimes out of safety, and sometimes simply because that's how things were done. But scholars such as Zora Neale Hurston and contemporary authors such as Luisah Teish inspired younger people to proudly explore Hoodoo practices. Workshops on rootwork appeared. Hoodoo-themed books found audiences. Shops owned by Black practitioners opened in cities and online.

Black women entrepreneurs led this revival's forefront, opening spiritual supply stores and botanical shops in Black neighborhoods and on the internet. They tapped into Hoodoo's health and wellness facets, presenting it as self-care and self-determination for modern times. They taught practices such as ancestral herb use for healing trauma and cleansing rituals for coping with racism-induced stress.

REMEMBER

The modern Hoodoo revival isn't about inventing something new. It's about reclaiming what was always there but hidden. Many practitioners are returning to practices their own families carried but didn't discuss openly.

Reclaiming cultural heritage

A beautiful trend has emerged in the modern revival of the Hoodoo tradition involving younger African Americans proudly sharing how they discovered a grandparent's mojo bag in a drawer, realized mom's "tea" for bad dreams was actually a rootwork remedy, or found a bottle for protection buried under the front porch of the family home.

These revelations bring families closer to their ancestry. Hoodoo is no longer a shameful secret, but a badge of cultural resilience. The same practices that grandparents hid are now being claimed with pride by grandchildren who understand what those practices meant and what they cost to preserve.

This reclamation has a healing dimension. For many African Americans, reconnecting with ancestral spiritual practices repairs the cultural severing that slavery and its aftermath inflicted. Learning that your family carried this knowledge — that your great-grandmother knew these things, that your lineage includes this wisdom — can be profoundly restorative.

The community is actively working to preserve Hoodoo's integrity while welcoming back African Americans whose families may have forgotten or suppressed the old ways. That inclusiveness has the clearest consensus: If Hoodoo is in your lineage, reclaim it. It's yours.

TIP

If you're African American and curious whether your family practiced, ask your elders about home remedies, dream interpretation, signs they watched for, or things they did for luck. Often the practices were there but weren't called Hoodoo.

Recognizing academic and artistic validation

Modern scholarship has vindicated Hoodoo's importance. What was once dismissed as superstition by mainstream academia is now recognized as a complex spiritual system with deep cultural significance. Research studies and artistic depictions frame Hoodoo as a national treasure of African American folklore and religion. It's viewed not a curiosity or embarrassment, but a sophisticated tradition worthy of serious study and respect.

Here are examples:

- Historians such as Tony Kail and Katrina Hazzard-Donald have traced Hoodoo's development in meticulous detail, demonstrating what casual observers missed. Kail's research in Memphis linked local practices directly to Kongo and West African traditions, showing the continuity from Africa to America that survived the Middle Passage. (See Chapter 7 for more information about the effects of the Middle Passage on Hoodoo.) Sociologist Sterling Stuckey argued that African cultural practices like the ring shout and conjure formed the core of Black American identity and fueled liberation movements.
- Artists have also engaged Hoodoo themes, further destigmatizing the tradition. Visual artist Renee Stout created acclaimed works like *The Rootworker's Table,* which incorporates conjure symbols and tools. Writers from Ishmael Reed (*Mumbo Jumbo*, 1972) to contemporary poets have woven Hoodoo lore into their work, presenting it as a source of creative strength rather than shameful primitivism.

REMEMBER

This academic and artistic recognition matters. It shifts Hoodoo from the margins to the center of African American cultural heritage, giving practitioners and descendants a framework for understanding the tradition's value.

Connecting Hoodoo to modern social justice

Unsurprisingly, Hoodoo and African spirituality have found places in modern activism, including the Black Lives Matter movement. Organizers have acknowledged the need for spiritual grounding in the work of fighting systemic racism. After incidents of police violence, some community gatherings have incorporated *libation ceremonies* — pouring water to honor the dead — and created altars at tragedy sites with candles, flowers, and personal items. In Ferguson after the 2014 unrest, activists cleansed streets with burning sage and laid offerings. These acts are rooted in ancestral traditions that never disappeared.

These public rituals represent a full circle: Where ring shouts and Hoodoo prayers once helped people endure slavery, descendants now consciously invoke those same energies to confront contemporary injustice. The tradition that sustained people through the Middle Passage, through slavery, through Jim Crow, and through the long struggle for civil rights, continues sustaining people through ongoing struggles today.

REMEMBER

Modern resistance to systemic bias underscores what I emphasize throughout this book. Hoodoo has always been about Black freedom, survival, and well-being. The modern application to social justice isn't a new use of the tradition; it's the tradition's original purpose, adapted to present circumstances. Hoodoo's connection to liberation isn't metaphorical or recent. The tradition was forged in resistance and has served resistance movements for centuries. Today's activists are walking a path their ancestors cleared.

Navigating digital Hoodoo

The internet is a big part of the modern revival and has transformed how rootworkers and eager newcomers learn, share, and practice Hoodoo. This transformation brings both opportunities and challenges, and you get a glimpse of the opportunities in this list:

- **The internet allows practitioners nationally and globally to connect, share knowledge, and correct misconceptions.** African American-led online forums, YouTube channels, podcasts, and workshops now teach Hoodoo practice, reclaiming the narrative from old stereotypes and non-Black commercialization.

- **Online spaces provide connection that wouldn't otherwise exist for practitioners in areas without local Hoodoo communities.** Someone in rural Montana or urban Seattle can learn from practitioners in New Orleans or the Georgia Lowcountry. The geographic isolation that once limited transmission has been partially overcome.
- **Social media enables collective spiritual work.** Practitioners can organize coordinated workings — protection for protestors, justice for victims, and healing for communities — across distances that would have been impossible to bridge a generation ago.

The internet's openness also creates problems for a practice like Hoodoo that's rooted in tradition. This list offers a look at some of these challenges:

- **Not everyone teaching "Hoodoo" online knows what they're talking about.** Some content creators package aesthetic and fragments of practice without understanding or context. Others actively spread misinformation, whether through ignorance or deliberate deception.
- **The online search algorithms don't distinguish authenticity.** You can get search engine results that mix links to a knowledgeable elder sharing authentic tradition and someone who learned everything from YouTube or TikTok videos last month. Popularity doesn't indicate accuracy. Aesthetic appeal doesn't indicate depth.
- **The public nature of social media can mean getting faulty content.** Hoodoo practices that were traditionally transmitted privately are now displayed for anyone to see — including people who will strip them of context, commercialize them inappropriately, or claim expertise they don't have.

WARNING

Having a large online following doesn't translate to accurate teaching. Vet online teachers carefully. Look for connection to lineage, consistency with documented tradition, and respect from other practitioners, not just video production quality or confident presentation.

Acquiring Materials and Adapting Workspace in the Modern Era

Traditional Hoodoo relied on locally gathered roots, herbs grown in kitchen gardens, and supplies obtained from practitioners who knew exactly what they were selling. Modern practice often requires different approaches to finding appropriate materials.

Also, Hoodoo developed in rural Southern contexts that included houses with yards, access to woods and crossroads, neighbors who minded their own business, and space to burn things and bury things without anyone calling the fire department or the landlord.

Modern practitioners often work in very different environments: city apartments, shared walls, smoke detectors, lease agreements prohibiting open flames, and no yard to speak of. Adapting the tradition to these circumstances requires creativity while maintaining the work's integrity.

Sourcing quality materials

You have several options for obtaining supplies in a more urban or suburban environment. Each option in this list has trade-offs:

- **Botanical shops and spiritual supply stores,** especially those owned by Black practitioners in Black communities, remain valuable resources where they exist. The staff working in these shops often know the tradition, can answer questions, and stock materials appropriate for actual practice rather than aesthetic display. If you have access to such a shop, support it.
- **Online retailers** have made supplies accessible to practitioners anywhere, but quality varies enormously. Some online shops are run by knowledgeable practitioners who sell quality materials. Others are drop-shipping generic herbs with Hoodoo-sounding names attached.

  TIP

  Do your research and learn to distinguish the good sources. Look for online shops with roots in the community, transparent sourcing, and good reputations among practitioners you trust.
- **Growing and gathering your own materials** connects you to the tradition's roots. Even a small container garden can produce useful herbs. If you have access to wild spaces, learning to identify and ethically harvest local plants builds relationship with the land and ensures you know exactly what you're working with.

Avoiding common problems with online supplies

Mass-produced spiritual oils and preparations are often more fragrance than function. A bottle labeled "Money Drawing Oil" from a novelty supplier may contain none of the botanicals (such as cinnamon and bayberry) traditionally used for that purpose. When possible, find out how to make your own preparations or buy from practitioners who make theirs properly.

Be cautious of products marketed with Hoodoo terminology but created by people with no connection to the tradition. The commercialization of Hoodoo has produced a flood of products trading on the aesthetic without delivering the substance. Also watch for ecological concerns. Some traditional materials are now endangered or unethically harvested. Responsible practitioners find substitutes or ensure their sources are sustainable.

TIP

When buying supplies online, search for the shop's name along with the term *review* in practitioner online communities. Don't just trust general retail review sites. Fellow practitioners can tell you whether the materials work.

Working in small spaces

You don't need a dedicated altar room to practice Hoodoo. A closet, a shelf, a corner of a dresser, or a cabinet that closes can serve that function. Some practitioners maintain portable altars that they can set up for work and store afterward. These portable altars are particularly useful if you have roommates or family members who wouldn't understand this part of your practice.

REMEMBER

Discretion was always part of the tradition. Your ancestors often practiced without anyone outside the household knowing. A small, private setup honors that history.

Managing smoke and scent

Burning herbs, incense, and candles can trigger smoke detectors, bother neighbors, and violate lease terms. Adaptations for practicing under these conditions include using electric oil warmers instead of burning incense, choosing smaller candles that produce less smoke, working near open windows or using fans, doing smoke-heavy work outdoors when possible, and using sprays or washes instead of smoke for cleansing.

Some practitioners do their burning work on balconies, in parks, or at actual crossroads rather than inside apartments. Others reserve smoke-intensive practices for times they can visit family with yards or take trips to appropriate outdoor spaces.

Disposing of ritual materials

Traditional methods for disposal of ritual materials, such as burying them at crossroads, throwing them into running water, or leaving them at specific locations, can be challenging in cities. You can adapt disposal methods by finding urban crossroads (anyplace where two roads cross works), identifying accessible bodies of moving water, using potted plants for burial when earth burial in a yard isn't possible, and disposing of materials in public trash receptacles away from your home, when appropriate.

REMEMBER

Some workings specify disposal methods that matter; others are more flexible. Learn which workings really require specific disposal, and stick to the requirements. You can adapt disposal for the flexible workings to your circumstances.

Cities have crossroads everywhere; any intersection counts. Parks, riverbanks, and urban green spaces can provide the natural elements that certain workings require. Railroad tracks still exist in most cities. Cemeteries remain accessible. The workings of Hoodoo adapt to where you are. Your ancestors practiced in whatever circumstances they found themselves, including circumstances far more constrained than a modern apartment. They adapted. You can too.

REMEMBER

FACING THE DEBATE ABOUT PRACTICING HOODOO TODAY

Increased popularity brings challenges in keeping Hoodoo true to its roots. Internet openness means many non-Black enthusiasts have accessed Hoodoo spells and practices, sometimes selling "Hoodoo kits" without understanding cultural context or the history that created them.

The question of who can practice Hoodoo is contentious. This book can't settle that debate, as outlined in Chapter 2, but it will give you knowledge to engage the conversation honestly and insightfully.

Here's where the debate gets less complicated: There's a long history of Hoodoo practitioners helping everybody who needed it. So even if there's debate about who can learn and claim the practice, there should be no debate about who practitioners can assist, given the centuries-long history that answers that question before it's asked today. Help yourself, help your community, help whoever needs it.

Finding Teachers and Community

Traditional Hoodoo passed from hand to hand, with a grandmother teaching a grandchild, an established rootworker taking on an apprentice, and knowledge flowing through family and community relationships. That model of teaching and passing on the tradition still exists but isn't available to everyone.

Vetting potential teachers

If you're seeking to learn Hoodoo practice from another practitioner, whether in person or online, look for these factors and ask these questions when you choose a mentor:

- **Lineage and connection:** Where did they learn? Who taught them? Can they trace their knowledge to documented tradition rather than books they read? This line of questioning doesn't require that the practitioner you're considering needs to be a famous teacher, but they should be able to articulate where their knowledge comes from. And transmission of knowledge through family counts.
- **Consistency with tradition:** Does what they teach match what's documented in historical sources, academic research, and the testimony of acknowledged practitioners? Everyone has personal variations in their workings, but wholesale contradiction of established practice is a red flag.
- **Respect from peers:** What do other practitioners say about them? Do respected voices in the community vouch for them, or do they operate in isolation, making claims no one else supports? Go the extra mile to find out whether other Hoodoo practitioners know and believe in their teachings.
- **Appropriate humility:** Anyone claiming to know everything, dismissing all other practitioners, or refusing to acknowledge the limits of their knowledge probably isn't trustworthy. The tradition is vast; no one conquers all of it.

Recognizing red flags

Be cautious of teachers who charge enormous fees for secret knowledge, claim exclusive access to authentic tradition that no one else has, pressure you to cut ties with other teachers or communities, make claims about their powers that seem designed to impress rather than educate, or can't answer questions about where they learned what they're teaching.

Hoodoo has always been practical and grounded. Teachers who emphasize drama, mystery, and their own importance over actual practical knowledge are often selling something other than authentic tradition.

Building genuine relationships

The best learning still happens through relationships. Even if you start with books or online content, eventually you need connection with practitioners who can answer questions specific to your situation, correct your mistakes, and pass on the intangible aspects of practice that don't translate well to written or video instruction.

TIP

Building these relationships takes time. Show up consistently. Demonstrate genuine respect. Don't demand teaching as if you're entitled to it. And let relationships develop naturally.

WARNING

Anyone who promises to teach you everything about Hoodoo in a weekend workshop is lying. The tradition takes years to develop comprehensive knowledge and skill. Be suspicious of shortcuts and instant expertise.

TAKING THE HOODOO TRADITION FORWARD

REMEMBER

This book teaches you the history of the Hoodoo tradition so you understand what you're engaging with. It presents techniques and knowledge for those who choose to practice. It emphasizes respect, context, and responsibility. It encourages you to listen to American Descendants of Slavery (ADOS) practitioners, especially elders. It asks you to examine your own motivations and relationship to the tradition.

What the book doesn't do is claim authority to decide who belongs in the practice and who doesn't. That's a community conversation, not an author's decree. As a living tradition, Hoodoo continues growing and adapting while maintaining the same purpose at its heart: empowering and healing Black people facing adversity. That purpose has carried it through four centuries. It will carry it through whatever comes next.

Hoodoo has survived everything history has thrown at it because practitioners have adapted while maintaining the tradition's core. Today's practitioners carry that responsibility to adapt what must change, preserve what must remain, and pass forward a tradition as vital as the one they receive. Hoodoo isn't a relic. It's a living practice, carried by living people, addressing living needs. Its future will be written by the practitioners who carry it forward, adapt it to new circumstances, protect its integrity, and pass it on. That's what living traditions do. They live.

IN THIS CHAPTER

» Knowing why accurate depiction of Hoodoo matters

» Countering the misrepresentation and harmful tropes

» Examining Hoodoo in music and film

» Analyzing examples of Hoodoo in entertainment

» Using entertainment as a gateway to deeper understanding

Chapter 17 Hoodoo in Entertainment

The television show *Supernatural* reintroduced many viewers to the word *Hoodoo*. They'd heard it before, usually in dismissive contexts — "That's a bunch of Hoodoo," meaning something not to be taken seriously. But watching the Winchester brothers use goofer dust and juju bags as practical tools made the word stick differently. For some viewers, including African Americans who'd grown up with certain family practices but never had a name for them, the show sparked recognition:

> Wait, that's what my grandmother was doing. She just never called it that.

This less-than-authentic portrayal of reality is the complicated gift of entertainment. A TV show created by people with no deep connection to Hoodoo can still, accidentally, open a door. The portrayal of the practice and tradition may be imperfect, stripped of cultural context, or flat-out wrong in places. But it can still send someone searching for the real story.

This chapter explores how Hoodoo has appeared in American entertainment — music, film, and television — from the earliest misrepresentations to the sophisticated, culturally grounded portrayals emerging today. In these pages, you can find out how to recognize both the harmful tropes and the authentic representations and come to understand why getting this depiction right matters.

Understanding Why Representation Matters

For most Americans, entertainment is the primary source of information about spiritual traditions outside their own experience. What people see on screen shapes what they believe is real, acceptable, and true. Here are some scenarios describing what people get from seeing Hoodoo through the entertainment lens:

- When Hoodoo appears in entertainment only as sinister magic wielded by villains, audiences absorb the message that African American spirituality is dangerous, primitive, or evil.
- When Hoodoo is confused with Haitian Voodoo and presented as a cult of possession and human sacrifice, audiences learn to fear rather than understand.
- When Hoodoo practices are played for laughs — the superstitious old Black woman with her potions and warnings — audiences learn to dismiss them.

These representations have real consequences. They shape how employers view job candidates who practice ancestral traditions. They influence whether children feel pride or shame in their family's heritage. They affect whether practitioners feel safe being open about their spiritual lives.

But representation can also heal. When audiences see Hoodoo portrayed as what it actually is — a sophisticated tradition of healing, protection, and survival developed by brilliant people under impossible conditions — something shifts. Descendants of practitioners feel seen. People outside the tradition gain respect. The centuries-long project of demonizing African American spirituality loses some of its power.

REMEMBER

Entertainment doesn't just reflect culture. It shapes it. How Hoodoo appears on screen affects how millions of people understand the tradition, including people who might carry it in their own family history without knowing.

Confronting the History of Misrepresentation

The entertainment industry's engagement with African-derived spirituality has a troubled history. Understanding that history helps you recognize harmful patterns that persist today. In this section, you find out about the wrong depictions of Hoodoo and how the industry is changing to correct its perspective.

Tracing early cinematic portrayals

Early 20th-century portrayals of Black spirituality were rooted in visual rhetoric of savagery. Comics, cartoons, and films depicted Black spiritual practitioners as witch doctors or cannibal kings, which projected racial anxieties onto an imaginary geography of Africanized horror. This graphic voodoo coincided with US military interventions in the Caribbean, linking Black ritualism to human sacrifice and gruesome imagery.

Hollywood learned early that voodoo, a catch-all term misapplied to any African-derived practice, could sell tickets through fear. The result was decades of films featuring evil dolls, cursing spells, and sinister priestesses. These images bore no resemblance to actual Hoodoo or Vodou practice but still became fixed in the American imagination.

Identifying persistent tropes

Several harmful *tropes*, commonly occurring motifs, themes, or character types, emerged from the history of encounters with African traditions and continue appearing in film and other media today. These misrepresentations include the following:

- **The Magical Negro** trope presents Black characters who exist only to help white protagonists through mystical means, with no inner life or agenda of their own. Their magic is in service to white stories.
- **The Voodoo Villain** trope presents practitioners as evil, using dark powers for selfish or malevolent purposes. The magic is always sinister, never healing or protective.
- **The Superstitious Primitive** trope plays Black spirituality for laughs. It's the uneducated believer whose practices are silly or backward, contrasted with rational white characters.

» **The Voodoo/Hoodoo Confusion** collapses distinct traditions into one scary black magic, usually featuring elements of neither Vodou nor Hoodoo but a Hollywood invention.

Recognizing counternarratives

Even in the early 20th century, Black filmmakers offered counter-narratives. The race film movement, led by pioneers such as Oscar Micheaux, depicted Black spiritual life with nuance and dignity. Spencer Williams's *The Blood of Jesus* (1941) integrated authentic religious practices — including communal prayer and spiritual combat — into its narrative, providing realism foreign to the white mainstream viewers.

These early Black films established an alternative tradition that contemporary creators continue: showing Black spirituality as lived reality rather than exotic threat.

WARNING

When you see imagery of voodoo in a film or show, ask this question: Is this media depicting Haitian Vodou, Louisiana Voodoo, Hoodoo, or a Hollywood invention that's none of the above? Usually it's the last option.

Embracing the rise of expert consultants

One of the most significant developments in recent entertainment is the emergence of expert consultants who can help ensure accurate Hoodoo representation. Engaging Hoodoo consultants in mainstream entertainment is a sign of progress. It means the industry is beginning to recognize that accurate representation requires insider knowledge, not just research.

Understanding what consultants do

Scholars such as Yvonne Chireau now serve as historical and cultural consultants for major productions. Their work ensures accurate representation of practices, materials, and cultural context. They help productions avoid harmful tropes while telling compelling stories.

Dr. Chireau, author of *Black Magic: Religion and the African American Conjuring Tradition*, worked with Ryan Coogler on the film *Sinners* to ensure accurate depiction of ancestral practices and physical construction of mojo bags. The filmmakers were careful not to disclose protected knowledge while allowing practitioners to see themselves represented with dignity.

This balance, authenticity without exposure of sacred information, is central to what consultants provide. They help creators understand not just what to show, but what should remain private.

Seeing the impact of the experts

The difference between productions that use consultants and those that don't is often visible on screen. Films and shows with knowledgeable guidance tend to present Hoodoo as complex, functional, and rooted in specific cultural context. Those without guidance often fall back on generic voodoo tropes (see the section "Identifying persistent tropes" earlier in the chapter) that could apply to any imaginary black magic practice.

The shift toward expert consultation represents growing industry recognition that getting representation right matters, both ethically and commercially. Audiences increasingly recognize and reject lazy stereotypes. If you're involved in entertainment production, hiring cultural consultants isn't optional for responsible representation. If you're a viewer, productions that credit cultural consultants are often more trustworthy than those that don't.

Welcoming new voices

The 2020s have brought a wave of new entertainment engaging Hoodoo with unprecedented sophistication and cultural respect. Beyond theatrical films like *Sinners* (see the section "Welcoming Sinners" later in the chapter), television shows and documentary media are also shifting the landscape.

Watching The Conjure Family

The Conjure Family, a 2025 reality series streaming on Apple TV, follows practitioner Lala Inuti Ahari and her daughters building a metaphysical business rooted in Hoodoo. The series explicitly places Hoodoo and African spiritual traditions at its center, reclaiming them as family legacy rather than outsider curiosity.

This kind of reality programming, where practitioners tell their own stories rather than being depicted by outsiders, represents a fundamental shift in who controls Hoodoo's narrative in entertainment.

Learning from documentaries

Documentary programming has also contributed to public education. PBS's *Ritual* series includes an episode specifically tracing Hoodoo from slavery to the present day, presenting it as ancestral practice rather than entertainment horror.

The *United States of Hoodoo* (2012) follows writer Darius James exploring the African and Caribbean bloodlines running through American culture. The documentary uncovers Hoodoo influences in everything from New York's African Burial Ground to the music of the Delta Blues, arguing that these traditions are central to American culture rather than marginal to it.

TIP Seek out documentaries and programming where practitioners speak for themselves. Entertainment made by community members typically offers more accurate and respectful portrayals than outsider productions.

Using entertainment as a gateway

If entertainment is where many people first encounter Hoodoo, how do you use that encounter productively? How do you move from what you see on screen to understanding the actual tradition?

TIP Keep a list of entertainment that depicts Hoodoo well versus poorly. Over time, you can develop an eye for authentic representation versus stereotyping. Share your assessments with others who are learning to navigate this landscape.

Watching critically

When you encounter Hoodoo in entertainment, watch critically and look for these qualities:

- Creators who have connection to the tradition or hire consultants who do
- Authentic depiction of actual Hoodoo or Voodoo practice rather than a Hollywood invention
- Portrayal of magic as healing and protective, not just as harmful
- Use of Black characters as agents in their own stories; they shouldn't exist only to serve white protagonists

Analyzing these qualities of the entertainment can help you sort authentic representation from stereotype and useful portrayals from harmful ones.

Following curiosity deeper

If something you see on screen sparks recognition or curiosity, follow it. If you see a TV show that makes you think of your grandmother's practices, do some research on what you saw. Talk to family elders. Look for books and resources by practitioners and scholars, not just entertainment producers.

Entertainment can be a door to discovery of hidden Hoodoo, but it's rarely the destination. Use it to find your way to deeper sources of understanding the tradition.

Honoring mixed feelings

It's okay to have complicated feelings about entertainment that depicts your Hoodoo tradition imperfectly. You can appreciate that a show introduces people to concepts they'd never encounter otherwise while also being frustrated by what the show got wrong. You can enjoy a film's craft while critiquing its cultural politics.

Hoodoo practitioners have long lived in a world that misunderstands and misrepresents them. Navigating that reality with clear eyes — taking what's useful, rejecting what's harmful, and always seeking deeper truth — is itself part of the tradition.

Engaging with Hoodoo in Music and Film

Music is arguably the most important medium for Hoodoo's survival in public consciousness. In Delta blues, Hoodoo wasn't metaphor; it was functional knowledge encoded in lyrics. And the film industry offers a primary site for both Hoodoo's misrepresentation and its authentic portrayal. Understanding specific examples of Hoodoo in music and film that I present in this section can help you recognize the real depictions.

Decoding the blues as Hoodoo archive

The acoustic blues of the early 20th century contains some of the clearest descriptions of Hoodoo materials and their uses. Songs by Tampa Red, Robert Johnson, Son House, and others serve as oral repositories for Hoodoo knowledge. Listen carefully to their lyrics, and you can hear references to mojo bags, black cat bones, High John the Conqueror root, and crossroads rituals.

Common Hoodoo references in traditional blues include these:

- **Mojo hand or mojo bag** as a charm bag for power and protection, appearing in lyrics as source of luck, sexual power, success
- **Crossroads** as an intersection where spiritual bargains occur, and a place of transformation and deal-making

UNDERSTANDING THE CROSSROADS MYTH

TECHNICAL STUFF

The myth of the crossroads deal, famously associated with Robert Johnson, is a direct appropriation of Hoodoo lore. In the tradition, a person goes to a crossroads at midnight to meet a spiritual figure who can grant specific abilities in exchange for something of value.

The Black Man at the crossroads in Hoodoo lore isn't Satan, a European Christian figure, but a spiritual gatekeeper. *Black Man* refers to a spirit, not a racial description. The crossroads itself represents a threshold between worlds, a place where normal rules suspend and transformation becomes possible.

When this imagery entered mainstream rock mythology, it lost much of its original meaning. But in its original context, the crossroads ritual was serious spiritual technology used by people seeking real change in desperate circumstances.

- **High John or John the Conqueror** as a root for overcoming obstacles and a source of victory and triumph
- **Black cat bone** as a charm for invisibility or luck, and used for protection, gambling luck, and romantic success
- **Goofer dust** as the graveyard dirt used in workings and associated with harmful magic and cursing enemies
- **Nation sack** as another term for mojo bag for personal power and "fixin'" situations

Including these mentions in blues songs wasn't just artistic license. Blues musicians often draw on practices they know firsthand or have witnessed in their communities. The music preserves knowledge that couldn't otherwise be written down safely or openly discussed.

Following the musical thread forward

The Hoodoo current in American music didn't stop with acoustic blues. The music carries the tradition forward even when listeners don't recognize what they're hearing. Here are examples:

- **Sister Rosetta Tharpe,** the godmother of rock and roll, brought the spiritual passion of the Church of God in Christ, a denomination founded by a known rootworker, into secular performance spaces. She was conjuring the divine in nightclubs and concert halls.

- **Jimi Hendrix** blended Afro-futurist imagery with Black American spiritual symbolism, continuing the tradition of the musician as shamanic figure.
- **Contemporary Southern hip-hop** encodes spiritual philosophies in discussions of survival and struggle, using poetic speech as the descendants of the linguistic practices developed by enslaved Africans to communicate in code.

TIP

If you want to hear Hoodoo in music, start with pre-war Delta blues. Listen for specific materials and practices mentioned in lyrics. You're hearing oral tradition preserved in song.

Critiquing The Skeleton Key

In the film arena, *The Skeleton Key* (2005) is a definitive example of how Southern Gothic horror uses Hoodoo to generate fear while offering some genuine complexity. The film follows a hospice nurse who becomes embroiled in what appears to be a Hoodoo ritual in a Louisiana plantation house.

The film accurately describes Hoodoo as an African American tradition of conjuring, which is more than many films manage. Its twist ending reveals that the apparent villains are actually original Hoodoo practitioners who survived their own lynching by transferring their consciousness into white bodies, a kind of ultimate resistance against racist violence.

However, the film ultimately frames Hoodoo as a boogeyman that requires the victim's belief to function. This disconnects the practice from its actual context as a tradition of healing and protection, positioning it instead as a source of nightmare.

Celebrating Daughters of the Dust

Julie Dash's *Daughters of the Dust* (1991) remains the gold standard for authentic Hoodoo representation in film. Set among the Gullah/Geechee people of the Sea Islands off the South Carolina coast, the film depicts rootwork and conjure as living tradition within a specific community.

The film shows bottle trees, protective charms, ancestral communication, and root medicine as natural parts of how the Peazant family lives. Nothing is sensationalized or played for horror. The spiritual practices are simply there as part of the cultural fabric that the film celebrates and documents.

Dash's film demonstrates the approach that Black-led cinema can provide: a layered portrayal that shows the tradition as its practitioners experience it, rooted in specific place, history, and community rather than generic "voodoo" imagery..

Welcoming Sinners

Ryan Coogler's *Sinners* (2025) represents a new high point for Hoodoo in mainstream film. The film centers on a Hoodoo conjurer named Annie who confronts supernatural threats in the Depression-era South. Coogler hired scholar Yvonne Chireau as the official consultant to ensure authentic representation.

The result is a film in which Hoodoo functions as it actually does — as healing, protection, and community resource — even within a horror framework. Practitioners can see themselves represented with dignity rather than as villains or curiosities.

Recognizing problematic film examples

The 2020 film *Spell* demonstrates that harmful tropes persist. Written by a screenwriter with no connection to the tradition, the film depicts a rural Hoodoo cult using dolls to torture the protagonist. Critics argued that it presented magic-practicing savages, reinforcing exactly the stereotypes Black creators have worked to dismantle.

The contrast between *Spell* and films like *Daughters of the Dust* or *Sinners* illustrates how much the perspective of the film's creators matters. The same genre, Southern Gothic with spiritual elements, can either perpetuate harm or provide nuanced representation, depending on who's telling the story and what they understand about what they're depicting.

TIP

When evaluating films that feature Hoodoo, ask these questions: Who made the film? Did they consult Hoodoo practitioners? Is the magic only evil, or does the film show its healing and protective dimensions? Does this portray a real tradition or a Hollywood invention?

Exploring Approaches to Hoodoo

Entertainers in many aspects of the industry share the responsibility and opportunity to present Hoodoo accurately and fairly. For example, Beyoncé's visual albums aren't documentaries about Hoodoo, but they draw extensively on its imagery and logic. They've introduced millions of viewers to symbols and concepts they might never otherwise encounter.

And the TV show *Supernatural* also introduced millions of viewers to terminology and concepts they'd never encountered. For some viewers, particularly African Americans who'd grown up with family practices they'd never had a name for, the show provided a vocabulary that sparked recognition and further investigation.

Watching Beyoncé conjure

In the 21st century, few artists have integrated Hoodoo and African diaspora symbolism into global pop consciousness more effectively than Beyoncé. Through her visual albums *Lemonade* and *Black Is King*, she performs what scholars identify as the Conjure Woman archetype, a figure who unearths and reclaims ancestral memory to heal modern trauma.

Reading Lemonade as conjure work

The album *Lemonade* is structured as a journey through grief, rage, and transformation, the same emotional territory Hoodoo has always addressed. The visual album deploys specific symbols such as these drawn from African diaspora traditions:

- **Water imagery throughout the work evokes Oshun, the Yoruba orisha of rivers, love, and fertility.** Beyoncé emerges from water, is submerged in water, and floods rooms with water. All of this suggests spiritual rebirth and the power of the feminine divine.
- **Plantation settings and Southern Gothic imagery reclaim spaces of historical trauma as sites of ancestral power.** Rather than fleeing these locations, the visual narrative transforms them through presence and ritual.
- **Lemons are traditional Hoodoo ingredients used to overpower negative energy and transform bitterness into something useful.** The folk saying referenced in the album — about making lemonade from life's lemons — has deeper roots than just positive thinking.

Recognizing Black Is King's visual vocabulary

The *Black Is King* album continues the work of *Lemonade* (see the preceding section) with even more explicit African and diaspora imagery. Haint blue, the protective color used in Lowcountry Hoodoo to ward off spirits, appears throughout. Cowrie shells, which are symbolic of wealth, creation, and femininity in multiple African traditions, adorn costumes and sets.

Choreography in several sequences has been described as intentionally "Hoodoo-inspired," using specific hand and body movements meant to evoke the grasping of personal power. Whether or not viewers consciously recognize these symbols, they're receiving a visual education in diaspora spiritual aesthetics.

REMEMBER

By bridging sacred Yoruba traditions with Southern rootwork, Beyoncé's visual work serves as a high-budget archive of African diaspora survival practices. It's entertainment, but it's also cultural preservation.

Analyzing Supernatural's complicated legacy

The long-running television series *Supernatural* offers a particularly interesting case study in how mainstream entertainment engages with Hoodoo — sometimes usefully, often problematically, and occasionally both at once.

Recognizing what the show got right

Unlike many of its contemporaries, *Supernatural* was one of the first mainstream series to depict Hoodoo as a functional, positive tool for its protagonists. The Winchester brothers use goofer dust, juju bags, curse boxes, and other elements drawn from actual Hoodoo practice to combat supernatural threats.

Missouri Moseley, a Black psychic who appears in early episodes, is shown creating protective juju bags and cleansing houses. That's practical Hoodoo work presented as legitimate and effective.

Acknowledging what the show got wrong

Supernatural also demonstrates the limitations of mainstream engagement with Hoodoo. The show rarely acknowledges the African American origins of the practices it depicts. Instead, Hoodoo gets filed under a generic hunter's manual alongside European folklore, treating it as just another weapon in an arsenal of the arcane.

Some specific details are simply incorrect. The show uses goofer dust as a protective ward against hellhounds, when traditionally goofer dust is a harmful substance used to curse enemies. The word derives from the Kikongo word *kufwa*, meaning to die.

There's also a profound meta-irony in the Winchesters' relationship with magic: They frequently utilize Hoodoo rituals in early episodes while harboring deep prejudice against witches. This reflects something real: Many Hoodoo practitioners don't consider themselves witches and would reject that label, especially those who identified with a religion that demonizes various types of magicians. The show doesn't explore this nuance consciously.

Accepting complicated gifts

Supernatural illustrates how entertainment can serve as an imperfect gateway. The show got enough right that it pointed some viewers toward authentic tradition, while getting enough wrong that it also spread misinformation.

For Hoodoo practitioners, this duality creates complicated feelings. It's frustrating to see your tradition stripped of context and inaccurately depicted. It's also strangely gratifying when someone says, "I started learning about real Hoodoo because of that show."

REMEMBER

Supernatural used Hoodoo as a practical tool, which was novel for mainstream TV, and reflects the approach of many of its practitioners. But it stripped the tradition of its cultural context and got some details wrong. It's a gateway, not a guide.

Celebrating P-Valley's authentic portrayal

Katori Hall's *P-Valley* drama series represents a significant departure from the scary-magic trope, offering a sophisticated and culturally grounded portrayal of Hoodoo through the character Diamond.

TIP

P-Valley is one of the most authentic portrayals of Hoodoo practice currently on television. If you want to see rootwork depicted as the tradition actually functions — healing, protective, connected to lineage — this show delivers.

Meeting Diamond the rootworker

Set in the fictional Mississippi Delta town of Chucalissa, *P-Valley* introduces Diamond as a former military man working as a strip club bouncer. As the series develops, he's revealed to be a rootworker and Hoodoo practitioner who views his practice as an extension of care.

Diamond's rootwork is portrayed with focus on its medicinal and communal roots. He gives a character a carnelian stone for courage. This stone is a healing crystal associated with inner strength. He uses an old remedy from his grandfather — crushed pepper and alcohol — to treat muscle soreness. This specific remedy is a direct reference to Zora Neale Hurston's anthropological documentation, demonstrating the show's commitment to historical accuracy.

Seeing Hoodoo as healing

Unlike the Magical Negro stereotype who exists only to serve white characters, Diamond's Hoodoo is a private, culturally specific source of strength that he uses to navigate his own trauma and protect his community. His magic isn't performed for outsiders' benefit — it's part of his personal spiritual life.

One particularly powerful scene shows Diamond magically removing seven pounds of pressure from a dancer's shoulder, a healing practice that addresses the physical and emotional weight carried by someone surviving difficult circumstances. This depiction shows Hoodoo as healing justice, not as entertainment spectacle.

The show emphasizes what this book has highlighted throughout: Hoodoo's longstanding relationship with Black Southern survival. Diamond carries forward a tradition his grandfather practiced, connecting contemporary Black life to ancestral wisdom.

Appreciating Queen Sugar's subtle approach

Ava DuVernay's *Queen Sugar* series takes a different approach than *P-Valley*. The show never uses the word *Hoodoo*, but its depiction of rootwork and ancestral spiritual practice is among the most nuanced and layered on television.

REMEMBER

Queen Sugar shows Hoodoo-derived practice as simply part of how its characters live — not exotic, not scary, not performed for outsiders. This normalization may be its most radical choice.

Following Nova Bordelon

The character Nova Bordelon, journalist, activist, and herbal healer, is the primary vessel for spiritual representation in *Queen Sugar*. Her identity as a healer is established in her first scene, where she prays over an elderly neighbor and provides herbal medicine for pain.

Nova's spirituality is presented as a way of life centering on her connection to Louisiana soil and African ancestral heritage. She maintains shelves of jars filled with herbs and remedies, serving as her community's herbalist. This role is a modern iteration of the conjure woman, though the show never labels it as such.

Complicating the healer's role

Queen Sugar complicates Nova's spiritual responsibilities by placing them in tension with her professional ambitions. When she publishes a memoir revealing family traumas, her relatives accuse her of betrayal, using their pain as material under the guise of public healing.

This narrative choice highlights a contemporary dilemma: the tension between the sacred secret of Black spiritual practices and modern demands for transparency and commercial visibility. Nova's story asks whether some knowledge should remain private, shared only within community and family.

The character also subverts traditional controlling images of Black womanhood. Though she nurtures her community, she's childless and queer, escaping the archetypes of Mammy or Matriarch. Her spiritual practice is a site of personal autonomy, not self-sacrifice.

Looking at the Future of Hoodoo in Entertainment

The future of Hoodoo in entertainment lies in the transition from othered horror to cultural technology — from something scary that happens to Black characters to something powerful that Black characters wield with agency and purpose. This shift is already underway. Black creators are increasingly telling their own stories, with Hoodoo as part of lived reality rather than an exotic backdrop. Expert consultants are ensuring accuracy. Streaming platforms are funding programming where practitioners control their own narratives.

The plasticized images of Hoodoo that once dominated entertainment are being challenged by narratives focusing on survival, healing, and ancestral wisdom. Whether through prestige television dramas, horror films that complicate rather than demonize, or documentaries letting practitioners speak for themselves, the American imaginary is slowly shifting.

Hoodoo has survived centuries of misrepresentation, and it will survive whatever Hollywood does next. But as representation of authentic Hoodoo improves, something valuable happens: Descendants of practitioners feel less alone, outsiders develop respect instead of fear, and a tradition that was forced into hiding can increasingly be practiced in the light.

REMEMBER

Entertainment shapes how millions of people understand Hoodoo. As representation improves, the tradition benefits. Support creators and productions that get it right, and don't be afraid to critique those that don't.

IN THIS CHAPTER

» Recognizing cyclical patterns in Hoodoo history

» Heeding fundamental conversations and timeless principles

» Embracing your responsibility in continuing the tradition

Chapter 18 Carrying Hoodoo Forward

The Hoodoo tradition I present in this book has survived four centuries, not by standing still, but by moving, adapting, transmitting, going underground when necessary and resurfacing when possible, and always serving the needs of the people who carry it.

This chapter looks at where Hoodoo has been and what it has always done. In this chapter, you get a glimpse of the patterns that repeat across generations and move into current happenings in the Hoodoo community. In Hoodoo's cyclical understanding of time, the future tends to echo the past.

More importantly, this chapter asks you to consider your role in carrying the tradition forward. Whether you're an American Descendants of Slavery (ADOS) descendant reclaiming ancestral practice, someone exploring your family's hidden history, or a respectful learner engaging from outside the tradition, you have a part to play.

Understanding Hoodoo's Link to Cyclical Time

Western culture tends to think of time as a line with the past in the rearview mirror, the future up ahead, and everything moving in one direction toward some destination. Hoodoo draws on African cosmological roots (see Chapter 2) and often relates to time differently.

For example, in Hoodoo's worldview, the ancestors aren't simply dead and gone. They're present, accessible, and actively involved in the lives of their descendants. When you call on them, they answer, not from some distant past but from a place that touches the present moment. See Chapter 7 for more information about ancestors and their place in the soul of Hoodoo.

This ancestral link means that the past isn't really past. The enslaved people who developed Hoodoo, the root doctors who carried it through Reconstruction and Jim Crow, the grandmothers who hid it, and the grandchildren now reclaiming it are part of one continuous thread. When you study Hoodoo, you don't study a historical artifact. You enter a living conversation that includes people who walked this earth centuries before you were born.

Seeing patterns that repeat

If the ancestors are present and time moves in cycles rather than lines, then the future isn't some unknown territory. It's a return of happenings that have different details but a familiar shape. Consider these examples of patterns that Hoodoo has faced and overcome:

- Suppression during slavery, reconstruction, and Jim Crow
- Commercialization, especially during the Great Migration, which threatened its core
- New technologies, including the railroad, the postal service, and the telephone, which sought to replace hand-to-hand knowledge transmission
- Debates about who belongs in the practice of Hoodoo and who doesn't

Throughout its four-century history, Hoodoo has survived to serve personal needs and collective liberation, often at the same time. Whatever comes next will involve some version of these same dynamics. The specific circumstances will be new. The underlying patterns won't be.

Seeing historical patterns in current trends

Everything happening in Hoodoo today has precedent. Recognizing the patterns helps you understand current developments as continuation rather than innovation.

REMEMBER

Hoodoo's cyclical understanding of time means that its future tends to echo its past. Knowing the history isn't just about understanding where the tradition came from. It's about recognizing what's happening now and what's likely to come. When current developments in Hoodoo feel unprecedented or threatening, look for historical parallels. Usually the tradition has faced something similar before and found ways through.

Reclamation has happened before

The current wave of African Americans rediscovering and proudly claiming Hoodoo isn't the first such movement. After Reconstruction, after the Harlem Renaissance, and after the Civil Rights era, each generation has had its moment of reaching back for ancestral traditions that had been suppressed or hidden.

What's different now is scale and visibility. The internet allows reclamation movements to connect across geographic distance in ways previous generations couldn't. But the impulse itself — the need to reclaim what was taken or hidden — is as old as the tradition.

Commercialization pressure isn't new

Debates about commercialization feel urgent today, but they're not new. The mail-order Hoodoo supply industry of the early 20th century generated similar concerns. Were these mass-produced oils and powders authentic? Were the companies selling them connected to actual tradition? Was making money from Hoodoo inherently corrupting?

The tradition survived that commercialization wave while practitioners continued doing their work. Some adapted by using commercial supplies. Others maintained entirely hand-prepared materials. The same range of responses exists today, and the tradition continues regardless.

Digital transmission is still hand-to-hand

The internet might seem to fundamentally change how Hoodoo transmits knowledge of materials and methods, but I challenge you to look closer. A YouTube teacher explaining rootwork to a subscriber isn't so different from a practitioner teaching someone who showed up at their door. The medium changed, but the relationship didn't disappear.

Yes, new challenges come with the landscape of the digital world. Misinformation spreads faster, context can be stripped, and people can claim expertise they don't have. But the digital medium also brings new opportunities. Isolated practitioners can find community online, knowledge becomes accessible to people without access to local teachers, and the tradition reaches descendants who might never have encountered it otherwise.

Previous technology shifts (literacy, postal service, telephone, and the automobile) created similar mixtures of opportunity and challenge. The tradition adapted then, just as it's adapting now.

Access debates aren't new either

Arguments about who can practice Hoodoo and who can't feel contemporary, but root doctors have always made decisions about who they would and wouldn't teach, serve, or welcome. The specific terms of debate shift, but the underlying questions about who belongs, who decides, and what obligations come with traditional Hoodoo knowledge have always been present.

The tradition has survived previous rounds of these debates without fragmenting into uselessness. It will survive this round too, even if resolution remains elusive.

Embracing what Hoodoo has done repeatedly

Across four centuries, regardless of external circumstances, Hoodoo has consistently performed certain functions. These aren't incidental features. Instead, they're the tradition's core that makes the practice Hoodoo rather than something else.

In this section, you can read about the consistency of Hoodoo. The functions of surviving, adapting, healing, protecting, seeking justice, and transmitting the tradition are what Hoodoo has always done. Any authentic continuation of the tradition will involve these same functions, whatever form they take.

Surviving

Hoodoo is survival technology. It was created by people who needed every possible edge to endure conditions designed to destroy them. That survival function has never stopped being central. When Black communities face threats, whether economic, physical, political, or spiritual, Hoodoo provides tools for making it through.

This survival orientation shapes everything about the tradition. It's why Hoodoo is practical rather than abstract, why it focuses on results rather than elaborate theology, why it adapts to circumstances rather than demanding circumstances adapt to it.

Adapting

Hoodoo has never been static. It incorporated Native American herbalism alongside African botanical knowledge. It wove in European folk magic and Christian scripture. It adapted to the Great Migration, moving from rural South to urban North. It shifted from local root doctors to mail-order catalogs to the internet.

This adaptability isn't weakness or lack of authenticity. It's core to what the tradition is. A practice that couldn't adapt wouldn't have survived slavery, wouldn't have survived Jim Crow, wouldn't have survived the 20th century's massive disruptions to Black life. Hoodoo survived precisely because it could change shape while maintaining essence.

Healing and protecting

Despite Hollywood's obsession with curses and hexes, Hoodoo has always been primarily about healing and protection. Root doctors were community healthcare providers when formal medicine was inaccessible or hostile. Protective work for individuals, families, homes, and communities has always been the tradition's bread and butter.

This healing function extends beyond physical ailments. Hoodoo addresses emotional wounds, spiritual damage, and the collective trauma of racism. It provides tools for putting yourself back together when the world tries to break you apart.

Seeking justice

When legal systems refused to protect Black lives and interests, Hoodoo provided alternative means of accountability. Court case work helped people navigate hostile legal systems. Retribution work ensured that harm didn't go unanswered even when official justice was impossible.

This justice function isn't about revenge for its own sake. It's about maintaining moral order in a world that denied Black humanity. When someone harms you and the law won't help, you still have options. That knowledge matters.

Transmitting

Throughout its history, Hoodoo has passed from person to person, hand to hand, and mouth to ear. Grandmothers taught grandchildren. Established practitioners mentored newcomers. Knowledge flowed through family lines and community relationships.

This transmission model means Hoodoo has never depended on institutions that could be shut down. There's no central authority to dissolve, no building to burn, no single text to ban. The tradition lives in people, and as long as people carry it and share it, it continues.

Continuing the cycles

The Hoodoo tradition doesn't need saving because it's not fragile. It has demonstrated resilience repeatedly across history. What Hoodoo needs is continuation: practitioners who do the work, communities that support them, and transmission that keeps the knowledge moving from those who know to those who need to learn.

The ancestors who created this tradition did so under conditions that people today can barely imagine. They had every reason to give up, but they didn't. They built something that outlasted the oppressive system. They passed it down so that their descendants — and others who would come to respect what they built — could benefit from their wisdom.

But the tradition is also made of individual practitioners doing individual work, connected to each other and to the ancestors through bonds of knowledge, practice, and spiritual relationship. You can be one of those persons, in whatever way is appropriate to who you are.

The historic cycle closes the circle when knowledge returns to those who need it. Maybe that's you. Maybe that's someone you teach, recommend a book to, or simply refrain from mocking when they mention their grandmother's practices.

REMEMBER

The tradition is bigger than any individual but made of individuals. Whatever your role, play it with honesty and respect. See the section "Embracing Your Responsibility to the Practice" later in the chapter. Participation is how Hoodoo continues — one person at a time, one generation at a time, one act of carrying forward at a time.

Engaging with Ongoing Conversations and Timeless Principles

The Hoodoo community is actively working through several conversations that don't have settled answers. You don't need final resolution to engage responsibly; you need awareness of the issues being discussed and willingness to confront the complexity. To engage with the questions around Hoodoo practice honestly, you must know your own position in relation to the tradition, listen to voices from within the community — especially elders, and be willing to accept boundaries even when they apply to you.

Consider these points about Hoodoo and its practice as the tradition moves forward:

- **Who can practice Hoodoo?** Chapter 2 explores this question in detail, and the community hasn't reached consensus. Some practitioners say the tradition is closed to non-ADOS people. Others welcome sincere learners who approach with appropriate humility and understanding.
- **How much can Hoodoo change and still be Hoodoo?** This question and others regarding Hoodoo's essential nature and adaptability are important to moving Hoodoo forward. The tradition has always adapted, but not every change is equal. Substituting locally available herbs for unavailable traditional ones is different from stripping out ancestor veneration because it makes non-Black practitioners uncomfortable. Where the lines that limit adaptation fall is genuinely contested.
- **Is Hoodoo's newly found visibility good, bad, or mixed?** Hoodoo survived partly by staying hidden. Now it's increasingly visible — in entertainment, on social media, in academic study, and in this book. More visibility means more people learning about the tradition, including descendants who might reclaim it. It also means more opportunities for appropriation, misrepresentation, and commercialization without connection to community.
- **What elements make Hoodoo practice authentic?** Different practitioners emphasize different elements, some of which appear in this list:
  - *Lineage* and learning from someone who learned from another in an unbroken chain
  - *Method* and using traditional materials and techniques
  - *Function* and doing the work the tradition has always done, even with adaptations
  - *Identity* and being part of the community that created and maintained the tradition

REMEMBER

Hoodoo has no governing body to issue definitive rulings. The conversations continue through practice, through community accountability, and through the slow work of tradition shaping itself across generations.

But beneath the conversations and adaptations, certain principles have kept Hoodoo alive across centuries. These principles will continue anchoring the tradition regardless of what specific circumstances arise. And the principles don't create a rigid system of adherence to historical forms. Whether the work does what it's supposed to do is the important part.

Following are some of the timeless principles that guide the practice of Hoodoo, now and going forward:

- **Practicality over purity:** Hoodoo has always prioritized what works over what's theoretically correct. If a technique gets results, it stays; if it doesn't, it goes. This pragmatism allowed the tradition to incorporate useful elements from multiple sources without worrying about categorical purity.
- **Community rootedness:** Hoodoo has never been a solitary practice disconnected from community. Root doctors served their communities. Knowledge of the tradition was transmitted through relationships. The tradition's survival depended on networks of practitioners, clients, and families who carried it forward together.

  TIP

  You can start learning alone, but you can't fully practice alone. Isolated, individual practice has limits. Eventually, authentic engagement requires connection to teachers, to other practitioners, and to the community the tradition serves.
- **Ancestor connection:** Ancestors aren't optional in Hoodoo. They're the source of the tradition's power, the ones who developed these techniques and passed them down, the cloud of witnesses whose presence makes the work effective.

  REMEMBER

  This principle creates genuine metaphysical questions for people without ADOS ancestry who want to practice Hoodoo. Those questions don't have easy answers, but you can't ignore them. Any authentic continuation of the tradition maintains ancestor connection at its core.
- **Resistance to oppression:** Hoodoo was forged in resistance. It provided tools for surviving and fighting systems designed to destroy Black life. That resistance function isn't incidental history; it's part of the tradition's core.

REMEMBER

The principles of practicality, community rootedness, ancestor connection, and resistance to oppression have kept Hoodoo alive. They'll continue doing so.

Embracing Your Responsibility to the Practice

Whatever your relationship to Hoodoo, you have a role in what happens as the tradition moves forward. That role depends on who you are and how you're positioned relative to the tradition.

TIP

Be honest about your position relative to the tradition. Different positions come with different responsibilities. Clarity about where you stand helps you engage appropriately. If you're positioned to practice, practice. If you're positioned to learn, learn. If you're positioned to support, support. If you're positioned to step back, step back with grace. Whatever your role, play it honestly.

If you're ADOS and reclaiming

If you're a descendant of American slavery and you're reclaiming Hoodoo as part of your heritage, you're doing something important by refusing to let the tradition disappear. You're healing breaks in transmission that oppression created. You're taking back what's yours.

Your responsibility is to learn deeply, not just superficially. Seek out elders and experienced practitioners. Study the history. Do the work, not just the aesthetic. And when you've learned enough, pass it on to your children, to your community, to the next generation of practitioners.

If you're within the broader Black diaspora

If you're Black but not ADOS — perhaps Caribbean, African, Afro-Latino, or from another branch of the diaspora — your relationship to Hoodoo is real but different. You share African roots and the experience of anti-Black racism, but this specific tradition developed in a specific place among specific people.

Your responsibility is to approach the tradition with respect for that specificity. Learn the history. Recognize what Hoodoo is and isn't relative to traditions from your own lineage. Engage as a loving and respectful relative, not as someone with automatic equal claim.

If you're not Black

If you're not Black, you can still gain something from reading this book: understanding, context, and appreciation for a tradition that has shaped American culture in ways most people never recognize. That knowledge is valuable.

Your responsibility is to respect boundaries. Some practitioners will welcome your interest; others won't. Neither response is wrong. Don't demand access to what isn't yours by birthright. Don't claim expertise you don't have. Don't strip practices from their context and repackage them. Support the tradition by supporting Black practitioners, buying from Black-owned shops, amplifying Black voices, and stepping back when that's what's needed.

Whatever your position

Regardless of your background, reading this book can help you now know more about Hoodoo than most people. That knowledge creates obligation. Correct misinformation when you encounter it. Push back against harmful stereotypes. Recommend accurate resources. Don't let people conflate Hoodoo with Hollywood "voodoo" in your presence without saying something.

The tradition survives because people carry it. Even if you never practice, you can contribute to an environment in which Hoodoo is understood and respected rather than feared and mocked.

Taking practical next steps

Here are concrete ways to continue your engagement with Hoodoo, appropriate to different levels of interest and connection.

Continuing your learning

This book is an introduction, not a comprehensive guide. To go deeper, seek out works by practitioners and scholars with roots in the tradition. Zora Neale Hurston's *Mules and Men* remains essential. Katrina Hazzard-Donald's *Mojo Workin'* provides rigorous scholarly grounding. Yvonne Chireau's *Black Magic* offers historical depth. Stephanie Rose Bird's work covers practical applications.

Be cautious about sources. Not everyone who writes about Hoodoo knows what they're talking about. Prioritize authors who have ancestral connection to the tradition and whose work is respected by other practitioners.

Finding community

Books can only take you so far. Eventually, you need people: teachers, fellow learners, and a community that holds you accountable and helps you grow.

Start with what's available. If you have family members who practiced, talk to them. If you can find practitioners in your area, approach them respectfully. If online communities exist that seem legitimate, observe before participating. Building genuine relationships takes time; don't rush it.

Starting practice (if appropriate)

If you're able to practice because of your heritage, because you've found teachers who welcome you, or because your relationship to the tradition makes it appropriate, start small. Do the foundational work of cleansing, protection, and ancestor veneration. Solidify those basics before attempting anything elaborate.

Pay attention to results. Hoodoo is practical; it's supposed to work. If what you're doing isn't producing results, you need to change something, whether it's your technique, your understanding, your spiritual preparation, or something else.

Supporting the tradition

Even if you never practice, you can support Hoodoo's continuation. Buy supplies from Black-owned businesses when possible. Support practitioners financially if you consult them. Share accurate information. Correct stereotypes. Recommend this book or others to people who are curious.

The tradition survives through community support, not just through individual practitioners. You can be part of that support network regardless of whether you practice yourself.

Part 6
The Part of Tens

IN THIS PART . . .

Discover ten everyday signs — from haint blue porch ceilings to the way your grandmother handled hair clippings — that reveal Hoodoo's quiet presence in ordinary Black American life.

Trace ten concrete moments where Hoodoo shaped history, from a 1712 New York uprising to a 21st-century NFL stadium ritual, and see the tradition's reach across three centuries.

IN THIS CHAPTER

- » Recognizing everyday practices with Hoodoo roots
- » Understanding the "why" behind rules you may have grown up with
- » Connecting family traditions to ancestral spiritual practice
- » Seeing how Hoodoo hides in plain sight

Chapter 19 Ten Signs You Might Have Grown Up with Hoodoo

Many African Americans grew up with certain rules, remedies, and rituals that were simply *just what* we *do*. No one called it Hoodoo. No one explained the history. Grandma just said don't do that, and you didn't do it.

But those rules weren't arbitrary. They came from somewhere. Specifically, they came from a tradition of spiritual protection, practical wisdom, and ancestral knowledge that survived slavery, survived the Great Migration, survived generations of suppression, and landed in your childhood home without a label attached.

This chapter offers ten signs that you may have grown up in a household where people practiced Hoodoo, even if no one ever used that word. If you recognize these practices, you're not just remembering family quirks. You're recognizing an inheritance.

REMEMBER

The practices presented in this chapter survived because they worked. Your ancestors weren't superstitious; they were strategic about using every tool available to protect their families and improve their circumstances. If you grew up with these practices, you grew up with Hoodoo, whether anyone called it that or not.

You Were Told Never to Put Your Purse on the Floor

"A purse on the floor is money out the door."

If you heard this growing up — or if you still feel uncomfortable setting your bag on the ground — you were taught Hoodoo without knowing it. This isn't just a tidiness preference. It's a principle of sympathetic magic: Your purse holds your money, your identification, and your personal items. Putting it on the floor symbolically lowers your finances, invites loss, and disrespects the energy of prosperity.

The rule reflects Hoodoo's attention to symbolic action. How you treat objects that represent important aspects of your life affects those aspects. Keeping your purse elevated keeps your money elevated.

The next time you automatically hang your purse on a chair instead of dropping it on the floor, know that you're practicing a form of money magic your ancestors would recognize.

Someone Told You Not to Sweep Their Feet

If you've ever been scolded for accidentally sweeping someone's feet with a broom — or if you instinctively avoid doing this — you've encountered one of Hoodoo's most persistent household rules.

Sweeping someone's feet is believed to sweep away their luck, their romantic prospects, or their ability to travel safely. For unmarried people, it supposedly means they'll never marry. The remedy for accidentally sweeping someone's feet is for them to spit on the broom. It's a way for them to reclaim their essence and break the accidental curse.

The broom itself has deep significance in African American spiritual tradition. It's used in cleansing rituals, in the wedding tradition of jumping the broom, and in sweeping negative energy out of a home (always out the door, never further into the house). The care around the use of and esteem for the broom reflects its power as a spiritual tool, not just a cleaning implement.

Your Porch Ceiling Was Painted Blue

Throughout the South, you'll see porch ceilings painted a distinctive shade of pale blue, sometimes called *haint blue* in Lowcountry Hoodoo (around New Orleans). Real estate agents might tell you it's to mimic the sky or to keep wasps from building nests. Those explanations miss the point.

Haint blue comes from Gullah Geechee tradition. *Haints* are restless spirits — ghosts that might cause trouble for the living. Blue represents water, and spirits can't cross water. By painting your porch ceiling blue, you create a symbolic barrier that prevents haints from entering your home through the front door threshold.

The practice was so widespread that it became just what people did in many Southern communities, Black and white alike. If your family painted porch ceilings blue, or if you feel inexplicably drawn to that color for your own home, you're participating in a tradition of spiritual protection that goes back centuries.

You Had Coins above Your Door

Did your family keep coins above the doorframe, under the doormat, or buried near the entrance to your home? This habit is classic Hoodoo protection and prosperity work.

Coins at the threshold of your house serve multiple purposes. They can attract money into the home. They can prevent poverty from entering. Silver coins, specifically, offer protection against negative spiritual influences because silver is considered a pure metal with protective properties.

Mercury dimes (minted before 1945) were particularly prized in Hoodoo work. Some practitioners wore them on ankle bracelets for protection, carried them for luck, or placed them in mojo bags. If your grandmother had strong opinions about keeping "real silver" around rather than modern coins, she knew something about their traditional uses.

The doorway to your home is a threshold: a place of spiritual vulnerability where influences enter and exit. Protecting and blessing the threshold protects and blesses everyone who passes through.

You Carefully Disposed of Hair and Nail Clippings

Were you taught to burn your hair from brushes rather than throwing it in the trash? Did someone carefully collect nail clippings rather than letting them scatter? Was there a sense that you needed to handle these things with intention?

In Hoodoo, hair and nails are powerful personal concerns. They're items that carry your essence and can be used in workings directed at you. Leaving your hair in a public trash theoretically makes it available to anyone who might want to work against you. Burning the hair destroys its usefulness for such purposes.

This practice reflects a Hoodoo understanding that you remain connected to parts of your body even after they're removed. Practitioners can use that connection for healing and blessing, but also for harm. Careful disposal isn't paranoia. It's basic spiritual hygiene.

If your family was particular about these things without explaining why, they were teaching you to protect yourself using principles they may not have named but definitely practiced.

Your Family Discussed Dreams as Real Communications

In some households, dreams are just random brain activity. In Hoodoo households, dreams are messages.

If your family took dreams seriously — discussing them at breakfast, interpreting their meanings, taking action based on what appeared in dreams — you grew up with one of Hoodoo's most important divinatory traditions. Dreams can carry warnings, guidance, communications from ancestors, or glimpses of possible futures.

This communication potential demonstrates why dream books were so central to the Policy game, which I discuss in Chapter 20. Dreams aren't seen as meaningless; they're seen as coded information that can be translated into practical knowledge, including lucky numbers.

If someone in your family was known for their prophetic dreams, or if you were raised to pay attention to what you dreamed and what it might mean, you were raised in a Hoodoo-informed understanding of consciousness and communication with the unseen world.

You Sipped Special Tea for Every Condition

Did your grandmother have a tea for upset stomachs, a tea for nerves, a tea for *female troubles*, a tea to help you sleep, or a tea to give you energy? Was the first response to any ailment putting on the tea kettle?

Root doctors were herbalists first and foremost. The *root work* in rootwork refers to actual roots — and leaves, barks, flowers, and seeds — used for healing. This knowledge passed through families even when the broader spiritual context was lost or hidden.

That nasty tea your grandmother made you drink when you were sick was likely a remedy with generations of use behind it. The specific knowledge of which plants addressed which conditions represents practical botanical wisdom refined over centuries.

If your family reached for herbs before reaching for pharmaceuticals — or alongside them — you inherited a fragment of the rootwork tradition that kept Black communities healthy when formal medicine was inaccessible or hostile to them.

Your Parents Sprinkled Salt in Corners or at Doorways

Salt is one of the most widely used protective substances in Hoodoo. If your family kept salt near the door, sprinkled it in corners of rooms, added it to cleaning water, or used it in ways that seemed like more than just seasoning, you witnessed everyday spiritual protection.

Salt purifies and protects. It also absorbs negative energy. Lines of salt across doorways can prevent unwanted spiritual influences from entering. Salt in corners captures negativity that accumulates in stagnant spaces.

Some families sprinkle salt around the perimeter of their homes after an argument, after bad news, or after someone who has bad energy visits. Others add salt to mop water for spiritual as well as physical cleaning. And some families keep a dish of salt near the home's entrance to absorb whatever negativity visitors might bring.

If salt in your household served purposes beyond cooking, you grew up with one of Hoodoo's most basic protective tools.

Red Brick Dust Lined Your Steps

In some Southern households, particularly in Louisiana and the Lowcountry, you might have seen red brick dust sprinkled across doorsteps, windowsills, or property lines. This wasn't decoration.

Red brick dust is a traditional Hoodoo substance used for protection. Scrubbing your front steps with water mixed with red brick dust creates a barrier against enemies and negative influences. The practice is often combined with other protective work — prayers, salt, or certain herbs — for a layered defense.

The color red carries protective properties in Hoodoo tradition. Red flannel wraps mojo bags. Red candles serve specific purposes. Red brick dust at the threshold combines the protective power of the color with the intention of keeping harmful influences out.

If you remember red-tinted steps or a grandmother who scrubbed her entrance with particular care using reddish water, you witnessed threshold protection that goes back to the earliest days of Hoodoo practice in America.

You Were Warned Never to Split the Pole

When walking with someone, did you ever hear "don't split the pole"? This means if you're walking together and a pole, post, or tree is in your path, you both go around the same side rather than separating and passing on opposite sides.

Splitting the pole is believed to split your relationship — to create division, bad luck between you, or separation. If you accidentally split the pole, the remedy is to say "bread and butter" to symbolically hold your connection together despite the physical separation.

This practice reflects Hoodoo's attention to the symbolic meanings of physical actions. Walking together represents unity; allowing an obstacle to separate you, even momentarily, symbolically threatens that unity. The physical world and the spiritual world aren't separate — what you do in one affects the other.

If you still feel uncomfortable splitting the pole, or you automatically say "bread and butter" when it happens, you're carrying forward a Hoodoo understanding of how the material and the spiritual interweave.

You Recognize Your Inheritance

If you recognized several of these practices from your own upbringing, you didn't grow up in a "superstitious" household. You grew up in a household where ancestral wisdom survived, even when its name and context were lost.

These practices aren't random. They're fragments of a coherent spiritual tradition that helped Black people survive and thrive under impossible conditions. Your grandmother may not have called herself a rootworker, but she was passing down knowledge that rootworkers would recognize.

TIP

Recognizing these signs of Hoodoo wisdom isn't about claiming expertise you don't have. It's about understanding that the tradition may already live in you, in ways you absorbed before you had words for them. That's how Hoodoo has always been transmitted: hand to hand, generation to generation, and often without formal articulation.

If this chapter sparked recognition, you have a choice. You can let these practices remain as things Grandma did. Or you can investigate further, learn the tradition more deeply, and consciously carry forward what was unconsciously given to you.

Either way, know that what you received was valuable. It kept people alive, families together, and hope possible. And now it's yours.

IN THIS CHAPTER

» Seeing how Hoodoo functioned in real historical moments

» Understanding Hoodoo as economic engine, resistance tool, and community practice

» Learning how the state lottery stole a Black institution

» Recognizing Hoodoo practitioners who shaped history

Chapter 20

Ten Historical Examples of Hoodoo in Action

Hoodoo isn't just something people believed in. It's something people did. Throughout American history, Hoodoo has been put into action to resist oppression, build economic power, protect communities, and shape events that made the history books even when the Hoodoo connection didn't.

From colonial-era uprisings to modern football stadiums, from Policy numbers to blue porch ceilings, these examples show Hoodoo as it has always functioned: practical, adaptive, and effective. The tradition isn't just about individual spells or private rituals. It's been woven into economic systems, resistance movements, architectural practices, and public ceremonies. It's shaped history, built wealth, protected communities, and preserved itself against every attempt at suppression.

This chapter presents ten historical examples of Hoodoo in action. Some incidents involve famous names. Others involve movements that changed American society. All demonstrate that Hoodoo has always been practical — a tradition that does things in the world, not just in the mind.

The Policy Game: How Black Communities Invented the Lottery

Did you ever wonder about the origin of the state lottery that millions of Americans play today? Black communities invented it. And then the government took it.

In the late 19th and early 20th centuries, an underground lottery called Policy became a cornerstone of Black urban life in Chicago, Harlem, Detroit, and other cities. Players selected three-digit numbers, often inspired by dreams, and small bets could yield substantial returns. In an era when Black Americans were systematically denied access to banking, credit, and legitimate economic opportunity, Policy became a vital financial institution. This development was Hoodoo in action; it represented not just magic, but strategic adaptation, economic creativity, and community resilience until the state decided to steal what Black people had built. Policy had these characteristics:

- **Hoodoo was woven throughout the Policy system.** Players used dream books, which were manuals that translated dream imagery into lucky numbers. The number 769 was widely recognized as the Hoodoo code for death. Players and runners alike carried mojo bags and lucky oils. The entire operation reflected Hoodoo thinking by using symbolic systems to navigate and influence material reality.
- **The money Policy generated stayed in Black communities.** Policy Kings and Queens, like the Jones Brothers in Chicago and Stephanie St. Clair in Harlem, became local celebrities and philanthropists. They funded Black businesses, newspapers, and political campaigns. Policy provided employment, informal credit, and community investment when white institutions provided nothing.

Then two things happened. First, the Italian Mafia muscled in during the 1940s and 1950s, using violence to seize control of the Policy racket from Black operators. Second, states realized they could legalize the game and take the profits for themselves. State lotteries launched in the 1960s and 1970s explicitly copied the mechanics of Policy's Pick 3 and Pick 4 games.

This takeover resulted in a community-owned capital generator becoming a regressive tax that siphons money from poor neighborhoods, offers worse odds than the original street game, and returns almost nothing to the communities that invented it. The Hoodoo-infused system that built Black wealth was transformed into a state revenue stream.

REMEMBER

Every time you see a state lottery, you're looking at a system that Black communities created, Hoodoo practices shaped, and government took over from Black control. The dream books and lucky numbers came first.

Peter Doctor and the 1712 New York Uprising

One of the earliest documented instances of Hoodoo used as a revolutionary tool occurred in 1712 in New York City.

Peter Doctor was a free Black man who was recognized as a practitioner of conjure. When enslaved people in New York planned an uprising to burn down the town and strike for their freedom, Doctor provided crucial spiritual support. He created a magical powder from his knowledge of botanical elements and African medicine and instructed the rebels to rub it on their clothing and bodies.

The powder, Doctor told them, would grant spiritual protection and make them invulnerable to their captors' weapons. This practice, using protective dusts and powders, has roots in West African tradition and remained central to Hoodoo practice for centuries afterward.

The uprising was eventually suppressed, and the colonial response was brutal. But Peter Doctor's role established something important: From the earliest days of African presence in North America, conjure practitioners served as tactical leaders and spiritual doctors for resistance movements. The Hoodoo practitioner wasn't just a healer of individual ailments; he was a revolutionary resource.

Gullah Jack and the Denmark Vesey Conspiracy

The 1822 planned insurrection in Charleston, South Carolina, remains one of the most significant slave revolts in American history, and Hoodoo was at its center.

Denmark Vesey, a free Black man, organized the conspiracy. But his co-leader was Gullah Jack Pritchard, an African-born conjurer from Angola who had been described as a *priest* in his own country. Jack carried his conjure bag throughout the Middle Passage and maintained his spiritual authority in the new world.

Jack used his reputation as an invincible spiritual figure to recruit fellow Angolan countrymen for the revolt. He distributed physical charms — specifically crab claws — to the rebels, instructing them to hold the claws in their mouths during the attack to prevent being wounded or captured. He mandated a ritual diet of parched corn and ground nuts for spiritual preparation.

Jack's spiritual power served a practical function: His ability to terrify others into silence through his reputation as a conjurer kept the conspiracy secret until just days before its scheduled start. The colonial government's response — executing Jack alongside Vesey — showed how seriously they took the threat of the conjure man as a leader of resistance.

Bras Coupé: The Conjuring Maroon of Louisiana

In the swamps outside New Orleans in the 1830s, an escaped, formerly enslaved man named Squire (later called Bras Coupé, meaning "cut arm" after he lost the use of one arm) became a legendary figure who terrified white Louisiana for years.

Bras Coupé was said to be a powerful conjurer whose magic made him impossible to capture. He lived in the swamps with other *maroons* — people who escaped enslavement and formed free communities in the wilderness — and reportedly led raids that struck fear into plantation owners.

The stories about Bras Coupé became embellished in the telling. He was said to be bulletproof and could appear and disappear at will. His conjure protected not just himself but his entire community. Whether these specific powers were real or legendary, the belief in them was real enough to shape behavior — making enslaved people hope and enslavers fear.

When Bras Coupé was finally killed in 1837, his body was displayed publicly for days. It was an attempt to prove that the conjurer was human after all, that his magic hadn't saved him. But the legend only grew. Bras Coupé became a symbol of freedom and resistance, and his story was told and retold for generations.

The story illustrates how Hoodoo functioned not only as individual practice but also as collective psychological warfare. The belief that conjure protected the maroons made resistance imaginable.

Zora Neale Hurston's Initiation

In the 1920s, a young anthropologist named Zora Neale Hurston did something remarkable: She was initiated into the practice of Hoodoo.

Hurston was already a trained academic when she traveled to New Orleans to document Hoodoo practice. But she understood that observing from outside would only take her so far. To truly understand the tradition, she had to enter it.

Her initiation with a root doctor involved lying naked on a couch for 69 hours without food, her navel touching a snakeskin. She reported being "struck by lightning" spiritually five times. She emerged with the status of a *two-headed doctor* — a practitioner with spiritual sight.

Hurston's willingness to undergo initiation transformed her research. Her books *Mules and Men* and *Tell My Horse* remain foundational texts because she wrote from inside the Hoodoo tradition and wasn't just telling about it. She witnessed and documented practices that might otherwise have been lost precisely because practitioners recognized her as one of them.

This example shows Hoodoo in action as documentation and preservation. Hurston's initiation wasn't just personal spiritual development. It was strategic positioning that allowed her to create a written archive that the tradition still draws on today.

TIP

Hurston's work at documenting the practice demonstrates that real understanding of Hoodoo requires more than intellectual study. She became a practitioner to become a proper witness.

Madame Stephanie St. Clair: Numbers Queen

Stephanie St. Clair, known as Madame Queen and Queenie, ran the most powerful numbers operation in Harlem during the 1920s and 1930s. She was also a well-known practitioner of protective spiritual work.

St. Clair arrived in Harlem from Martinique and built her Policy empire from nothing, eventually controlling much of the neighborhood's gambling economy. She employed hundreds of Black workers, invested in Black businesses, and became a political force who openly challenged police corruption and organized crime.

When the Italian Mafia, led by Dutch Schultz, tried to take over Harlem's numbers racket, St. Clair fought back both practically and spiritually. She reportedly used Hoodoo protection work alongside more conventional resistance. She also worked with the police and the press, taking out newspaper advertisements denouncing Schultz and corrupt cops.

When Dutch Schultz was finally shot in 1935, St. Clair reportedly sent a telegram to him as he lay dying with the message "As ye sow, so shall ye reap." Whether this reflected her spiritual work against him, simple satisfaction, or both, the timing was noted.

St. Clair's story demonstrates Hoodoo integrated with business acumen, political savvy, and community defense. Her spiritual practice was one tool among many in building and protecting Black economic power.

The Great Migration Spiritual Shops

When millions of Black Southerners moved north during the Great Migration, Hoodoo moved with them and adapted.

Practices that had been conducted in woods, at crossroads, and by rivers now had to work in apartment buildings and city alleys. The root doctors who had gathered their own materials from familiar landscapes now lived far from those sources. Something had to change.

The answer was the spiritual supply shop. Businesses such as King Novelty Company in Chicago and various botanicas in NY Harlem, Detroit, and other cities began selling what practitioners could no longer gather for themselves: roots, herbs, oils, candles, and prepared products. Dream books proliferated, guiding Policy players in their number selection.

Some practitioners bemoaned this commercialization, and legitimate concerns existed about quality and authenticity. But the shops also made Hoodoo practice possible for people who would otherwise have been cut off from their tradition. A factory worker in Chicago couldn't walk into the woods for High John root, but she could buy it at a supply shop.

REMEMBER

The birth of spiritual shops due to the Great Migration represents Hoodoo's adaptive genius. The tradition didn't die when its people moved. It built new infrastructure. The same practical, survival-oriented mindset that created Hoodoo in the first place found ways to maintain it in radically different circumstances.

Haint Blue across the South

Drive through the South Carolina Lowcountry, coastal Georgia, or parts of Louisiana, and you'll notice something: blue porch ceilings, blue window frames, blue shutters, and blue doors. This isn't a decorating trend. It's Hoodoo made visible in architecture.

Haint blue as a particular color comes from the Gullah Geechee word for ghost: *haint*. The color represents water, which the ghostly spirits can't cross. By painting your porch ceiling blue, you create a symbolic barrier that prevents restless spirits from entering your home.

What makes haint blue remarkable is its spread. The practice began in Gullah communities but expanded across racial lines throughout the South. White families adopted it too — sometimes knowing its purpose, sometimes just knowing "that's what you do." Paint companies such as Sherwin Williams and Benjamin Moore continue to sell colors that they specifically market as haint blue.

This example represents Hoodoo in action as material culture that reshapes the built environment. The tradition isn't just in people's minds or private practices. It's visible in thousands of houses across multiple states, declaring protection to anyone who knows how to read the signs.

WARNING

The prevalence of haint blue colors used on porch ceilings shows how Hoodoo practices can move into mainstream culture while their origins are forgotten or obscured. The real estate agent who tells you blue porch ceilings keep wasps away is passing on a fragment of something much deeper.

The Clementine Barnabet Case: Hoodoo as Accusation

Not every historical example shows Hoodoo used successfully. Some show how accusations of Hoodoo were used against Black people by a hostile legal system.

In the early 20th century, Clementine Barnabet of Louisiana confessed to a series of gruesome murders, claiming membership in a group called the Church of Sacrifice. She said she used conjure bags to make herself invisible to authorities.

The media of the time seized on the *voodoo* angle, characterizing the case as evidence of negro barbarity and conflating Hoodoo, Voodoo, and any African-derived practice into a single menacing cult. The coverage reinforced stereotypes that white Americans were eager to believe.

However, later historians noted problems with the case. The "conjure bags" Barnabet possessed, which were two crossed needles bound in thread and wrapped in red flannel, were common healing charms used to treat rheumatism, not tools of murder. The sensationalized coverage ignored evidence that didn't fit the voodoo-killer narrative.

The Barnabet case illustrates how Hoodoo has been weaponized against Black people. Accusations of voodoo connections served to criminalize Black spirituality and justify harsh treatment. The moral panic around Hoodoo often had less to do with actual practice than with white anxiety about Black spiritual autonomy.

WARNING

When you see historical accounts of voodoo crimes, approach the accounts with skepticism. The legal system has a long history of using Hoodoo accusations to demonize Black defendants and sensationalize cases.

Removing the Superdome Curse

For over three decades, the New Orleans Saints football team failed to win a playoff game. Fans attributed this losing streak to the "Curse of the Superdome." The stadium had been built near the site of the old Girod Street Cemetery, and disturbing the dead, as any Hoodoo practitioner knows, invites trouble.

In 2000, before a crucial playoff game, the team did something unusual: They hired Voodoo priestess Ava Kay Jones to perform a ritual cleansing of the stadium. With a boa constrictor around her neck, Jones prayed and called upon the spirits before a capacity crowd.

That night, the Saints won their first-ever playoff game, defeating the St. Louis Rams.

Critics might dismiss this as coincidence or spectacle. But for the people of New Orleans, a city where spiritual traditions are woven into public life in ways unusual for America, the event was a public acknowledgment of something that had been obvious all along. The curse was real because enough people believed it was real. The cleansing worked because the community witnessed it and accepted it.

This instance is Voodoo in action in the 21st century: public, unapologetic, and effective. It demonstrates that African-derived spiritual traditions, whether Hoodoo or Voodoo, have not retreated from public life and can still operate at the level of community ritual, addressing collective problems — even lighthearted ones like football curses — with collective spiritual solutions.

Appendix

In this appendix, you can find helpful references for purchasing Hoodoo supplies, finding Hoodoo communities online and in person, and understanding the meaning of everyday elements (days of the week, moon phases, and so on) as they relate to Hoodoo. You also find sections with good advice for spotting fake versus authentic Hoodoo practitioners and answers to common questions about Hoodoo.

Spiritual Suppliers and Botanicas

REMEMBER

When purchasing spiritual supplies for your Hoodoo practice, prioritize Black-owned businesses that have authentic roots in the tradition. Many non-Black merchants have profited from selling Hoodoo supplies while giving nothing back to African American communities. When Black-owned suppliers aren't available in your area, botanicas — storefronts rooted primarily in Latino spiritual traditions such as Santería and Espiritismo — often carry herbs, candles, oils, and ritual supplies that overlap with what Hoodoo practitioners use and can be a practical alternative. Buying from practitioners within the tradition, where and when possible, keeps resources circulating where they belong.

For an online curated starting point, Shoppe Black at `shoppeblack.us/black-owned-hoodoo-shops/` maintains a list of Black-owned Hoodoo suppliers vetted by the platform's editorial team.

TIP

Look for suppliers who are transparent about the tradition their products come from, employ or are owned by practitioners, and don't appropriate imagery or terminology from other closed traditions for marketing purposes.

Organizations and Communities

Embodied community is irreplaceable in Hoodoo. Online spaces have made Hoodoo more accessible than ever, but they vary widely in quality and authenticity. When engaging with online communities, look for spaces centered on African American practitioners and elders, that discourage appropriation and predatory behavior, and that emphasize relationship and lineage over consumption.

These are a few communities that are worth your exploration:

- **Professor Chireau's Academic Hoodoo** (`https://academichoodoo.com`), a research blog, offers rigorous, scholar-grounded writing on Hoodoo's history and living tradition.
- **The Hoodoo Society** (`https://hoodoosociety.com`), rooted in the Chesapeake-Tidewater region, centers community, ancestral reverence, and environmental stewardship.
- **Conjure Cleaning** (`www.conjurecleaning.com`), founded by practitioner James E. Stewart, offers both services and community engagement grounded in documented Hoodoo practice.
- **The Hoodoo Nerds community** (`hoodoonerds.org`) provides ongoing education through videos, online community, podcasts, and written curriculum exploring Hoodoo's history and cultural breadth.

REMEMBER

In-person communities, where they exist, offer something that no digital space can replicate. If you have access to a rootworker, spiritual community, or elder willing to teach you about Hoodoo, that relationship is worth cultivating with patience, respect, and reciprocity.

Timing and Correspondences in Hoodoo

The following reference material describes the timing frameworks and symbolic correspondences that Hoodoo practitioners use. Timing strengthens work but doesn't determine it. *Correspondences* are tools observed over time, not cosmic laws. When in doubt, work when you need to.

REMEMBER

Understanding timing and symbolic correspondences helps you recognize patterns in practitioner work and in the tradition's material culture. It's reference material for learning about how the tradition operates, not a practice guide.

Days of the week

Here are the circumstances and situations that correspond to days of the week for specific types of working in Hoodoo practice:

- **Sunday:** Success, victory, solar power, ambition, career advancement.
- **Monday:** Emotions, intuition, dreams, psychic work, domestic matters, women's concerns.
- **Tuesday:** Courage, conflict, legal battles, overcoming enemies, protection.
- **Wednesday:** Communication, travel, education, divination, crossroads work.
- **Thursday:** Prosperity, abundance, business, expansion, luck.
- **Friday:** Love, beauty, pleasure, reconciliation, attraction.
- **Saturday:** Banishing, binding, endings, protection, ancestral work, uncrossing.

Moon phases

Phases of the moon are powerful in Hoodoo practice and correspond to particular types of Hoodoo work:

- **New Moon:** New beginnings, planting intentions, starting fresh.
- **Waxing Moon:** Drawing things toward you, such as money, love, success, healing, and growth.
- **Full Moon:** Peak power for all work; especially potent for divination and spirit communication.
- **Waning Moon:** Sending things away. Examples are banishing, uncrossing, ending situations, and removing obstacles.

Colors and their meanings

This list helps you recognize the colors that have specific meanings in Hoodoo:

- **White:** Purity, protection, peace, spiritual clarity, ancestors.
- **Red:** Passionate love, courage, power, strength, sexual attraction.
- **Pink:** Gentle love, friendship, emotional healing, reconciliation.

- **Green:** Money, prosperity, growth, abundance, employment.
- **Yellow/Gold:** Success, confidence, solar power, attraction, mental clarity.
- **Blue:** Peace, healing, protection, calm, fidelity.
- **Purple:** Spiritual power, psychic ability, wisdom, justice.
- **Orange:** Road opening, opportunity, attraction, legal matters.
- **Black:** Banishing, binding, protection from harm, absorbing negativity.

Numbers in Hoodoo

These numbers correspond to circumstances and situations in Hoodoo:

- **3:** Manifestation, the trinity, completion of a cycle.
- **7:** Luck, spiritual completion, widely considered the most powerful number in Hoodoo.
- **9:** Endings, completions, the highest single digit; used in banishing and binding work.
- **13:** Powerful and traditionally lucky in African American Hoodoo, despite European associations with misfortune.

Red Flags: Spotting Scams and Fake Practitioners

Hoodoo's decentralized nature and the vulnerability of people in spiritual distress make the practice a target for exploitation. Knowing what to look for to identify fake or predatory practitioners can protect you.

Immediate red flags

You need to run away quickly if you face any of these immediate red flags:

- **The curse removal scam:** A reader tells you that you're cursed, hexed, or have "black magic" on you, and only they can remove it, usually for hundreds or thousands of dollars in escalating payments. If you didn't suspect that you were cursed, you probably aren't. Through the Hoodoo lens, real curses have symptoms. Real practitioners teach you to protect yourself rather than creating dependency.

- **Financial information requests:** No legitimate practitioner needs your bank account numbers, credit card details beyond a standard payment, or financial passwords. Full stop.
- **Guaranteed specific outcomes:** No practitioner can guarantee that a specific person will love you, that you will win a specific lawsuit, or that a specific outcome will materialize on a specific date. Hoodoo works with spiritual forces, not vending machines. Anyone guaranteeing specific outcomes is likely lying or delusional.
- **Pressure tactics and fear-mongering:** If someone tells you that terrible things will happen if you don't pay immediately, or uses urgency and fear to push you toward a decision, walk away. Legitimate practitioners don't operate through manufactured panic.
- **Requests to break the law:** If a practitioner asks you to do anything illegal as part of spiritual work, refuse and disengage. Legal risks are yours alone, and this is manipulation.

Warning signs

If you encounter any of these situations, proceed with extreme caution:

- **Wildly out-of-range pricing: As of 2026,** Hoodoo divination readings generally run $25–$150. Custom mojo bags are typically $50–$200. Candle services are $35–$100. Major workings might reach $300–$1,000 or more. Extreme outliers in either direction warrant questions. Experienced practitioners with proven results often charge more; some offer sliding scale. But if the price feels designed to exploit rather than compensate, trust that feeling.
- **No clear explanation of the work:** Legitimate practitioners explain what they'll do, what materials they'll use, how long it will take, and what you should expect. Vague promises of "powerful magic" without specifics are a concern.
- **Endless follow-up work required:** Sometimes work genuinely requires multiple approaches. But if you've paid for five different workings and nothing has manifested, a good practitioner would reassess the situation, not sell you more work.
- **No explanation of their connection to the tradition:** A legitimate practitioner (not necessarily a supplier) should be able to tell you how they came to Hoodoo: family lineage, a specific elder or teacher, a community they're part

of. Some practitioners learned primarily through self-study, and that's a valid path, but they should say so honestly rather than being evasive. Vagueness about how someone learned Hoodoo practice is different from humility about how much they know.

- **Creating dependency:** If someone tells you that you need to check with them before any decision or implies you can't handle your own spiritual life, that's a problem. Good practitioners empower. They may work on your behalf, but they're strengthening you, not making you dependent.

Good Signs: What Legitimate Practitioners Do

Legitimate practitioners tend to share certain qualities regardless of their specific style or tradition:

- They're clear about their pricing and what services include.
- They're realistic about outcomes and honest about limitations.
- They empower clients rather than cultivating fear or dependency.
- They assess a situation before recommending or selling services.
- They maintain professional boundaries with clients.
- They're part of a community and can be verified through that community.
- They respect your autonomy and don't insist that you can't function without them.

The best path for finding a legitimate practitioner is through community. Someone who comes recommended by a person you trust, who's known and verified within a community, is far more likely to be genuine than someone you found through a cold internet search.

Ask these questions before hiring a practitioner:

- How did you learn? Who taught you?
- What tradition or lineage do you work within?
- What does this service include, and what does it cost?

- What can I realistically expect, and when?
- Can you provide references, or are you known within a community I can verify?

TIP Referrals from trusted community members are the gold standard for finding an authentic Hoodoo practitioner. African American spiritual and cultural organizations, botanicas and spiritual supply shops with ties to the community, and established online communities centered on Black practitioners are reasonable starting points. Trust your instincts in the first interaction. If something feels off, it probably is.

Common Questions and Concerns

In this section, you can find common questions and concerns that people have regarding Hoodoo and its practice.

"How do I know if I'm actually cursed?"

Real *crossed conditions* that indicate a curse tend to show consistent patterns:

- Sudden and unexplained reversals across multiple areas of life simultaneously
- Persistent bad luck that defies probability
- Physical symptoms without medical explanation
- Recurring nightmares or sleep disruption
- A feeling of heaviness or interference that practitioners describe as "something being on you"

REMEMBER Having one bad week doesn't indicate that you have a curse on you. But ongoing bad luck that clusters and resists practical solutions is worth investigating. Get a reading from a trusted practitioner before assuming you're crossed and before paying anyone to remove a curse.

"Can I do Hoodoo if I'm not Christian?"

People of many faiths practice Hoodoo. Christianity is deeply woven into the tradition's history, and many practitioners are devout Christians. But Hoodoo has no doctrinal requirement. The tradition has always been religiously flexible, adapting to the spiritual lives of the people practicing it. Non-Christian practitioners, including those who are Muslim, Jewish, practitioners of African traditional religions, or non-religious, have practiced Hoodoo throughout its history.

"Will I go to hell for practicing Hoodoo?"

The question of going to hell is a theological one that falls outside this book's scope, and it's one only you can answer within your own faith tradition. What history does show is that generations of deeply devout African American Christians practiced Hoodoo without experiencing it as incompatible with their faith. They read the Psalms as working texts, understood the Holy Spirit as active spiritual power, and saw no contradiction between their Christianity and their conjure. Your own discernment matters here more than any outside answer.

"What if my work doesn't manifest?"

Several possibilities are worth considering if you find that your Hoodoo work isn't manifesting. In order of consideration, these are the possibilities:

- **The work needs more time.** Spiritual work doesn't follow clocks.
- **You need to take practical action alongside the spiritual work.** Hoodoo supports effort; it rarely replaces it.
- **Your intention wasn't clear.** Revisit what you actually asked for.
- **You may be crossed or blocked.** A cleansing before new work is always advisable.
- **This particular outcome may not be available to you right now.** That's a hard truth, but a real one.

"Can Hoodoo backfire on me?"

Potentially, yes, Hoodoo can backfire. This happens particularly if you work while you're already crossed, if your intentions are unclear, if you haven't fully thought out what you want to happen, or if you're careless with the spiritual forces you're working with. Prevention is straightforward: Cleanse yourself before major work, be specific about your intentions, protect yourself, and follow through on any promises made to spirits. If work does go wrong, uncross immediately, make offerings to any spirits you may have offended, and seek guidance from an experienced practitioner if needed.

"What if I accidentally disrespect a spirit or ancestor?"

Don't panic if you think that you've accidentally showed disrespect to a spirit or ancestor. In Hoodoo, it's understood that spirits generally understand mistakes and learning curves, especially when intentions are good. Acknowledge what happened, apologize sincerely, make an appropriate offering, and recommit to the relationship. Ancestors who chose you want you to succeed. Approaching with humility and genuine respect goes a long way.

"Do I need to be initiated?"

You generally don't need initiation for Hoodoo. Unlike sibling traditions such as Santería or Haitian Vodou, which have formal initiation structures, Hoodoo is historically accessible without them. Most practitioners learned from family, elders, or community, and not through initiation ceremonies. Some contemporary practitioners and lineages do use initiation, and for specific types of work, formal training or apprenticeship may be appropriate. But the tradition itself doesn't require it.

"Someone is practicing Hoodoo against me. What do I do?"

First, verify whether someone is practicing a working against you. Not every misfortune is a spiritual attack. Get a reading from a trusted practitioner before assuming that you're being worked against. If attack is confirmed, the response generally follows this sequence:

- Cleanse yourself thoroughly by using a spiritual bath with hyssop or rue, a salt scrub, or a floor wash formulated to remove crossed conditions.
- Strengthen your protections by refreshing any protective items at your thresholds, feeding your mojo if you carry one, or working a protection candle.
- Consider counter efforts, such as *return-to-sender* work, which redirects a spiritual attack back toward its source, if that's appropriate to your ethics.
- If the situation seems serious or dangerous, engage an experienced practitioner to help you.

TIP

Fear is the enemy when you're the target of Hoodoo work. Calm, methodical protection work is the answer, and it is worth remembering that in Hoodoo, protection has never been purely self-interested. You protect yourself so you can remain present, capable, and useful to the people who depend on you.

Recommended Reading

The following titles represent a range of scholarly, practitioner, and historical perspectives on Hoodoo and related traditions. Some are academic; some are practitioner-authored; all are worth your time.

- *Mules and Men* by Zora Neale Hurston (1935): Firsthand accounts of Hoodoo rituals, formulas, and ceremonies by a practitioner-scholar who was herself initiated.
- *Hoodoo in America* by Zora Neale Hurston (1931): Hurston's foundational scholarly survey of the tradition.
- *Mojo Workin': The Old African American Hoodoo System* by Katrina Hazzard-Donald (2012): A rigorous scholarly reconsideration of Hoodoo's origins and structure.
- *Conjure in African American Society* by Yvonne Chireau (2003): Essential academic treatment of Hoodoo's religious and cultural dimensions.
- *Hyatt's Hoodoo, Conjuration, Witchcraft, Rootwork* by Harry M. Hyatt (5 vols., 1970–1978): The massive primary-source archive of practitioner interviews collected across the American South in the 1930s.

Index

A

B

D

E

F

N

O

P

Q

R

S

T

U

V

W

Y

Z

About the Author

Nathaniel "Nth" Bar-Fields is a practicing Hoodoo spiritual worker, the founder and chief visionary officer of Elysian Trust, and the creator of Hoodoo Nerds, a multimedia platform exploring the cultural, historical, and scientific dimensions of Hoodoo and its intersecting traditions. His work is grounded in the conviction that understanding Hoodoo is inseparable from understanding the Black experience in America.

He holds a certification from the US Navy Nuclear Power Propulsion School, is an Ashoka Changemakers Scholar, and is a TANDO Fellow. For 20 years, he served as an ESP test subject at UC Berkeley's Psychophysiology Lab, MIT's Corkin Lab, and the University of Virginia's Department of Perceptual Studies.

He splits his time between California, Massachusetts, and Texas.

Dedication

To my grandparents, Odessa Olivier and J. C. Coleman, who raised me in a tradition they never once called Hoodoo. My grandfather had a remedy, a root, or a concoction for every ailment you could name. My grandmother didn't have psychic visions: God simply told her things. Because of my family, I was deep in the work long before I had a word for it. This book is, in many ways, just me finally finding the words.

Author's Acknowledgments

Five generations ago, my ancestors were enslaved people in the Carolinas and Virginia, carried to Louisiana and Texas in one of the great forced migrations that also carried Hoodoo westward. Writing this book sent me deeper into that history than I expected. DNA testing connected me to relatives I never knew I had: people from different regions of Africa, communities across Europe and the Middle East, and Native American relatives across the Americas. Everything I learned about the tradition taught me something about myself, and everything I learned about myself taught me something about the tradition.

Special thanks to Dr. Holly Mathews, whose research on lay midwifery and root doctors in the American South provided essential scholarly grounding for some of this book's most important material.

To my cousin Dr. Kiana Long, DO, whose conversations with me about folk medicine and the granny wife tradition sharpened that same material from the inside.

To Earnest L. Hudson Jr., whom I first met as a fellow member of SoulSIG, Mensa's African American special interest group. He became a long-time friend and fellow traveler in African Traditional Religion scholarship, and I later discovered that he is also my cousin by blood.

My deepest professional gratitude goes to Dr. Yvonne Chireau, scholar of African American religion, one of the most incisive thinkers working in this space, and the source of my Wiley connection. Years of conversation with her sharpened every idea in these pages.

Thank you to Alicia Sparrow, who conceived of this book and brought it into the *For Dummies* series; to Leah Michael, whose editorial instincts and genuine patience made this manuscript better at every stage; to Karen Davis, whose meticulous copy editing caught what the rest of us missed; and to the full team at Wiley who believed a *For Dummies* book could hold this much history.

Publisher's Acknowledgments

Associate Acquisitions Editor: Alicia Sparrow

Project Manager and Development Editor: Leah Michael

Copy Editor: Gill Editorial Services

Editorial Assistant: Shannon Kucaj

Managing Editor: Murari Mukundan

Production Editor: Magesh Elangovan

Cover Image: © FuzullHanum/stock.adobe.com